LABOR,
FREE AND SLAVE

Labor, Free and Slave

Workingmen and the Anti-Slavery Movement in the United States

by

Bernard Mandel

Introduction by
Brian Kelly

University of Illinois
Urbana and Chicago

Library of Congress
Cataloging-in-Publication Data
Mandel, Bernard, 1920–
Labor, free and slave : workingmen and
the anti-slavery movement in the United States /
Bernard Mandel ; introduction by Brian E. Kelly.
— Paper ed.
p.   cm.
Originally published: New York :
Associated Authors, 1955.
Includes bibliographical references and index.
ISBN-13: 978-0-252-07428-8 (paper : alk. paper)
ISBN-10: 0-252-07428-9 (paper : alk paper)
1. Antislavery movements—United States—
History—19th century. 2. Slavery—United
States—History—19th century. 3. Working class—
United States—History—19th century. 4. Labor
movement—United States—History—19th century.
5. United States—Race relations—History—
19th century.
I. Title.
E449.M25   2007
326.973—dc22   2006029414

To
My Parents

———

CONTENTS

INTRODUCTION
TO THE ILLINOIS EDITION

Brian Kelly

Bernard Mandel was born in Cleveland, Ohio, to Jewish immigrant parents of some means on January 4, 1920. By the time Bernard reached his tenth birthday, his father, Max, had managed to set aside enough of his earnings to go into the grocery business, move his family to the city's comfortable East Side, and take on a live-in domestic servant.[1] The entrepreneurial Mandels were both religiously observant and politically conservative, having fled Poland to escape Bolshevism, and it "mortified" them to discover sometime in the mid-1930s that their son was involved in establishing a branch of the Young Communist League at Cleveland Heights High School. Determined to bring a halt to Bernard's early foray into left-wing politics, Max made the mistake of hauling him before the rabbi at the Temple Tifereth Israel, apparently hopeful that a stern scolding from the local religious authority would "straighten Bernard out and get him out of all this radical thinking." The rabbi—something of a maverick himself—was unenthusiastic about being called upon to proscribe the younger Mandel's encounter with radicalism, however, spurning Max's appeal with the explanation that he was "not sure he had brought [his son] to the right place." Although the immediate crisis between father and son would subside, the rift evident in this early confrontation would persist, deepening in the years ahead and eventually compelling Bernard to sever relations with his parents.[2]

It is unclear exactly what circumstances first brought Mandel around left-wing politics or whether the apprehension with which his father treated Bernard's adolescent radicalism was based on actual involvement or mere paternal overreaction, but by the time of their early spat the emergence of the Committee for Industrial Organization—later the Congress of Industrial Organizations

(CIO)—and the vibrant oppositional culture to which it gave rise had begun to register among working-class communities across the Midwest traumatized by the depression. In the spring of 1934, Toledo's Auto-Lite plant had witnessed a remarkable strike that helped pave the way for organization of the automobile industry and the rise of the CIO. The innovation critical to turning the tide there was the success of socialists and communists in organizing the unemployed in support of striking auto parts workers. Mass pickets of upward of ten thousand workers rendered it impossible for the company to restart production with strikebreakers, and when eventually the National Guard was dispatched to take the situation in hand, soapbox agitators bombarded them with appeals to refuse orders. Those unmoved by their pleas were forced into a "six-day pitched battle" with strikers and their supporters.[3]

The Associated Press disseminated blow-by-blow accounts of the cathartic developments in Toledo across the world's wire services, and the spirit of working-class militancy infusing the Auto-Lite strike was replicated in a series of explosive confrontations that erupted across Ohio and the Midwest over the next several years. Within days of the Toledo settlement, some of the strike's most prominent organizers were thrown into another sharp confrontation, this one pitting members of the Guard and racist vigilantes against mainly Mexican and Appalachian migrant farmworkers harvesting onions to the south in Hardin County.

Months later the insurgency spread to Cleveland, where a handful of left-wing militants who had been carefully laying the foundations for organization in the auto industry from the early 1930s began to see their work come to fruition. In early 1936 John L. Lewis addressed a mass meeting of five thousand workers organized by the Cleveland Auto Council in the city's public auditorium (his "first attempt to speak directly to the workers in the mass industries," according to a leading CIO activist), and within days news came from downstate that workers had initiated the first in a rash of effective sit-down strikes in Akron's rubber plants. By the end of the year the steady preparatory work in Cleveland's auto industry was consummated by seven thousand workers at Cleveland's Fisher Body plant, who launched a forty-four-day occupation, in turn touching off a chain reaction in Flint, Michigan, and the wave of sit-down strikes that secured unionization of the automobile industry and which constitute the greatest upheaval in American industrial history.[4]

In Cleveland, this powerful insurgency was pushed forward by a vibrant and relatively nonsectarian Left with substantial roots in a racially and ethnically diverse working class. Robert Zieger acknowledges that the CIO's developing organizational apparatus "itself played a limited role in the actual conduct" of the early industrial revolt and that a small core of rank-and-file activists provided "day-to-day-leadership" in these strikes. In Ohio that mostly left-wing leadership included Bob Travis, a former preacher and leading Toledo militant, and Wyndham Mortimer and Henry Kraus, both based in Cleveland. Earlier the city had acquired a reputation as something of a "stronghold" for the left wing of the Socialist Party, whose influence was embodied in the figure of Max S. Hayes, an early founder of Cleveland's labor press and an energetic critic of Samuel Gompers within the AFL who "came to life with the beginning of the drive for industrial unionism and supported it vigorously." It was home as well to a talented cadre of workplace-based Trotskyists and to an effective Industrial Workers of the World (IWW) local, both of which played significant roles in the local labor movement throughout the 1930s. But the dominant force on the Cleveland left during the CIO upsurge was the Communist Party. Led by autoworker Mortimer and Kraus, Mandel's future publisher who in 1934 founded the *United Auto Worker* newspaper, communists had built a solid presence in the local auto industry, reaching out to the "hunkies" ignored by the AFL and spreading the infectious hope of industrial unionism. The Party would play a leading role in organizing the Fisher Body strike. Together all of this meant that to an extent perhaps unmatched anywhere else in the United States the CIO operation in Cleveland "faced an alternative 'industrial unionism' that seemed . . . to pull it leftward."[5]

The communists' influence extended beyond the city's workplaces into important community-based struggles involving substantial participation from Cleveland's black residents. Mortimer recalls that "demonstrations of ten thousand people were not unusual in the Cleveland Public Square" in the mid-1930s and credits the Party with organizing "the only effective struggles against unemployment and evictions" during that period. His recollections are largely confirmed by Kimberley L. Phillips in *AlabamaNorth,* an important study of black working-class politics in early-twentieth-century Cleveland. "The newly formed Unemployed Councils, established by the local CP," she writes, "elicited considerable participation from African Americans." On at least one occasion police attempts to suppress a rally ended in the deaths of two black demonstrators whose funeral in the heart of the black community several days later (conducted to the strains of *The Internationale*) was attended by "thousands." On the basis of such activity the Party established a fighting reputation in Cleveland's African American community, winning to its ranks a number of prominent black activists, launching the interracial Cleveland Workers' School, and helping along the already advanced process of galvanizing black working-class politics in the city.[6]

Almost certainly, Bernard Mandel had no direct involvement in Cleveland's industrial agitation or in the string of confrontations that rippled across the Midwest in the mid-1930s. Nor can it be definitively established that he took part in any of the important struggles taking place in the streets and workplaces of the very city in which he lived. But there can be little doubt that the convulsions swirling around him lent powerful authority to the socialist critique of American society that Mandel would soon embrace or that the mobilization of large numbers of working people under the banner of the CIO could capture the imagination of socially conscious, intellectually curious young people in a city like Cleveland. Perhaps, as his father suspected, Mandel was in touch with the local Party leadership about building a Young Communist League branch at school. He seems to have been on the margins of the Party throughout the 1950s, although those who worked alongside him later in life remember him as an undogmatic and independent socialist.

Whatever Mandel's formal relationship with the CP, it seems not to have prevented him from developing close working relationships with those outside its ranks. Sam Pollock, like Bernard the Cleveland-born son of Jewish immigrants, had played a central role in the Toledo Auto-Lite strike as leader of the Lucas County Unemployed League and was a member at that time of the American Workers' Party.[7] Later, after the formative period of CIO organizing, Pollock would serve as a state official for the Amalgamated Meat Cutters and Butcher Workmen, encouraging Mandel to contribute to the union journal and advertising his seminal biography of Samuel Gompers when it was published in 1963. From 1953 onward Pollock served as president of the Amalgamated's successor, Cleveland's United Food and Commercial Workers Local 880. Throughout the 1950s and 1960s he and Mandel worked together in United Labor of Ohio, formed initially to fight the imposition of right-to-work legislation in the state, and in Cleveland's chapter of the Congress of Racial Equality (CORE), in which Mandel played a central role. Nor was Pollock the only non-party contact with whom Mandel regularly collaborated. From the early 1960s he appears to have developed a close working relationship with the Socialist Workers' Party (SWP) in Cleveland, speaking regularly at their Militant Forum and at SWP and Young Socialist Alliance summer schools.[8]

Although his political activity through the 1930s and 1940s is difficult to reconstruct, we know that Mandel enrolled at (Case) Western Reserve University in Cleveland in the late 1930s, graduating in 1941 and enlisting in the U.S. Army within a week of the bombing of Pearl Harbor. Discharged with the rank of captain in 1946, he returned to part-time study, teaching in the Cleveland public school system while completing a master's degree, and later his doctorate, at Western Reserve.[9] For the next thirty years Mandel taught in the city's public schools, spending the majority of his tenure teaching history and social studies at segregated, all-black Rawlings Junior High School. At Rawlings, and later as a part-time instructor in labor and African American history in the night school at Fenn College, Mandel found an institution where his intellectual abilities and activist commitment were both desperately needed.[10]

Undoubtedly, it was in his role as a public school teacher and member of Cleveland Teachers' Union Local 279 that Mandel managed to most effectively draw together the various strands of his public and intellectual life, where he succeeded most completely in linking class politics and antiracist activism, and where he lived out his deep commitment to the fight for social justice. The political climate confronting Mandel upon completion of his dissertation may have rendered it difficult to land a permanent university post, but there is no evidence that his decision to spend his professional life teaching in a rundown, segregated public school system was based on anything other than a deep sense of political commitment. "Based on everything I know of him," his daughter Ann Garson speculates, he "probably chose to be 'in the trenches.'"[11]

Like many inner-city public school systems throughout the northern United States, Cleveland in the mid-twentieth century consigned African American students to dilapidated and overcrowded facilities and deprived them of the fundamental elements for a decent education. A core group of dedicated teachers, most of them black, did their best to compensate for the lack of resources but faced a daily struggle against adversity. As the black freedom movement in the South demonstrated its resolve to push ahead in the face of racist brutality it inspired African Americans in northern ghettos to press their own grievances. In Cleveland, where segregation meant that "white" schools operated at less than 50 percent of capacity while "black" schools faced severe overcrowding, a campaign initiated by black working-class parents began to take shape in the late 1950s. By the fall of 1963, "inspired by the direct action protests in the South," black Clevelanders organized the United Freedom Movement (UFM); brushed aside the conservative, middle-class leadership that had represented the city's African American community since the decline of working-class radicalism in the late 1930s; and launched a year-long, militant campaign to overturn de facto segregation. Galvanized by Cleveland's CORE chapter, parents, students, and teachers organized to confront the school board. Tensions exploded when twenty-seven-year-old Bruce Klunder, a white Methodist minister and CORE activist, was crushed to death by a bulldozer during a protest against the construction of a new school, which, black parents charged, would reinforce the isolation of their children within the bleak confines of an impoverished ghetto.

Outraged parents declared a school boycott to begin on April 20 and "called for all students in the school system, black and white, to stay away from school," the most thorough account of the campaign records. "Instead, children would attend freedom schools set up throughout the city." Launching the boycott, CORE director Ruth Turner declared, "Every child will be a freedom soldier and will learn something about himself and his struggle." "The revolution has come to town," UFM president Harold Williams announced. "[L]et's hit the streets like one mighty wave." A few of the most prominent individuals in the city's black middle class succumbed to pressure from white civic leaders and expressed opposition to CORE's strategy but recanted when activists threatened to publish their names in the African American press. Mass rallies of up to two thousand students were held in the run-up to the boycott, and on April 20 black students left the schools en masse.[12]

Mandel's role in the boycott, although little known, was substantial. His critical biography of the architect of AFL "business unionism," Samuel Gompers, had consumed him in the years since publication of *Labor, Free and Slave: Workingmen and the Anti-Slavery Movement in the United States,* and it finally appeared in print just as tensions between black parents and the Cleveland School Board were about to explode.[13] Mandel was active in CORE from its founding and through it had helped organize a series of militant rent strikes in Cleveland's "rat infested, poverty strickened [*sic*], overcrowded ghetto," an area that would go up in flames during riots in the summer of 1966.[14] He had been arrested in early January along with Ruth Turner while intervening against police harassment of a black man in the heart of the city's African American community and charged with "abusing two police officers attempting to make an arrest." Mandel's lawyer, however, protested that "the only reason he was arrested . . . was because 'he was talking to a colored woman on Hough Avenue.'"[15]

Like much of Cleveland's poor black community and many of its white allies in civil rights agitation, Mandel endured considerable harassment during this period. His daughter Ann, whose mother, Janet Hanson, was involved in CORE alongside Bernard, recalls their "house being broken into and completely torn apart" twice between 1963 and 1966. "Furniture [was] broken, closets emptied, bookcases overturned, cupboards emptied and the contents thrown around the house, every piece of glass broken, etc., and 'Nigger Lover' written on the walls in ketchup."[16]

The pressure that such incidents brought to bear on a couple with an infant in the house need hardly be spelled out, but in the end they failed to deter Mandel from playing a central role in the school boycott.[17] An active member of the Teachers' Union local, he was involved not only in organizing its membership to take part in the boycott but also in directing the alternative Freedom Schools CORE organized to replace the regular curriculum. "Within days of the boycott, more than nine hundred teachers, one hundred school locations, and a complete schedule and curriculum were organized," and Mandel was responsible for much of that success.

With a "curriculum centered on African and African-American life, history, and culture," Cleveland's Freedom Schools were attended by 92 percent of all black students in the city system. Bonnie Gordon, the daughter of well-known Cleveland labor militants, was herself prominent in civil rights and tenant rights agitation.[18] It was Mandel, she recalls, who came up with the idea that "upon 'graduation' from the Freedom School, students would be presented with a slip of paper explaining that they had missed classes because they were 'Sick. Sick of segregation.'" These letters of "excuse" would then be presented to public school teachers upon the students' return to regular classes. Gordon remembers "Bernie" as a "modest participant in all these activities." Although "serious about everything he did," she recalls, "he was friendly and listened carefully to those he worked with."[19]

In spite of its impressive organization, the Cleveland boycott ended ambiguously, without a clear victory for the black community.[20] The conditions under which black students were compelled to seek an education disgusted Mandel, however, and he continued to write and organize against inequality in the classroom. He concluded a comprehensive article on racism for the NAACP's *Crisis* magazine in 1955 with a denunciation of segregated schools. "Until their adulthood, and sometimes later, most Negroes never know any white people except those who exercise authority over them . . . or who exploit them," he wrote. "And most white children never know any Negroes except those whom they see employed as menial workers or those they see in movies (etc.) and these are generally represented as menials or clowns." He was a founding member and the first president of the Cleveland Negro History Association and an organizer of the city's Negro History Week program. Three years after the boycott Mandel published a "Young People's History of the United States" through Rawlings Press (presumably a low-budget publication produced at the junior high school where he taught), and into the early 1970s he continued to publish articles with such titles as "How English Teachers Destroy Black Children" and speak in public forums on "Black History and White Racism," "The Writing of Negro History," "Black History in the Schools," "Education in Inner-City Schools," and "Our Racist Schools."[21]

Having witnessed firsthand and over a protracted period the staggering effects of racism in Cleveland, Mandel responded with enthusiasm to the emergence of Black Power out of the crucible of civil rights agitation in the early 1960s. At the height of the Cleveland boycott movement he published "The Freedom Struggle" in the Trotskyist *International Socialist Review*. In that article he welcomed "the determination to reject white leadership" evident in the new militancy among black working-class youth. "The movement has reached a stage where the black freedom fighters insist on developing their own programs and having their own spokesmen," Mandel wrote, a turn that he considered "beneficial in many ways." But he tempered his enthusiasm with a cautionary note about the lack of clarity among those seeking to topple the "white power structure." "In the past few years this expression has come to be almost universally employed . . . as to be almost a cliché," he observed, to the point where "[t]he most conservative Negro spokesmen roll it off their tongues glibly." Ultimately, he argued, the movement must turn toward a root-and-branch confrontation with the "whole structure" of capitalism. Otherwise "the Negro revolt will peter out in a sickening acquiescence in tokenism [or] the rebellion will be drowned in blood."[22]

It was during the aftermath of the Cleveland boycott, and against the backdrop of massive social and cultural upheaval in American society at large, that Mandel underwent a process of deep personal and political transformation. He continued throughout the end of the 1960s to speak at public forums organized by the Marxist Left, developing a close working relationship with the Socialist Workers' Party, whose members he had organized alongside in CORE and which had developed a vibrant branch rooted in Cleveland's labor and civil rights movements. Although direct evidence about the character and extent of this collaboration is lacking, it seems likely that the SWP's attempt to face the new turn in African American militancy with a serious reconsideration of the catalytic power of the black revolt was compatible with the evolution of Mandel's own thinking. Certainly, he would have disassociated himself from the CP's "undisguised hostility" toward renascent black nationalism, its refusal to acknowledge the "new . . . sweep and quality" of the movement of the mid-1960s. From the early 1970s onward Mandel attempted to combine the class-based politics he had espoused since youth with a passionate embrace of black nationalism.[23]

In 1966, two years after the end of the school boycott and almost simultaneously with the outbreak of week-long rioting in Cleveland's densely packed Hough Avenue neighborhood, Mandel married Althea Warner.[24] Warner, an African American who held a doctorate in early childhood education, was at the time director of the day nursery at Karamu House, a community and performing arts center that had played a vital role in sustaining African American art and culture in Cleveland since the facility's founding in 1915.[25] Althea and Bernie would share a remarkable and intensely active life. Much of their early relationship was spent touring before they finally settled in Africa, where tragedy would intervene and compel them to return to the United States.

In an interview published in the *Cleveland Press* in 1969 under the heading "A White Man Becomes Black," Mandel declared himself a "black man," insisting that his marriage to Althea was "not an interracial marriage, because I am black too." In remarks that anticipate more recent debates about the social construction of race, he explained that "[s]cientists have told us that there is no such thing as race biologically. It is a distinction that society has created." In the context of "a growing move toward pride and identification with being black," reporter Bob Williams explained to his readership, Mandel's outlook regarding his racial identity had undergone a dramatic transformation. "[M]y concern is primarily over how a person views himself," Bernard declared. "When blackness was associated only with color or ancestry, I could not, of course, be a

Negro or an Afro-American. But today . . . blackness has become a sociological and psychological quality."[26]

For many years Mandel's social, working, and activist lives had been spent predominantly in the company of African Americans, and by 1969 he had completely cut (or lost) all ties with his parents despite living within a few miles of them. Whatever the reaction of his remaining white friends and comrades to his new orientation, the mutual friends whom he and Althea shared in the city's black community seem to have been neither shocked nor perturbed by Mandel's revelation. African American press coverage of the "bon-voyage" dinner given in their honor when the couple moved to Nairobi in 1974 noted that "everyone [who sees] Dr. and Mrs. [sic] Mandel . . . understands that they personify the slogan, 'Black is beautiful.'"[27]

Mandel's role as a public intellectual from 1969 onward reflected this dramatic shift in self-perception along with a more pronounced intellectual eclecticism and a keen enthusiasm for research related to his newfound interest in African history and culture.[28] In addition to the many articles and lectures he continued to produce exposing inequality in the classroom, Mandel published a short biography of Max S. Hayes, like him a homegrown Ohio socialist.[29] He also presented a talk to the Cleveland Socialist Summer School on "The Civil War and Reconstruction." Along with those projects, consistent with his intellectual output over many years, Mandel composed a poem, "For Sékou Touré," in tribute to the leader of the resistance to French colonial rule in Guinea and an article entitled "A Glimpse of West Africa," presumably based on his impressions during a visit there with Althea in 1971.[30] Other public talks were on "Black History and Black Power" and "African Culture." He and Althea made themselves fluent in Swahili in preparation for a move to Africa, and over the next fifteen years Mandel would make a major contribution to intellectual exchange between black America and the African continent by translating and publishing a large volume of African American literature in

Swahili. His first project, completed before the couple relocated abroad, was a translation of Alex Haley's *Roots,* but over the course of a prolific career his work would include translations of writing by W. E. B. Du Bois, Langston Hughes, and many others.[31]

There is no reason to doubt that Mandel retained his lifelong commitment to socialist politics and, throughout the latter period of his life, his faith in the potential of a multiracial working class to transform American society. His desertion of whiteness (although it is unlikely he would have called it that or loaded the term with its current connotations) in terms of his personal identity should not be read as an endorsement of the notion of "white skin privilege" then popular among sections of the New Left. In an article provocatively entitled "Race Supremacy—Curse of the Master Race," published in 1955, Mandel had written that although racism and inequality bore down hardest on African American victims, "[r]ace supremacy is . . . a curse on the 'superior' race as well as on the suppressed race." Expanding on the materialist line of reasoning that provided the foundations for *Labor, Free and Slave,* he asserted that it was "important for this fact to be understood, for people are more prone to act from self-interest than from altruism or an abstract sense of justice." The notion that white workers had a direct stake in the fight against white supremacy—powerfully expounded by the Communist Party from the 1930s onward—was one Mandel espoused forcefully and consistently throughout his life. Illustrating his point with historical examples—including the experience of non-elite whites under slavery—Mandel suggested that white working people "will have a quicker interest in the campaign for full freedom when they recognize that this is not only a campaign to elevate one-tenth of the nation, but to advance the interests of all the people of our country." In 1964, at the height of tensions surrounding the desegregation struggle in Cleveland, he published an article arguing for black and white unity, asking "Can Ten Percent Win?" One of the last public lectures he delivered—a seminar paper at the University of Nairobi in 1975—pursued the same theme under the title "Black and White Workers—Allies or Enemies?"[32]

Bernie and Althea visited Africa twice in the early 1970s, but when, after thirty years of teaching in the Cleveland public schools, Mandel retired in 1974, they relocated to Kenya "permanently," full of enthusiasm and hopeful that they could make a meaningful contribution during an important historical juncture for postcolonial Africa. Bernie found steady (voluntary) work as a teacher at a private academy and was, initially, a frequent guest lecturer in the history department at the University of Nairobi. Althea made use of her background in early childhood education as a volunteer in pre-primary schools and kindergartens and a teacher trainer in Nairobi city schools. Seven years later, looking back upon their experience in Africa, the couple emphasized that they had not "depended on the government of Kenya for our living costs" but lived off "a pension from the State of Ohio Department of Education and our savings. . . . We hope," they wrote, "that the lives of those we touched have been made richer by our contacts with them."[33]

Although the memoir of their sojourn accurately conveyed both the energetic commitment that Bernard and Althea brought to their work in Nairobi and the sense of fulfillment that they found there, it vastly understated the tragic aspect of their experience abroad. In 1975, while waiting to cross a busy street in Nairobi, Mandel was involved in a debilitating accident when a double-decker bus swerved into him and knocked him unconscious. He never fully recovered. After spending four months in a coma and undergoing brain surgery, Mandel finally regained consciousness, but much of his memory had been lost. "He had to learn everything all over again," Ann Garson recalls, "how to dress, bathe, use a fork, etc. Althea took amazing care of him but he was never quite the same." They returned together to Cleveland in 1981, where Althea looked after him with infinite love and unwavering loyalty until her own health began to fade.

The one skill that seemed not to have been taken from Bernard Mandel was his proficiency in Swahili. He compiled a Swahili-

English dictionary that is "probably the most complete of any ever published," and he would continue to translate African American literature for "five hours a day, every day" until six months before he died, on November 10, 2004. Bernard Mandel—"kind and gentle, a seeker of justice"—was eighty-four. He passed his final days within walking distance of many of those now aging veterans who fought the good fight alongside him and still remembered him as a long-time stalwart in Cleveland's working-class and antiracist movements. Their names and faces, however, he no could no longer recall.[34]

* * *

"Unquestionably," Bernard Mandel insists in the opening chapter of the study that follows, "the most persistent, thorough, and effective anti-slavery force in the nation was the slaves themselves" (23). The assertion that the four million or so African Americans held as chattel in the southern United States played the central role in their emancipation is by now a staple of Civil War historiography, but in 1955, when the author penned these words, they could still generate hostility from what remained an overwhelmingly white, male, and socially exclusive guild of professional historians.[35] A handful of brilliant, committed scholars had taken aim at the racial assumptions embedded in conventional wisdom about the causes and significance of the war, but important though their challenge was it had not yet managed to dislodge the conscience-salving interpretation constructed for the nation by the professoriate. Most serious historians had by then distanced themselves from the gratuitously offensive "scholarship" of William E. Woodward, who had written famously that "American Negroes [were] the only people in the history of the world . . . that ever became free without any effort of their own," but elements of that perspective lingered until the black freedom struggle and the broader social upheaval that it set in motion shook the academy from its stupor in the 1960s.[36]

The residual power of this mythology of Yankee deliverance combined in the mid-1950s with more general pressures for intellectual conformity emanating from the cold war to stifle dissident young scholars whose work veered too far from the prevailing consensus. Although the central arguments in his own work did not touch directly upon the questions surrounding emancipation, Mandel's focus on the labor movement and its relationship with antislavery placed *Labor, Free and Slave* clearly outside a mainstream saturated with anticommunist hysteria. Others, including Arthur M. Schlesinger Jr., the dean of cold war liberal historiography, had written favorably of prewar antislavery activity, and among labor historians the relationship between chattel and wage slavery had attracted the interest of no less prominent a figure than John R. Commons, the architect of the institutional approach driving what is now regarded as the "old" labor history.[37] Mandel's study differed significantly from these, however, in that his was an attempt to make sense of this period through the framework of historical materialism and make his findings accessible to left-wing labor militants. Although the book does not suffer from the flagrant presentism that other studies of the same period by Party-affiliated historians exhibit, Mandel was clearly drawn to the problem of labor and its relationship to abolition because he believed that it had something to say about the world in which he lived.

This kind of engaged scholarship was anathema to a profession increasingly committed to closing ranks behind the cramped vision of a just society propounded by advocates of Western free-market capitalism. Mandel owed his success in publishing *Labor, Free and Slave* to the extraordinary efforts of a group of left-wing intellectuals who committed themselves explicitly to challenging the debilitating effects of McCarthyism on "unknown artists and young writers," those upon whom "the general climate of self-censorship and repression fell hardest." The Austrian Jewish exile Gerda Lerner, instrumental in that effort, recalled the difficulties left-wing academics at the beginning of their careers faced in trying to see their work into print. "Publishers were careful to avoid printing anything that might make them subject to the charge of pro-Communism," she observed in *Fireweed: A Political Autobiography.* "Controversial topics were taboo, as were topics pertaining to working people, unions, or racial problems." Taking their lead from blacklisted artists and intellectuals who had "fought back by organizing a sort of semi-underground cultural movement," a handful of communists and fellow travelers led by Henry and Dorothy Kraus organized a cooperative publishing house, settling on the name Associated Authors.[38]

Organized and self-financed by a collective membership of six, Associated Authors was launched on an abundance of commitment but negligible financial resources. The collective planned to solicit subscriptions for a select group of titles before they went to print and try to convince a sympathetic mailing list to pay for books in advance. "If we did not get enough advance orders within a given period," Lerner recalled, "we would refund the subscription." Of the dozens of manuscripts submitted to them after the announcement of their project, *Labor, Free and Slave* was one of four accepted for publication along with Lerner's semiautobiographical *No Farewell,* advertised as "a novel of young love and family conflict in prewar Vienna," and Estolv Ward's *Piecard,* a "novel of trade union struggles in the New Deal era."[39] The fourth, a manuscript by Philip Stevenson (writing under the pseudonym Lars Lawrence), was held in the wings to see how the venture would fare.[40] The intended audience for these publications would have included left-inclined academics, but in the main Associated Authors aimed at bringing this work into the more socially diverse radical milieu that had developed from the late 1930s onward around the margins of the Communist Party and the broader Popular Front.

The rigor of the editing process at Associated Authors is difficult to determine. Angus Cameron, an accomplished former editor-in-chief at Little, Brown who had fallen victim to McCarthyism, was drafted to aid in the selection process.[41] It is not known, however, whether he—or anyone aside from the authors themselves—copyedited the manuscripts to prepare them for publication. In revising

Labor, Free and Slave Mandel relied mainly on the scrutiny and editorial advice of the faculty with whom he had worked at Western Reserve—especially the pioneering labor and immigration historian Carl Wittke, who had overseen his graduate work, and Harvey Wish, who was instrumental in laying the foundations for African American history there well before it became an established field nationally. Mandel's study was constructed around three articles he had published previously—two in the *Negro History Bulletin* and a third in *Science and Society*—and the finished work did not entirely succeed in eliminating the structural inconsistencies and overlaps that such a format often generates.[12]

Of the four manuscripts accepted, just two—Mandel's study and Lerner's *No Farewell*—found their way into print before the publishing collective was compelled to close shop. The relative success of *Labor, Free and Slave* was mainly down to Mandel himself, who sent out hundreds of promotional leaflets and followed them up with "a personal letter and often a visit." He and Lerner devoted considerable time to informal book readings in the homes of sympathetic readers, in union halls, and before branches of the American Labor Party before its collapse in 1956. Despite the financial difficulties, Gerda Lerner considered the effort to have been worthwhile. Though Associated Authors failed to establish itself as a permanent entity and was unable even to see through its modest plans for publishing the four manuscripts it had originally accepted, she was satisfied that "we had brought two books to life that otherwise would have been unborn and with it, we had saved their authors." But the accomplishment amounted to more than mere charity work for worthy academics. Labor historian David Montgomery recalls that although it "did not circulate widely," Mandel's work was "important to my generation." The print run for *Labor, Free and Slave* is impossible to establish, but presumably Mandel's study sold somewhere in the vicinity of the 2,500 copies that Lerner managed to distribute of her own work.[43]

The atmosphere into which this study was born reflected a so-

ciety at the crossroads of upheaval and change. The challenge to
segregation was gathering momentum in the mid-1950s, made
possible by the massive social transformations that the American
South had undergone in World War II and boosted by the decision of the U.S. Supreme Court in *Brown v. Board of Education*
(1954). Intellectually, the shift was most apparent in a gathering
revisionist assault on the racist, Dunningite interpretation of the
Civil War and Reconstruction. The "rectification of the racist writing of Negro history" initiated earlier in the century by Carter
G. Woodson had gathered pace by mid-century and was moving
outward from its home in the *Journal of Negro History,* where, as
Mandel put it, "a generation of young Negro and white humanist
(mostly Marxist) scholars . . . rewrote the tragic and heroic history
of black America," to find a wider academic audience. George
Brown Tindall recalls that his *South Carolina Negroes, 1877–1900*
(1952) found its way into print "at a time when the legal assault
on Jim Crow and the white primary were scoring their first major
triumphs and when the revisionist history of Reconstruction was
very much in the air and beginning to be in print." These were
exhilarating times for an activist-scholar hopeful that his intellectual labors might resonate among a generation at the crossroads
of change, and few were more enthusiastic about the potential for
a break with the past than Bernard Mandel.[44]

Early reception to *Labor, Free and Slave* reflected the contested
nature of this historiographical terrain at the commencement of
the postwar challenge to Jim Crow. Mandel's work drew several
favorable reviews, most notably in *Phylon,* the quarterly "review
of race and culture" founded by W. E. B. Du Bois in 1940, and in
the *New England Quarterly,* where William Lloyd Garrison's biographer, Walter M. Merrill, lauded Mandel's ability to "marshal all
the scholarly paraphernalia to analyze the complex forces which
involved both the abolition and the labor movements" in making
a "convincing" argument. On the whole, though, *Labor, Free and
Slave* met with marked hostility, reflecting the persistent racism

and intellectual narrow-mindedness that gripped university life in the heyday of McCarthyism.[45]

Predictably, at least one reviewer rejected the basic premise that slavery was the cause of the war, describing it instead as a mere "politician's trick" conjured up to bring the North and the West together against an aggrieved region. Herbert R. Northrup, then a corporate industrial relations consultant who had not yet begun his academic career at the Wharton School, regarded the book as "extremist in nature." "Predicated on and written in Marxist terms," he wrote, Mandel's "often questionable interpretations" were buttressed by "frequent quotations from such like-minded writers as Philip Toner [sic] and Herbert Aptheker."[46]

Columbia professor Richard B. Morris began his review more charitably, acknowledging that the author had "read thoroughly in the literature of labor and widely in contemporary newspapers" and that his "central thesis, if presented in moderate terms, would be acceptable to most historians." But he, too, argued that ultimately "Mandel's subjective approach has colored his treatment of virtually all phases of his subject," citing the author's elevation of the slaves' role as the book's most glaring transgression. "He makes the slave a central figure in the abolition movement [and] contends that 'the Negro played a decisive role in the struggle for emancipation,'" Morris objected, declaring it a "pity" that the author "did not keep to his central thesis instead of wandering off into thickets where truth and fiction are hopelessly entangled."[47]

Taking the full measure of Bernard Mandel's life as a scholar and an activist, one cannot help but speculate that he would have borne the derision of his mainstream contemporaries with equanimity and perhaps even a sense of accomplishment. The challenge that he set himself in researching and writing *Labor, Free and Slave* was to grapple intellectually with the fundamental contradiction that he, in common with so many American radicals, confronted at a practical level over a lifetime of activism: the historically rooted divergence between organized labor's fight against exploitation and the African American freedom struggle. Ironically, given the focus of objections to his study, Mandel was not primarily concerned with asserting slave self-activity. A handful of African American and left-wing historians had been doing that for almost a half century by the time his work appeared in print, and the author did little more than assimilate their most valuable insights into a study whose real focus lay elsewhere. Mandel's main concern was to examine the complicated and often fractious relationship between the antislavery campaign and the mid-nineteenth-century labor movement. At its most basic level the book was an attempt to move beyond evaluating abolitionism and northern labor solely in terms of rhetoric and instead attempt to ground a discussion of their mutual estrangement in the social relations prevailing during the period leading up to the outbreak of civil war.

One revealing measure of the ideological ground that American historiography has traversed in the half century since the book first appeared can be discerned in the fact that *Labor, Free and Slave*, criticized on publication for its exaggerated estimation of African American agency, has more recently been characterized by a leading advocate of "whiteness studies" as one of the two "classic works" of the "white-labor apologists." In *How the Irish Became White*, Noel Ignatiev holds up Mandel's study alongside German American socialist Herman Schlüter's *Lincoln, Labor and Slavery* as archetypes of a dubious attempt to "establish the antislavery record of the (white) labor movement."[48] Critical issues are at stake in the debate over the relationship between labor and abolition as well as in the more general critique of historical materialism raised by Ignatiev and others, to which I will return shortly. For now it is sufficient to register my judgment that although few works of historical scholarship can hold up to critical scrutiny, fully intact after a half century in circulation, on the whole Mandel's study has weathered the years well and may even offer something of a corrective to current trends in scholarship on the tangled relationship between race and class. The suggestion

xxx   INTRODUCTION TO THE ILLINOIS EDITION

that Mandel was engaged in apologetics is easy to disprove and a lamentable indication of the degree to which sanctimonious, less-white-than-thou moralism has displaced conscientious scholarship in some quarters.[49]

"The antislavery movement," Mandel insisted, "can be understood and evaluated only by analyzing [the 'social and economic forces that operated in nineteenth-century America'], their effect on the material conditions and ideology of the various classes, and the resulting actions of these people" (22). *Labor, Free and Slave* was, in other words, Mandel's attempt at a materialist explanation of the estrangement between northern labor and abolition. The most significant previous exploration of that relationship was to be found in Schlüter's study, published just after the turn of the century, and a number of relevant seminal articles had appeared in the *Journal of Negro History* and elsewhere, but none was based on the thorough immersion in the labor press that Mandel brought to bear, and no previous scholar had undertaken the extended, in-depth treatment that this study represents.[50]

The absence of a large body of academic scholarship on these questions did not leave the author without significant intellectual resources with which to construct an interpretation, however. Mandel was no doubt well acquainted with the considerable body of writing by Marx and Engels on the significance of the American Civil War and the implications of northern victory.[51] Neither left anything more than a few scattered comments on the specific relationship between the American labor movement and abolition, but these—particularly Marx's incisive conclusion that "[l]abor in white skin cannot emancipate itself where in the black it is branded"— illuminated the basic relationship between the struggles against chattel and wage slavery. Moreover, the general framework they developed for understanding the social upheaval unleashed by the war, based on a close and detailed familiarity with events as they unfolded between the late 1850s and the early period of Reconstruction, provided Mandel with a solid foundation upon which to build his own study. At a time when liberal historians inclined toward superficial explanations for the outbreak of sectional hostilities (lamenting, for example, the "tragic" inability of politicians to strike a compromise that would have averted war), the penetrating analysis contained in Marx's and Engels's writings made it possible to cut through the academy's trivialization of the revolutionary significance of these events. In common with the most far-sighted abolitionists, Marx expressed continual frustration with Lincoln's attempt to prosecute the war with the question of slavery pushed to the side. But neither he nor Engels ever doubted that the North would eventually be compelled to prosecute the war along revolutionary lines or that once the turn had been made, the fate of the slaveholders' rebellion would be sealed.[52]

This rich intellectual legacy bequeathed to Mandel a useful general framework for approaching his material but on its own could not furnish him with answers to the specific problems he set out to examine. One of the striking features of the scattered body of Marxist historiography on this period is the way in which interpretive revision reflected the historical evolution of the organized Left. Schlüter's early *Lincoln, Labor and Slavery* is in many ways a remarkable work, superior in places to earlier attempts by left-wing scholars and to the scholarship emanating from historians affiliated with the Communist Party during the period of the Popular Front a quarter century later.[53] Schlüter understood the Civil War in the classical Marxist sense as the completion of the bourgeois revolution in the United States—a revolution compelled to draw to its side the expectant slaves of the South and a majority of the working classes of the North but that did so only incidentally in its drive to vanquish rivals at the South and concentrate national power in the hands of the northern bourgeoisie. He was thus able to acknowledge Lincoln's important role in securing the ascendancy of free-labor capitalism over the regressive system represented by the southern slaveocracy without casting him in the role of a champion of labor, as one hyperbolic declaration from the First International had erroneously suggested and as Popular Front historians would later undertake to prove more systematically.[54]

This critical attitude to Lincoln and the bourgeois radicals manifest in Schlüter's study was a staple of Marxist historiography throughout the first third of the twentieth century, evident in publications emanating from the communist Left. In his *History of the American Working Class,* published by International Publishers in 1927, Anthony Bimba explained that he had "dwelt extensively upon the attitude of Lincoln . . . for the reason that the bourgeois historians and the trade union and socialist leaders almost worship [him] as the emancipator of the slaves. The Negro masses are made to believe that the representative of the northern bourgeoisie led them like a Moses, from the land of bondage to the land of freedom [but] if events had developed the way Lincoln desired the world would never have heard of the Emancipation Proclamation."[55]

A significant shift away from this shared historiographic perspective became discernible after the mid-1930s. By 1937 historians closely associated with the Communist Party had begun to revisit the history of the Civil War, and their attitude toward Lincoln and the wartime Republicans underwent substantial transformation in line with a fundamental revision of the Party's political orientation. Subordinating prospects for building an independent working-class political opposition in the United States to wartime defense of the USSR, the Party moved rapidly from a position of extreme hostility to Roosevelt and the New Deal toward pursuit of a Popular Front with all "progressive forces" in the country.[56]

Animated by the slogan "Communism Is Twentieth-Century Americanism," sympathetic historians set about to demonstrate that the Party was the repository of the revolutionary traditions of earlier American history, and in this exercise the distinction between bourgeois and proletarian revolutions fundamental to the Marxist understanding was blurred to the point of almost completely vanishing.[57] "The revolution during the Civil War," Herbert Morais, writing under the pseudonym Richard Enmale, explained, "was essentially the work of a broad and progressive coalition of wage-earners and farmers who after four years of bitter struggle crushed the counter-revolution and brushed aside an antiquated social order." Lincoln the reluctant bourgeois, compelled by the force of events to vanquish adversaries by revolutionary means, became in this new configuration scarcely distinguishable from the Great Emancipator who figured so prominently in mainstream accounts. Lincoln's estimation changed in one other important respect: his reputation as a "friend of the working man" was revived, in contrast to the critical earlier assessment shared by Schlüter and Bimba, among others.[58]

This bowdlerization of radical American historical writing still lingered when Mandel was beginning to formulate his thoughts on the key questions involved in his project. Although *Labor, Free and Slave* has a definite feel of Popular Front historiography about it, to his credit Mandel steered clear of the worst excesses of Party-inspired historical writing and defined himself largely in opposition to these trends. One small example of his willingness to defend an independent position was his response in 1955 to Philip Foner's excessively generous characterization of the celebrated speech that Abraham Lincoln had given during a strike by New England shoe workers at New Haven in March 1860. Mandel was prepared to "grant that Lincoln was much more liberal in his attitude toward labor than were many employers and the newspapers controlled by them," and he concurred with Foner's understanding of the Republicans as a "coalition of the classes which opposed the extension of slavery . . . the industrial capitalists, farmers and workingmen." But, he insisted, "the party was dominated by the capitalist class and was its instrument for gaining control of the federal government." Foner's "failure to give sufficient recognition to the negative aspects of the Republican party and its standard-bearer" led him, in Mandel's estimation, "to place a one-sided interpretation on Lincoln's utterances. . . . I have no desire to belittle Lincoln or his tremendous contribution to the progress of the United States

and the establishment of our democratic traditions," Mandel concluded, "but I feel it is a mistake to try to make him more than he
was."[59]

The corrosive power of Stalinist revisionism would have effects
beyond the narrow issue of Lincoln's legacy, bearing important
implications for the historiography of abolitionism. Ironically, in
light of Herbert R. Northrup's criticism that he had borrowed
heavily from Herbert Aptheker, Mandel's study in some ways
constitutes a direct challenge to that author's manifest attempt to
recast the abolitionist movement as an early embodiment of the
Popular Front and to gloss over its shortcomings regarding the
"labor question." Where Aptheker asserts that the abolitionist
press was "filled with condemnation of the frightful conditions
existing among working people both in the United States and in
Europe" and that the movement as a whole was "aware of the
close relationship between its effort and that of the working-class
movement," Mandel more accurately suggests that in their urge to
uphold "the nobility of free labor" abolitionists exhibited "almost
without exception, a blind spot for the ills that beset the working
men, except as the abolition of slavery would benefit them" (89).
This position was reminiscent of Schlüter's finding that "[t]he question of the Abolition of wage slavery [and] the demands of the labor
movement in general met with far less understanding among the
Abolitionists than the question of the abolition of chattel slavery
among the workingmen." Although alert to the effects of pervasive
racism in holding northern white workers aloof from organized
abolitionism, Mandel insisted that its inability, or unwillingness,
to combine an antislavery message with a critique of free labor
capitalism closed possibilities that might have existed for building
a more influential strand of labor abolitionism.[60]

That basic line of argument has been articulated in more nuanced
form (and with the added authority of a generation of subsequent
research) by Eric Foner in his indispensable essay "Abolitionism
and the Labor Movement."[61] Foner reiterates the distinction that

Mandel made between "the labor movement's response to abolition [and] its attitude toward slavery." Garrisonian abolitionism comes in for harsh criticism in Mandel's study, mainly for its obliviousness to the difficult conditions with which northern workers had to contend, but this study would have benefited from the measured assessment advanced by Foner, whose evenhandedness renders his critique no less penetrating. "It will not do," he cautions, "to 'defang' the abolitionist crusade: it was indeed a radical impulse, challenging fundamental aspects of American life (and none so deeply embedded as racism). But in its view of economic relations [the movement spoke] the language of northern society." It "understood slavery not as a class relationship, but as a system of arbitrary and illegitimate power exercised by one individual over another." This "liberal, individualistic definition of personal freedom" asserted by the abolitionists had a debilitating effect upon their ability to engage those on the bottom of northern society, those most affected by the negative features of the free labor vision they espoused. Such limitations "not only cut abolitionists off from the labor movement," Foner suggests, but also "prevented them from making a meaningful response to the economic condition of the Irish, despite a principled effort to overcome nativism and reach out for Irish-American support in the 1840s."[62]

For Mandel, the Garrisonian faith in moral suasion, generating a propagandist strategy predicated on the abolitionists' steady accumulation of numbers and influence as individuals became convinced of the righteousness of their position, was inadequate for winning northern workers to the struggle against slavery. This approach, underpinned by a conspicuous ambivalence over growing inequality in the "free labor" North, rendered it difficult if not impossible for mainstream abolition to win an audience among non-elite whites. And yet, Mandel contends, by the outbreak of hostilities substantial numbers of northern white workers had been won to antislavery and in some areas composed the backbone of public opposition to the Slave Power.[63]

How did this transformation occur? For many historians the key to the revolution in northern public opinion was the intensification of sectional hostility and the growing realization that slavery posed a tangible, direct threat to the freedom, status, and livelihood of white northern workers. "[E]vangelicism could not make of abolition a majority sentiment," Foner writes. Instead it was the "emergence of opposition to the expansion of slavery as the central political question of the 1840s" that transformed antislavery from a marginal force into a "truly mass movement."[64] "The aggression of the slave-power, and its impact on American life and politics," Mandel argues similarly, "cut the ground from under the position that the labor movement had maintained until 1845 and created the conditions which made possible" (133–34) an alliance between labor and abolition.

This trajectory, and the relationship between sectional polarization and northern consciousness that drove it, has been confirmed in a number of seminal studies of the period. Before the early 1850s, Bruce Levine suggests in his authoritative study of mid-nineteenth-century German immigration, "putting an end to slavery seemed to most German-Americans a matter of little personal urgency. The great majority of them settled in states in which slavery was already prohibited, and most . . . were preoccupied with matters that appeared to affect them more immediately. . . . It took the Kansas-Nebraska Act of 1854," he contends, "to transform widespread but generally passive antislavery sentiment in the north, and among German immigrants in particular, into overt, organized, and eventually partisan action." This qualitative transformation was only made possible by moving beyond moral suasion and "fusing the issues of free soil and antislavery with those of land reform and free labor in the West." Iver Bernstein argues similarly in his authoritative study of the New York City draft riots that northern labor's ambivalence about escalating tensions with the slave South, palpable as late as the early 1850s, became "difficult to sustain . . .

in 1854 as the question of slavery's status in the territories took precedence over all others." Labor's *Voice of Industry* grasped clearly in July 1848 the scale of the shift underway in northern politics and its implications for working people: "Every succeeding day only renders this question of slavery more vexing. Its ugly face peers up to view from every cranny and dog-hole into which it is attempted to hide it. . . . You cannot touch a single question of general policy in which slavery does not get some moral thrust. It cannot be avoided. Slavery must be extinguished. . . . We go for direct and internecine war with the monster."[65]

In this context the rise of "political antislavery," first in the form of the land reform movement and later in the Liberty Party, Free-Soil, and finally the Republican Party, played a central role not only in crystalizing this emerging sentiment but also in making it relevant to substantial numbers of northern workers. The Irish-born political economist John E. Cairnes observed that by 1862 "a political and social antagonism had developed" that "tended constantly to bring [abolitionists and broader antislavery forces] into closer relations" until they had "begun to act habitually together, and for practical purposes [constituted] a single party. . . . Already," he wrote, "the anti-slavery feeling is fast gaining on the mere unionist feeling, and bids fair ultimately to supersede it." Remarkably, however, as Bruce Laurie has noted, this evolution of a mass antislavery movement is typically presented as "a declension narrative, a retreat from high-minded egalitarianism to . . . opportunism" and an abandonment of the "racial idealism" that suffused abolitionism in its more pristine Garrisonian form.[66]

Questionable assertions about the "white supremacist" basis of the Liberty Party and its successors denigrate the fundamental contribution that they made to extending the social basis of the antislavery constituency. Mandel contends that under its authority "for the first time a serious and practical appeal was made for united political action by the workers and the abolitionists. 'In

asking you to assist us in vindicating the claims of the oppressed
colored man,'" the party assured disaffected northerners, "'we do
not ask you to stand neutral or non-committal, in your political
activity . . . in respect to the wrongs, greater or smaller, of any other
class of men. . . . We will hold no truce with a *Northern* Aristocracy
for the purpose of checkmating the *Southern* one'" (138–39).

Here, in contrast to the defensiveness over mounting social inequality evident in *The Liberator*, was an appeal that offered poor
and middling northern whites a meaningful basis for a united
effort to bring down the Slave Power. David Roediger's assertion that "working class abolitionism was limited because it asked
white workers to organize energetically on the Black slave's behalf"
might someday be borne out empirically, but whatever truth that
it illuminates will have to account for the fact that it was appeals
like this one—generated from outside the ranks of mainstream
abolitionism—which came closest to demonstrating that the emancipation of white northern free labor was inextricably linked to the
emancipation of black labor in the slave South. If white workers
"never viewed slavery as part of the labor question," as Ignatiev
asserts (despite his grudging admission that "some went so far as
to sign abolitionist petitions and join . . . societies as individuals"),
surely the responsibility for that failure must be a shared one.[67]

It is indisputable, of course, that Democratic Party demagogues
and secessionist propagandists who cared little about the plight of
labor in any skin went to great lengths to extend the gulf between
abolitionism and the northern working classes, a development
Mandel acknowledges here and which others, including Philip
Foner, have discussed at some length.[68] It is incontestable, too, that
some labor leaders who "pictured the lot of the slave in such glow-
ing terms that it would seem that they were pro-slavery" took
advantage of this estrangement to rationalize their unprincipled,
often racist abstention on the question of slavery. But it is also true
that there were energetic land and labor reformers whose commitment to exposing the plight of northern laborers did not blunt,

and in some ways sharpened, their denunciation of chattel slavery at the South. "[I]t was possible," Bruce Laurie writes, "for some ordinary men and women to be aware of the injustice of the mill and of the plantation—to support one another and to sympathize with the slaves."[69]

Their spirits lifted by the revolutionary upheavals unfolding across the Atlantic, the New England Workingmen's Association met in 1848 to denounce both the "despotick attitude of the *Slave Power* at the *South*" and the "domineering ascendancy of a *monied oligarchy* in the *North*," concluding with a commitment to the "destruction of all White and Black Slavery." Significantly, these attempts to make tangible the shared interests of free and slave laborers in both sections resonated among a number of individuals prominently involved in organized abolitionism, people prepared to acknowledge the shortcomings of a strategy that disdained a class appeal. "I believe that one reason why the working classes of the whole country have not come up by instinct and in masses, to the support of Freedom," Dr. William E. Channing told an audience in Boston in May 1850, "is that our Anti-Slavery friends have not gone far enough in showing that man is man everywhere. They have not carried their doctrine of equality in its application to our social usages." Similarly, Edward West expressed confidence that "if the working people of the states could be brought, by lectures delivered to them by working men, or by other means, to understand this encroachment upon their fair earnings, how few among them, especially the Irish portion, would by their votes sanction the longer continuance of slavery."[70]

The approach evident in various attempts to retrace the circuitous route by which antislavery found a mass audience among ordinary white northerners and to capture the contradictory consciousness—including ideas about race—manifested at all stages in that evolution have been eclipsed in more recent scholarship by the remarkable ascent of "whiteness" as an all-encompassing explanatory paradigm. It is unsurprising therefore that Mandel's work ends up on Ignatiev's hit list. Although emanating from individuals like Ignatiev, David Roediger, and Theodore Allen who have identified themselves formally with a revamped Marxism insofar as its practitioners share a consistent framework, whiteness scholarship exhibits an extreme philosophical idealism more in common with the moralist temperament of mid-nineteenth-century evangelicals than with Marxist materialism.[71] Strident in its espousal of the "abolition of whiteness" and the "creation of a culture of working-class non-whiteness," its approach to social transformation bears a marked resemblance to the Garrisonians', for whom, as Laurie puts it, "the reformation of the self had to precede . . . collective action in general."[72]

Starting from the conviction that historical materialism cannot adequately account for the pervasiveness of racism among white workers in the United States, whiteness scholars who have written at length on this period have produced a body of work that eschews the attempt to ground an understanding of racial antagonism in social relations generally or detail the relationship between popular consciousness and the ideological apparatus that dominant classes (and their institutions) generate at particular junctures in order to defend the status quo. "Reflecting a broad-based, ongoing shift in the historical profession from social to cultural history," Peter Kolchin explains, Roediger and others are "more comfortable discussing 'tropes' than actual social relations, and they display notable unease about coming to grips with class, interest, and power[,]" leading them to "[back] away from examining race 'within social formations' and [to] imply that it has intrinsic meaning apart from specific relations of power." This "assertion of the autonomy of race," Gregory Meyerson has written, constitutes the "distinctiveness of Roediger's position," but it is a tendency even more apparent in Ignatiev's work.[73]

The detrimental effects of this mystification of the relationship between popular culture, consciousness about race, and class power for reconstructing the past are most evident in writings about Irish immigrant workers and their ostensibly calculated embrace of whiteness in the mid-nineteenth-century urban North. In emphasizing "the agency of the [white] working class in the social construction of race," Ignatiev and Roediger systematically understate the much more impressive power of the dominant classes and their established institutions in determining the environment in which the relatively powerless maneuvered. Thus Ignatiev's seemingly generous offer to "make [the Irish immigrant working class] the actors in their own history" in reality amounts to obscuring the much greater agency of institutions like the Democratic Party and the Catholic hierarchy (not to mention urban employers with commercial ties to the slave South) in shaping immigrant attitudes toward slaves and free blacks. Gregory Meyerson notes the peculiar way in which Roediger frames the role of these powerful institutions. At most the Church can be charged with "not questioning the whiteness of the Irish"—"reflect[ing] the racial attitudes of its members" or "reproduc[ing] existing white supremacist attitudes without challenging them." Framing the relationship between powerful institutions like the Church and its flock this way, Meyerson suggests, "biases the argument about the construction of whiteness in favor of the Irish proletariat themselves, as if the Irish proletariat first asserted this whiteness and this was not questioned."[74]

Some scholars have emphasized that the close proximity of Irish and African Americans in some northern urban neighborhoods provided a basis for "polyvalent" relations marked by both conflict and cooperation.[75] Contemporary sources are unanimous, however, as are modern-day historians, that racial hostility toward blacks was more visibly manifest among the Irish immigrant poor than among any other segment of northern society. Their prominence in the horrific New York draft riots, with such obvious racial overtones, illustrates the depths that hostility could plumb in moments of serious strain. What is at issue among those trying to interpret this phenomenon is not whether such antagonism existed but how to explain why that was the case. For some, their oppression under

British rule in Ireland ("a country in which," Ignatiev writes, "Irish Catholics formed an oppressed race") would seem to have made the Irish natural allies of the slaves.[76] For others, their poverty and exploitation on arrival in the United States might have better disposed them toward proletarian solidarity with black chattels in the South. I will discuss the validity of these assumptions later, but here it is only necessary to point out that Roediger and Ignatiev have advanced significantly different explanations for the pervasiveness of this sentiment than many other historians—explanations in which their interpretive predispositions figure prominently.

Although Mandel addresses this problem only briefly in the study that follows, he sets out an argument that contrasts markedly with those advanced by Roediger and Ignatiev. Ignatiev in particular is oblivious in *How the Irish Became White* to the class limitations of organized abolitionism identified in the range of scholarship I have discussed earlier. In his enthusiasm for Daniel O'Connell's intervention on behalf of the Garrisonians (consummated in 1845, before the main influx of famine refugees had begun), Ignatiev seems to suggest that an ethnic appeal devoid of any meaningful attempt to redress the social and economic inequalities facing the immigrant poor should have been sufficient to win them over to antislavery. Its failure meant, for him, that the "Irish faded from Green to white, bleached by . . . something in the 'atmosphere' of America."[77]

Mandel proceeds from a different basis. He begins by remarking upon the relative *failure* of the Democratic campaign to influence northern labor.[78] Yet he acknowledges that Copperhead propaganda "undoubtedly did influence many of the unskilled and unorganized workers, whose economic conditions were the worst, who did not have the guidance of the most advanced working class leaders and the labor press, and who were still attached in large numbers to the Democratic party." It was, in fact, "to this group [that the] . . . Negrophobes directed their propaganda, and they used with greatest force the old tactic of frightening the workers with exaggerated predictions of the free Negroes flooding the Northern labor market" (184). In such a situation it was the Irish poor, seemingly trapped at the bottom of northern society, who "felt the competition of free Negro labor more acutely than any other group and were more sensitive to [such] propaganda." They were "even more susceptible to this propaganda," Mandel writes, "because of the sources from which it emanated: the Democratic party and the Catholic Church" (68). The draft riots, he concludes, were a "blind revolt against class legislation, against strike-breaking, against intolerable economic conditions, against the orgy of profiteering and speculation at the expense of the workers and soldiers . . . nourished on the white supremacy propaganda of politicians . . . and the divisive policies of employers . . . [and] stimulated by treasonous agents of the slave power" (191).[79]

Anxious to distance themselves from what they regard as a crude economist explanation for racial hostility, Ignatiev, Roediger, and Allen are at pains to discount the significance of black competition with Irish immigrant labor as a factor in fostering racial antagonism, particularly as a precipitating factor in the New York riots. The massive influx of incoming Irish had only a short time earlier displaced smaller numbers of black workers in certain sectors of employment, they point out. In some cities the Irish faced more serious competition from Germans and other Irish immigrant workers than from African Americans, they argue—again with some validity. But the overall argument that labor competition played a negligible role in solidifying racial antipathy can be sustained only if one substitutes a crass, economic determinist caricature for the more nuanced argument that earlier historians have deployed in highlighting the effects of this rivalry. The problem is compounded by omitting from serious consideration those exerting the most influence in shaping immigrant attitudes toward African Americans in the late antebellum period and during the war itself: employers, the Democratic Party, and the Catholic hierarchy.

In his essay "Irish-American Workers and White Racial Formation" Roediger acknowledges that "Irish workers . . . fought to keep away Blacks as job competitors and as strikebreakers," but he argues that to proceed from this "to the proposition that Irish racism was really a cover for job competition is an economic determinist misstep that cuts off important parts of the past." Similarly, in noting elsewhere the incidence of wartime race riots fueled by "white workers' fears of job competition even in cities where [an exodus of freedpeople] was highly unlikely," Roediger cautions that "it would be a mistake to focus exclusively on job competition and to ignore the wider uses of declaring oneself a white worker. . . . Even if we allow" that there existed among northern white workers genuine fears about "competition with nearly four million freedpeople," he writes, these were "consistently alloyed with other fears, ranging from political equality to sexual amalgamation and even to the peculiar terror that white women would begin to 'friz' their hair, '*a la d'Afrique*.'" Equally determined to exclude economic competition as an element in racial antagonism, Theodore Allen asserts that "'fear of Negro job competition,' so much favored as an explanation of the concentration of Irish-American workers' hostility on the African-American minority of their non-Irish competitors . . . had no basis in actual fact . . . nor did the existence of such fears qualify a 'white' pogrom against Negro men, women and children in July 1863 as a 'working-class movement.'"[80]

There are a number of points worth taking up in these passages, but the logical place to begin is to ask where in the historiography the facile economic determinist assertion that "Irish racism was really a cover for job competition" appears. Who is it that focuses "exclusively" on job competition? Which of the prominent historians who have written on this period assert the significance of competition to "qualify" the draft riots or describes them simply as a "working-class movement"?[81]

It was Albon Man Jr. who, in a 1951 article, asserted most explicitly the centrality of labor competition between blacks and whites as a factor in wartime racial antagonism, but the argument he advanced at even that early date bears no resemblance to the caricature held up by scholars associated with whiteness studies. Introducing his thesis with a fairly detailed discussion of the displacement of African Americans in menial labor by incoming Irish who "offer[ed] to work for any wages they could obtain . . . reduc[ing] the Negro's earnings drastically and depriv[ing] many of employment," Man places the onus for stoking fears of black competition squarely on the Democratic press, which by and large eludes responsibility in more recent accounts.[82] He goes further, highlighting a point almost completely absent from whiteness literature: "How did Republicans and Abolitionists deal with these predictions of their opponents? In 1860 and 1861 they failed to answer them at all. In 1862, however, they began to grasp the fact that the labor competition argument was making a deep impression upon working people of New York, particularly the Irish, and that it could no longer be allowed to go unchallenged. . . . Greeley . . . declared that it was the most common argument advanced against the abolition of slavery."[83]

Summarizing his thesis, Man writes that "Democratic leaders and newspapers . . . constantly harped upon the note that if the slaves were freed, they would flock north and take away the jobs of Irish laborers. The election campaigns of 1860, 1861, and 1862 and Lincoln's emancipation program were the occasions for their heaviest barrages of propaganda," which "Republicans and abolitionists were slow to answer." In early 1863, "the longshoremen of New York went on strike after strike for increased pay, only to see their places filled by colored men working for less money under police protection. . . . white labor on the waterfront was obsessed with the fear of competition from Negroes which needed only the commencement of the draft to be transformed into *wholesale murder.*" That hardly qualifies as an attempt to justify or evade the racial aspect to the New York riots. Elsewhere, Man writes that "in addition to the fear of black labor competition, an important influence upon the draft rioters was the position of the Catholic clergy and press," with the Church especially being "the one institution of preeminence that they had known in the old country."[84]

Surely the question of why it was that deep anxiety and anger over the inequitable conduct of the war on the northern homefront could so easily become directed at vulnerable African Americans is a problem demanding close examination, and Roediger is completely justified in insisting that sustained attention to the racial consciousness enabling such an evolution is essential. But that should not prevent historians from being able to weigh the relative importance of profound socioeconomic tensions, the power and motives of dominant institutions, and "terror" over white women's preference in hairstyles. To take just one example, Iver Bernstein manages to integrate a fairly comprehensive discussion of racial paranoia and sexual anxiety among whites and their role in shaping the draft riots into a thesis that rests on a full account of the complex political and economic backdrop against which the upheaval occurred. It is the systematic attempt to detach popular consciousness from its moorings in social relations and its reflection in class conflict and formal politics—not the attempt to interrogate consciousness itself—that limits the explanatory power of cultural studies constructed around "whiteness."[85]

How can one hope to explain these tensions if the most influential elements in northern society are set aside as central actors in their perpetuation? In common with others who wrote on the question, Mandel acknowledged that anxiety over the impending influx of freed slaves to compete with northern white workers emanated mainly from the Democratic press and that its dimensions were exaggerated for demagogic purposes, but he insisted that the threat of competition was a real one and not mere fantasy. "Although the Democrats magnified and embroidered the problem," he writes, "a problem did exist—not in emancipation, but in the anti-labor and anti-Negro policies of employers who could be counted on to create divisions and to employ Negroes in order to depress the wage standards of both white and Negro workers" (186–87). Sumner Eliot Matison argues along similar lines in relation to debates that arose in the ranks of northern labor during

Reconstruction. The "question of the relationship of Negro and white, of competition or cooperation, was not merely a theoretical one," he insists. "The danger to the organized labor movement from the actual and potential use of Negroes as strike-breakers was pointed up by bitter experience."[86] As Matison carefully points out, strikebreaking had cut both ways in the antebellum period. Moreover, not only have black workers exercised no monopoly on strikebreaking in the century and a half since, but also, in some situations as late as the 1960s, white workers have enthusiastically offered themselves as strikebreakers to obstruct black advance. It is quite clear, however, that during the Civil War northern employers began to deploy black strikebreakers systematically in order to break strikes by whites, a development that would evolve toward a coherent strategy in later decades.

Scholars of whiteness, by investing white workers with extraordinary agency in the "creation" of white supremacy and consistently understating the determinative capability of the dominant classes, ascribe conscious deliberation to a process marked by contradiction and largely directed by forces outside the control of ordinary whites. Roediger's disappointment that new scholarship has not produced "many class-specific studies of racism" is likely to grow deeper unless scholars are able to make a convincing argument that "working-class racism" arises or develops in hermetic isolation from the general discourse about race that dominates society at any given moment.[87] This is a discourse overwhelmingly shaped, then and now, by political and economic elites with infinitely greater resources at their disposal than working-class people. Kevin Kenny, in his revisionist survey of the Irish experience in the United States, identifies a number of flawed assumptions embedded in Ignatiev's work in particular but points to one critical defect in the voluntarist assumptions animating whiteness scholarship more generally. "[T]o argue," he suggests, "that the Irish 'opted for' or 'chose' whiteness, deliberately distancing themselves from African Americans in order to advance themselves socially, seems unnecessarily abstract and

tends also to overestimate the degree of conscious agency involved
in the process." Kenny makes clear his aim is

> not to downplay the extent of Irish-American racism in the nineteenth cen-
> tury, which was undeniably considerable, but simply to call for a better histori-
> cal explanation of that racism—one that shifts at least part of the focus away
> from individual agency and toward the wider social and cultural structure in
> which both Irish immigrants and African Americans operated. . . .Irishmen
> who drove black workers from the docks . . . knew what they were doing,
> and they doubtless advanced their assimilation by doing so. But the American
> Irish did not create the social and racial hierarchy into which they came, and
> to expect them to have overturned this hierarchy in the course of putting food
> on their tables is surely unrealistic.[88]

Although Mandel's *Labor, Free and Slave* was not intended primarily as a sustained examination of the pervasiveness of racism
among white workers in the Age of Emancipation, together with
a number of articles written by his contemporaries and some of the
more recent literature discussed earlier it does offer elements of
a basic framework for grasping the roots of the problem without
succumbing to the tautological allure of whiteness. Irrefutably,
the defects in certain of the arguments Mandel advances in this
study, now in print for more than a half century, have been exposed
by more recent scholarship carried out this side of the defeat of
Jim Crow. On the whole, however, what is most striking about
Mandel's work is the degree to which its basic elements have been
confirmed in the most penetrating recent work in the social history
of the mid-nineteenth-century United States.

As any serious engagement with it will confirm, the book is
emphatically not a work of apologetics. The author's insistence
on grounding his study of northern labor during the Civil War in
prevailing social and economic conditions does not restrain him in
the least from placing a substantial onus for difficulties in building
black and white unity on the wretched, debilitating traditions that
a "spurious pride of caste" encouraged among white workers. The
existence of slavery was "the most decisive factor" in ensuring that

"the revolutionary working-class movement of 1848 in Europe had no counterpart in the United States" (21–22). Divisions in the antebellum working class were the result, Mandel insists, "not only of the prejudices of employers but of the [white] workers also, who found themselves pitted against the Negro workers and taught that their own prosperity depended on the adversity of others. . . . By failing to unite with the Negroes in a common struggle to improve their conditions, they were forced into a mad strife for jobs, [and] in this brutish contest, the weapons of the brute were employed" (66). It was a "rare labor leader," he wrote, "who had the insight to comprehend that the labor movement could not achieve a really independent position until the field had first been cleared by the final overthrow of the slave system" (82).

Schlüter had written that at the war's end "no labor movement was to be thought of in the land of the emancipated slaves."[89] In contrast, Mandel (clearly benefiting from the work of Du Bois and others) argued that "[e]ven more for the Negro workers . . . emancipation inaugurated a new stage in their fight for freedom. [Being the] most exploited of laborers [they] began to organize trade unions and to strike for higher wages. In 1867 a wave of strikes, particularly among Negro longshoremen, swept over the South [and the] agrarian laborers . . . the bulk of the freedmen, began to organize" (206, 207). Finally, in his assessment of National Labor Union's emergence immediately following the war, Mandel writes that while it "represented a step forward," the new movement "also reflected the persistence of prejudice against the Negroes, the desire to protect white labor against their competition, and the refusal to accept them as equals in the labor movement" (215, 216).

Published on the cusp of an emerging public challenge to Jim Crow and ten years before the power of the social movements of the 1960s began to compel a fundamental reassessment of the American past, Mandel's *Labor, Free and Slave* reflects the intellectual and political horizons of the world in which it was constructed, limitations that left their stamp on the left-wing milieu to which its author belonged. In the text, Mandel continually touches upon the tension between the material circumstances that would seem to propel white workers, north and south, toward antislavery and the enduring ideological power of white supremacy, which pointed them elsewhere. Although in places he advances incisive explanations for the persistence of racism among working-class whites, these take the form of cursory summaries rather than extended analytical treatments. In short, Mandel never offers the kind of sustained examination of these tensions to which, whatever their shortcomings, leading whiteness scholars have in recent years directed our attention. The question that historians of the American working class should bear in mind while reading the text that follows is whether, in his general approach to the problem of racial antagonism, Mandel offers elements of a corrective to the antimaterialist framework so fashionable at present.

Whatever its limitations from the vantage point of the early twenty-first century, *Labor, Free and Slave* demonstrates the extraordinary prescience of a generation of paid and unpaid scholars influenced by Marxist materialism in anticipating the most compelling problems driving scholarship in the post–civil rights era. "[M]ore than is acknowledged," Christopher Phelps has written in relation to another important contribution from this milieu, the "Old Left . . . pioneered what the new Left would call 'history from below.'"[90] Although it can certainly be improved upon, and although details of the interpretation advanced in the pages that follow have been superseded or disproved in the half century since this modest book first saw the light of day, it is difficult to conceive how any attempt to grapple with the complex issues thrown up by this critical period in American working-class history can fail to benefit from its enduring insights.

Acknowledgments

Labor, Free and Slave was one of a handful of studies in American history written by radical and Marxist historians that made it possible to keep my bearings in graduate school, and I am grateful that Laurie Matheson and the University of Illinois Press saw the merit in bringing it back to life. I began research for this project while a fellow at the National Humanities Center in North Carolina, and it benefited from the immense generosity of my colleagues there and from the legendary expertise of its library staff. Betsy Dain, Jean Houston, and Eliza Robertson helped me gather much of the biographical material on Mandel, and this project would have gathered dust on the shelves without their encouragement and commitment.

Despite their efforts, I was unable to locate Bernard until several months after I'd returned to Belfast, when his obituary appeared in the Cleveland *Plain Dealer*. I regret very much that I was unable to speak with Mandel before he died, but that disappointment was relieved by his daughters, Ann Garson and Anita Austin, who reminded me that he was much more than a mere historian. David Montgomery was an early and avid supporter of this project, and no one who has worked with him will be surprised to know that much of what I was able to discover about Cleveland's labor Left came from advice offered by him. He introduced me to Jean Tussey and, indirectly, to her daughter, Bonnie Gordon, both of whom shared memories of Mandel with me. Nishani Frazier, who is engaged in a project on Cleveland CORE, corresponded with me over the course of a year and a half about the school boycott movement and put me in touch with Ruth (Turner) Perot. A long list of historians, including Bruce Laurie, Paul Buhle, David Gleeson, Mike Goldfield, Kevin Kenny, David Brundage, Gerda Lerner, Bruce Levine, and Mark Lause, offered useful critical advice on the research and historiography.

My son Oisín came into the world in time to bring the project to a slow crawl in its final stages. I am grateful for his daily reminders that there is much more to life than work, even when one is fortunate enough to love what one is engaged in. This small labor is dedicated to him and to his mother and my great love, Jennifer.

Notes

1. *Fifteenth Census of the United States: 1930* (Cleveland Heights, Ohio District 580), sheet 24–A, lines 43–46. The Mandels' house servant, a twenty-year-old female Austrian immigrant, is listed on sheet 12–A, line 45.
2. Ann Garson recalls that "Dad retold this story a lot and always with a smile on his face." Rabbi Abba Hillel Silver's expression of solidarity notwithstanding, Mandel rejected religion at a young age for atheism—a development that did not prevent him from teaching Jewish history at synagogue later in life. His break from Judaism was likely one factor that lead to his breaking relations with his parents, although his daughter Anita recalls that Mandel's decision around 1960 to move to an integrated neighborhood in Cleveland "met with disdain [in the] extended family." "A White Man Becomes Black," *Cleveland Press,* Feb. 14, 1969; Anita Austin to Author, Jan. 3, 2005.
3. Art Preis, *Labor's Giant Step—the First Twenty Years of the CIO: 1936–55* (repr. New York: Pathfinder Press, 1994), 23. Preis reports that veterans of the Toledo confrontation involved in a strike at the Pressed Steel Company in Defiance, Ohio, a year later discovered that "eight percent of the strikers had been National Guardsmen serving in uniform during the Auto-Lite strike."
4. Preis, *Labor's Giant Step,* 53; Edward Levinson, *Labor on the March* (repr. Ithaca: ILR Press, 1995), 141. On the relationship between rank-and-file organization and the Cleveland CIO see Wyndham Mortimer, *Organize! My Life as a Union Man* (Boston: Beacon Press, 1971), 55, 78–79, 99.
5. Mortimer, *Organize!* 98; Robert H. Zieger, *The CIO, 1935–1955* (Chapel Hill: University of North Carolina Press, 1995), 51; Theodore Draper, *American Communism and Soviet Russia* (New York: Vintage Books, 1986), 54. On Hayes see Mortimer, *Organize!* 257–58. Observations on Trotskyist and IWW influence in Cleveland labor from are from my conversations with veteran SWP leader Jean Tussey and are in David Montgomery to Author, April 22, 2005. On Mortimer, see Preis, *Labor's Giant Step,* 52. The Krauses discuss their role in Neil O. Leighton and William J. Meyer, "Interview with Henry and Dorothy Kraus," Paris, May 5, 1982, University of Michigan-Flint Labor History Project, Genesee Historical Collections Center, Frances Wilson Thompson Library, http://lib.umflint.edu/archives/kraus. html. Henry Kraus offers an endearing portrait of Travis in *The Many*

and the Few: A Chronicle of the Auto Workers (Urbana: University of Illinois Press, 1985), 31–32.

6. Phillips uncovers a vibrant black working-class politics that predated, but sometimes merged with, Party-led agitation. In relation to industrial unionism, she finds, black workers organized in the Future Outlook League were compelled to challenge both the anti-union orientation propounded by the city's black middle class and the indifference and exclusionary disposition of organized labor. Nishani Frazier, whose dissertation on Cleveland's CORE is forthcoming from Columbia University, considers it likely that FOL activity fed directly and indirectly into early CORE activism in Cleveland. Nishani Frazier to Author, Oct. 10, 2005. Quotations are from Mortimer, *Organize!* 53, 52; Kimberley L. Phillips, *AlabamaNorth: African-American Migrants, Community, and Working-Class Activism in Cleveland, 1915–1945* (Urbana: University of Illinois Press, 1999), 200, 201, 202.

7. Preis acknowledges Pollock's significant role in the Toledo events and in *Labor's Giant Step* (21–22) reproduces his letter defying an injunction against mass picketing.

8. Ann Garson to Author, Dec. 30, 2004; Bernard Mandel, curriculum vitae courtesy of Ann Garson, copy in author's possession.

9. Mandel's M.A. thesis was entitled "Religion and the Public Schools of Ohio." His Ph.D., completed under the supervision of Carl Wittke, was entitled "Labor and the Anti-Slavery Movement."

10. Fenn College was reorganized as Cleveland State University after 1964. "With several prestigious private colleges, including Case Institute of Technology and Western Reserve University nearby," a history of the college explains, "Fenn . . . focused on students for whom college otherwise would be financially unattainable by offering a low-cost quality education." "A Brief History of Cleveland State University" at http://www.clevelandmemory.org/csu/.

11. Ann Garson to Author, Jan. 19, 2005.

12. I owe my understanding of the 1963–64 campaign mainly to Leonard Nathaniel Moore's comprehensive account in "The School Desegregation Crisis of Cleveland, Ohio, 1963–1964: The Catalyst for Black Political Power in a Northern City," *Journal of Urban History* 28 (Jan. 2002): 135–57; the quotations in this and the preceding paragraph from are 136–37, 137, 151, 152–53, 142, and 153. On CORE in Cleveland see also "Affirming Action: Barbara Reskin's Work Is Informed by Activist Background," *Harvard University Gazette,* May

21, 1998. I am grateful also to Nishani Frazier and CORE veterans Bonnie Gordon, Jean Tussey, and Ruth (Turner) Perot for sharing their knowledge of the events.

13. Described by one reviewer as an "almost steady biographical warfare" against Gompers, Mandel's monumental study devoted considerable attention to relations between black workers and the AFL, castigating Gompers for "his advocacy of exclusion of Chinese and Japanese immigrants" and for "[making] peace with segregation and anti-Negro discrimination." In an interview with the *Cleveland Plain Dealer,* Mandel claimed that the book involved six years of research, during which he had read nearly a million letters in his subject's correspondence. A reviewer in the same newspaper described the study as "perhaps the best work on Gompers that we shall ever read through twentieth century eyes." Bernard's daughter Anita recalls having spent three consecutive summers in Washington, D.C., while her father was engaged in research at the Library of Congress. *Samuel Gompers: A Biography* was advertised in the *Butcher Workman* at a "pre-publication rate [of] five dollars per copy." The *Summit County Labor News* credited Mandel with explaining how Gompers' "views on race helped pave the way for today's pickets on the construction sites." Howard H. Quint, *American Historical Reviews* 72 (April 1967): 1111–12; Herbert Shapiro, *Journal of Negro History* 50 (Oct. 1965): 283–85; "Researcher Casts Fresh Light on Gompers," *Cleveland Plain Dealer,* Oct. 10, 1957; Todd Simon, "Cleveland Teacher Pens Gompers Life," *Cleveland Plain Dealer,* Sept. 2, 1964; Anita Austin to Author, Jan. 3, 2005; "Life of Gompers," in *Butcher Workman,* n.d., and *Summit County Labor News,* ca. 1964, in box 9, folder 12, Sam Pollock Collection, MS-468, Center for Archival Collections, Bowling Green State University.

14. Walter Johnson's vivid eyewitness account of the 1966 riots includes a powerful description of the horrific social conditions under which black Clevelanders lived and the aggressive racism pervading the city and its police force in the mid-1960s. "The Night They Burned Old Hough" at http://www.nhlink.net/ClevelandNeighborhoods/hough/Eyewitness2.htm.

15. "Teacher's Case Goes to Jury," *Cleveland Press,* May 4, 1964.

16. Ann Garson to Author, Dec. 30, 2004.

17. Garson, the daughter of Bernard Mandel and Janet Hanson (who never married), was born in 1963. Mandel also had two daughters from his first marriage, Anita and Carla, who lived with their mother, Emily.

18. Gordon's mother, Jean Tussey, was a Cleveland-based trade unionist and an SWP activist of national standing, the editor of an important collection of Eugene Debs's speeches, and founder of the Cleveland Labor History Society. Her father, Richard (Dick) Tussey, was a central figure in Metal and Machine Workers Industrial Union No. 440, the last IWW local in Cleveland. After its collapse in the late 1950s Tussey joined the staff of the Amalgamated Meat Cutters and Butcher Workmen (later the United Food and Commercial Workers).
19. Bonnie Gordon to Author, Sept. 2, 2004.
20. Moore, "School Desegregation Crisis of Cleveland," 135.
21. Bernard Mandel, "Race Supremacy—Curse of the Master Race," *The Crisis* 62 (June–July 1955): 343–50, 381; Mandel curriculum vitae.
22. Bernard Mandel, "The Freedom Struggle: Revolt to Revolution," *International Socialist Review* 25 (Spring 1964): 44, 63.
23. On the CP and black nationalism, see Robert Vernon, "Race and Radicalism: Review of Wilson Record's *Race and Radicalism: The NAACP and the Communist Party in Conflict*," *International Socialist Review* 25 (Fall 1964): 122–24.
24. Walter Johnson recounts the beginning of the riots as follows:

On July 18, 1966, at dusk of a steamy hot Monday, someone posted a sign outside the 79'ers bar, situated on the southeast corner of E.79th Street and Hough Avenue. The sign read, "No Water For Niggers." To make matters more difficult, the bar manager and a hired hand, who both happened to be white, patrolled the front of the bar, with shotguns, to show that they meant business. Hough's population was almost ninety thousand, over seventy-eight thousand of whom were African-American, all living in an area that stretches from E. 55th to E. 105th Streets. . . . A crowd of over three hundred people gathered at the crossroads in a matter of minutes.

The Cleveland Police Department arrived, in force, to diffuse the situation. However, [its] presence . . . only intensified the crowd's anger. Rocks and bottles began to take flight, someone fired a shot or lit a firecracker and police responded by firing volleys overhead to disperse the crowd. This tactic backfired setting off a wave of firebombings and arsons. . . .

When firefighters arrived to put out the flames, snipers disrupted firefighter and police activities. Sporadic sniper fire . . . caused delays and even pullouts for safety's sake. This caused massive fire damage and heavy losses. The action also brought aggressive police response. Homes and apartments were busted into with Gestapo-style search and seizure tactics. On the streets, police shot out the street lights for cover and began returning fire to suspected sniper positions. Joyce Arnett, a twenty-six-year-old mother of three, was shot dead, when calling out a window, trying to get permission to go home and check on her children. Johnson, "Old Hough" at http://www.nhlink.net/ClevelandNeighborhoods/hough/Eyewitness2.htm.

25. Founded by Presbyterians as the "Playhouse Settlement" in 1915, Karamu was intended to "[promote] interracial activities and cooperation through the performing arts" and assist the city's "growing African-American population . . . in their transition from rural Southern life to an urban setting." It was renamed Karamu House in 1941 and hosted work by a number of notable artists and playwrights, including Langston Hughes, whose career was launched there. Karamu House Records, 1914–1980, Western Reserve Historical Society. Karamu represented "an important exception to [segregationist] trends" in Cleveland settlement work, "struggling to fend for itself [while] it remained independent from the strong arm of the [Welfare Federation of Cleveland]" (Phillips, *AlabamaNorth,* 158).

26. "A White Man Becomes Black." Mandel acknowledged that "[h]is marriage contributed to transforming his identity by making it more personal and complete."

27. Roland Forte on "Bon Voyage Dinner Party," untitled clipping, ca. 1974, courtesy of Ann Garson, copy in author's possession.

28. This eclecticism wasn't completely new for Mandel. Both he and Sam Pollock were passionate Cleveland Indians fans, and in addition to being an avid statistician Mandel tried his hand at sports writing on several occasions. He reviewed the blacklisted writer Bucklin "Buckie" Moon's "Champs and Bums" in *Sports Review* 19 (May 1959): 165, and wrote two articles ("What Price Home Runs?" and "Percentage Baseball") for the *Cleveland Plain Dealer* in 1960 and 1961.

29. Hayes, the "most visible spokesperson for the Socialist Party in the AFL," tried several times to unseat Gompers as head of that body. He was founder and editor of the labor-affiliated *Cleveland Citizen* and in 1920 was the vice-presidential candidate on the Farmer-Labor Party's ticket. I am grateful to David Montgomery for information on Hayes's background. See also Mortimer, *Organize!* 98, 255–56.

30. In 1958 Ahmad Sékou Touré was the only West African leader to reject French president Charles DeGaulle's offer of autonomy within

a French-African commonwealth in favor of independence, declaring that Guinea preferred "freedom in poverty to liberty in chains." Portugal led a failed invasion of the country in December 1970, and Mandel's eulogy may have been written in response to several reported attempts on Touré's life by Portuguese agents in 1969 and 1970. Mandel, "For Sékou Touré," *Vibration 2* (July–Aug. 1970).

31. Mandel curriculum vitae.
32. Mandel, "Race Supremacy," 343 (quotation)–50, 381; Mandel curriculum vitae.
33. "Statement of Dr. Bernard Mandel and Mrs. H. Althea Mandel," 1981, copy in author's possession.
34. Ann Garson to Author, Dec. 30, 2004.
35. It is "important . . . to recall," Eric Foner and Manning Marable write in the introduction to a collection of Herbert Aptheker's writings, "that ideas central to Aptheker's scholarship . . . were radical and widely dismissed by established historians when he first advanced them." Herbert Aptheker, *The Aptheker Reader,* edited by Eric Foner and Manning Marable (Urbana: University of Illinois Press, 2005), 9.
36. William E. Woodward, *Meet General Grant* (New York: H. Liveright, 1928), 372.
37. Arthur M. Schlesinger Jr., *The Age of Jackson* (Boston: Little, Brown, 1945); John R. Commons, *Races and Immigrants in America* (New York: Macmillan, 1907).
38. Gerda Lerner, *Fireweed: A Political Autobiography* (Philadelphia: Temple University Press, 2002), 342.
39. Lerner, *Fireweed,* 344. Ward had been a reporter for the *Oakland Tribune* when the San Francisco General Strike broke out in July 1934. He was the author of biographies of Harry Bridges and Tom Mooney.
40. Stevenson was a blacklisted screenwriter whose first novel, *Morning, Noon and Night* (later reissued in Berlin under the title *Storm Out of New Mexico*), told of the efforts of a group of blacklisted Mexican American miners to organize in the face of company-sponsored vigilante violence. The manuscript adopted by Associated Authors (but presumably published elsewhere after the collapse of the venture) was probably one of the subsequent volumes in his trilogy, *The Seed. Morning, Noon and Night* (pt. 1, vol. 1) was published by Putnams' in 1954, as was *Out of the Dust* (pt. 1, vol. 2) in 1956. International Publishers brought out *Old Father Antic* (pt. 2, vol. 1) and *The Hoax*

(pt. 2, vol. 2) in 1961, one of which was probably the manuscript that Associated Authors had accepted. "New Mexico Fiction," Santa Fe Public Library at http://www.santafelibrary.org/nmfict3.html. Michael Denning writes that Stevenson (Lawrence) had been "part of the Taos circle of radical artists and writers in the early 1930s" and was responsible for bringing out the *California Quarterly*. Denning, *The Cultural Front: The Laboring of American Culture in the Twentieth Century* (London: Verso Press, 1998), 225.

41. In 1947 Cameron decided to resign when the publisher demanded that he clear outside political activities in advance after Arthur Schlesinger accused him of being "a supporter of several organizations close to the American Communist Party." Schlesinger continues, "Soon afterwards the right-wing magazine *Counterattack* claimed that thirty-one of Cameron's authors were 'fellow-travellers.'" "Angus Cameron" at http://www.spartacus.schoolnet.co.uk/USAcameronA.htm. His biographer Jonathan Coleman told *The Nation* that Cameron was "sympathetic to Communist Party values but not party discipline and was a strong anti-Stalinist." "Literary Hero," *The Nation,* Dec. 30, 2002 (Cameron's obituary).

42. Bernard Mandel, "Slavery and the Southern Workers," *Negro History Bulletin* 16 (Dec. 1953); Bernard Mandel, "Anti-Slavery and the Southern Workers," *Negro History Bulletin* 17 (Feb. 1954): 99–105; Bernard Mandel, "Calhoun, Lincoln and Labor," *Science and Society* 18 (Summer 1954): 239.

43. Lerner, *Fireweed,* 345; Montgomery comments in Laurie Matheson to Author, Feb. 26, 2004.

44. Mandel, "The Freedom Struggle," 43; George Brown Tindall, *South Carolina Negroes, 1877–1900* (repr. Columbia: University of South Carolina Press, 2003), xiii. On the wartime transformation of the South, see Numan V. Bartley, *The New South, 1945–1980: The Story of the South's Modernization* (Baton Rouge: Louisiana State University Press, 1995), 1–38.

45. Edward B. Williams, *Phylon* 16, no. 3 (1955): 315–16; Walter M. Merrill, *New England Quarterly* 29 (Sept. 1956): 417–20. On the cold war and its impact on the American historical profession, see Peter Novick, *That Noble Dream: The "Objectivity Question" and the American Historical Profession* (New York: Cambridge University Press, 1998), 320–32. On the cold war and university life generally, see the fine collection of essays in Noam Chomsky et al., *The Cold War and the University: Toward and Intellectual History of the Postwar Years* (New York: New Press, 1997).

46. Herbert R. Northrup, review in *International Labor Relations Review* 9 (Jan. 1956): 302–3. By my count, in some 490 endnotes citing well over a thousand primary and secondary sources, Philip Foner's work is cited just sixteen times (two of these are actually quotations from his edited collection of Frederick Douglass's writings) and Aptheker just four times.

47. Richard B. Morris, review in *Mississippi Valley Historical Review* 42 (Dec. 1955): 569–70. David L. Smiley objected to the book's focus on slavery in the *Journal of Southern History* 21 (Nov. 1955): 536–38.

48. Herman Schlüter, *Lincoln, Labor and Slavery: A Chapter from the Social History of America* (New York: Socialist Literature, 1913); Noel Ignatiev, *How the Irish Became White* (New York: Routledge, 1995), 213n72.

49. Ignatiev elaborates on a point made by Theodore W. Allen in *The Invention of the White Race: From Racial Oppression to Social Control* (London: Verso Press, 1994), 1:288n39. Allen credits Schlüter with "founding the 'Marxist' white-labor apologist school of American labor historiography." More charitably, Paul Buhle describes Schlüter as the "most profound of the Debsian historians" and considers *Lincoln, Labor and Slavery* "a more balanced account than later Socialist and Communist works, which almost invariably failed to treat white workingmen's racism." In Buhle's estimation, Schlüter's study was "outstanding" in its "serious and undemagogic efforts to place the American working class in a historic and political context, to reflect honestly upon some of its tensions, and to reconcile history written for laboring men with history which dealt rigorously with the class structures of society." Buhle, "American Marxist Historiography, 1900–1940," *Radical America* 4 (Nov. 1970): 8, 9, 10.

50. Williston H. Lofton, "Abolition and Labor," *Journal of Negro History* 33 (July 1948): 249–83; Sumner Eliot Matison, "The Labor Movement and the Negro during Reconstruction," *Journal of Negro History* 33 (Oct. 1948): 426–68.

51. For Marx, who followed events in North America closely during this period, the war represented "a conflict between two social systems, slavery and free labor" that could "no longer live peacefully side by side on the North American continent": it could end "only in the victory of one system or the other." Although led by bourgeois radicals inclined, at times, to "half measures" and to frittering away "the principle of the war and to spar[ing] the enemy's most vulnerable spot . . . *slavery itself*," Marx never doubted the war's profound significance. "Events themselves push toward the promulgation of the decisive slo-

gan—*emancipation of the slaves,*" he wrote in October 1861, and when two years later Lincoln was finally compelled to adopt abolition as a war aim, Marx wrote that "never has such a gigantic transformation taken place so rapidly. It will have a beneficent effect on the whole world." Marx, "The Civil War in the United States" and "Letter to Lion Philips," in *Karl Marx on America and the Civil War,* edited Saul K. Padover (New York: McGraw-Hill, 1972), 93, 272.

52. Here their conclusions contrast sharply with the argument Anthony Gronowicz advanced in his useful but uneven study of antebellum New York: "the Civil War was a sectional and not a class war, and where black troops were involved, a race war." Gronowicz, *Race and Class Politics in New York City before the Civil War* (Boston: Northeastern University Press, 1998), 170. Quotation from Karl Marx, "The Eight-Hour Working Day," in *Capital* (repr. New York: International Publishers, 1984), 1:284.

53. Schlüter's study moved beyond the economic determinist framework that led others on the Left, including Algie M. Simons and Anthony Bimba, to ignore the slaves' role in emancipation. In common with the Progressive historians Charles and Mary Beard, Simons asserted that the Civil War was "simply a contest to secure possession of the 'big stick' of the national government," involving primarily "northern capitalists" and "southern chattel slave owner[s]" and only peripherally involving slaves, whose status was changed "as an act of war, just as the southern ports were blockaded and southern railroads destroyed." Bimba's account was more positively hostile to any notion of slave self-emancipation: "The majority of [slaves] were so backward, so ignorant and so oppressed," he wrote, "that they did not even dream of living as free people." Except for a small "vanguard," he insisted, the slaves "worked hard and bowed low before their masters." Algie M. Simons, *Class Struggles in America* (Chicago: Charles H. Kerr Publishers, 1906), 66–67; Anthony Bimba, *The History of the American Working Class* (New York: International Publishers, 1927), 122.

54. For all its considerable strengths Schlüter's work was infused with the sense of historical inexorability common to German social democracy. The workers' movement in the United States, he suggested, would develop in perfect sync with the tempo of industrialization ("the rise of capitalist industry in the North and the concomitant growth of an industrial working class with separate class interests and separate class feelings, developing into perfect class consciousness with the advent

of greater intelligence") and take power so soon as workers' representatives won an electoral majority. Schlüter concluded his otherwise thoughtful study by posing the question of whether "the peaceful and orderly victory of the working class at the polls—*an event as sure to occur as was the victory of the Republican party in 1860*—[would] be followed by armed revolt on the part of the industrial overlords and their conscripts?" Schlüter, *Lincoln, Labor and Slavery,* 34–35, 237 (emphasis added).

55. Bimba, *The History of the American Working Class,* 122, 134–35.
56. Richard H. Pells describes the evolution in Party policy brought on by the rise of Hitler. "Following the defeat and suppression of the German Communist party in 1933," he writes, "the Soviet Union began to reappraise its hostile stance toward capitalism and the Western democracies. As the country most endangered by Nazi Germany and therefore most in need of allies, Russia appeared increasingly eager to strike a bargain with the bourgeois states against the day when Hitler should decide to launch his anti-Bolshevik crusade. Gradually, Moscow moderated its rhetoric and revised its policies so that they would seem more palatable to liberal tastes." In the United States this meant that although "on the one hand, the Communists tried desperately to preserve the pose, if not the substance, of socialist militancy[,]" on the other they "emphasiz[ed] the degree to which everyone—democrats and Marxists, reformers and revolutionaries, the middle class and the workers—had a stake in fighting fascism." Pells, *Radical Visions and American Dreams: Culture and Social Thought in the Depression Years* (Middletown: Wesleyan University Press, 1973), 293–94.

The effects of such dramatic shifts in policy among rank-and-file Party members is less clear. Irwin Wall suggests a high degree of continuity in the political outlook of Communist Party rank-and-filers in "Front Populaire, Front National: The Colonial Empire," *International Labor and Working-Class History* 30 (Fall 1996): 32–43. For an intriguing argument about the way Party-affiliated union organizers manipulated the related "no-strike pledge" during World War II, see Rick Halpern's *Down on the Killing Floor: Black and White Workers in Chicago's Packinghouses, 1904–54* (Urbana: University of Illinois Press, 1997), 179–82. For an assessment of the contradictory impact of Popular Front policy on the Party's periphery in Harlem during this period, see Mark Naison, *Communists in Harlem during the Depression* (repr. New York: Grove Press, 1983), 169–92.

57. "There is a kinship in the words of Jefferson and Lincoln with those of Engels and Stalin," Herbert Aptheker wrote in one especially unfortunate passage, "because the liberation of the working class and of all humanity—the victory of Socialism is in direct line with, an extension of, a leap forward from the limited liberating results of bourgeois-democracy." Aptheker, "Walter Lippmann and Democracy," in *History and Reality* (New York: Cameron Associates, 1955), 72.

58. Karl Marx and Frederick Engels, *The Civil War in the United States,* edited by Richard Enmale (New York: International Publishers, 1937), xxiv–v. For a scathing if somewhat superficial critique of the Party's Civil War historiography, see C. L. R. James [J. Meyer], "Stalinism and Negro History," *Fourth International* 10 (Nov. 1949): 309–14. For an extended, more penetrating critique of this writing that analyzes both revisionist and Stalinist scholarship, see Peter Camejo, "Racism and Historical Mythology," in *Racism, Revolution, Reaction, 1861–1877: The Rise and Fall of Radical Reconstruction* (New York: Monad Press, 1976), 207–27. The effects of the Popular Front policy on Communist Party historical writing are discussed in Buhle, "American Marxist Historiography," 20–22.

59. Bernard Mandel, "Communications," *Science and Society* 19 (1955): 56–63.

60. Herbert Aptheker, *Abolitionism: A Revolutionary Movement* (Boston: Twayne Publishers, 1989), 41; Schlüter, *Lincoln, Labor and Slavery,* 39.

61. Eric Foner, "Abolition and the Labor Movement," in *Politics and Ideology in the Age of the Civil War* (New York: Oxford University Press, 1981), 57–76.

62. Foner, "Abolitionism and the Labor Movement," 60, 63, 65. See also Bruce Laurie, *Beyond Garrison: Antislavery and Social Reform* (New York: Oxford University Press, 2005). Laurie rejects the conventional view that "moral suasion . . . represented a more exalted order of activity than political action did" (2) but acknowledges the importance of organized abolitionism generally, as well as the contribution of Garrison in particular, of whom he is in other respects highly critical: "Garrison's relentless agitation in the name of equal rights shook a nation that needed plenty of shaking. He tried hard to make antebellum Americans aware of the contradiction between the nation's lofty ideals enshrined in the Declaration of Independence and its disgraceful treatment of African Americans, as well as make them aware of

the complicity of Northerners and their institutions—including the Protestant churches—in the maintenance of Southern slavery" (5).

63. Schlüter distinguishes between "the working classes of the purely industrial centers, especially of New England, [who] took a more decided stand against Negro slavery," and "those of the large cities like Boston and New York, where Democratic influences were active . . . and where, through commerce, various economic considerations tended to dispose the workingmen in favor of Negro slavery" (*Lincoln, Labor and Slavery*, 70). In his discussion of the relative *failure* of Copperhead attempts to win workers over to a pro-Confederate position, Mandel acknowledges that they "did influence many of the unskilled and unorganized workers, whose economic conditions were the worst, who did not have the guidance of the most advanced working class leaders and the labor press, and who were still attached in large numbers to the Democratic party" (184).

Bruce Laurie's close study of the social composition of antislavery in Massachusetts confirms that "wage-earning workingmen and workingwomen were a significant segment of a larger social configuration of middling people[;] mechanics, small retailers, and petty professionals" (*Beyond Garrison*, 7). John B. Jentz argues that the composition of the antislavery movement in New York City "changed significantly over time" and that during the formative decade of the 1830s activists in the city's workingmen's movement formed "a consistent part of the antislavery constituency." Jentz, "The Antislavery Constituency in Jacksonian New York City," *Civil War History* 27 (June 1981): 122, 118. See also Edward Magdol, *The Antislavery Rank and File: A Social Profile of the Abolitionists' Constituency* (Westport: Greenwood Publishing Group, 1986).

64. Foner, "Abolitionism and the Labor Movement," 72.

65. Bruce S. Levine, *The Spirit of 1848: German Immigrants, Labor Conflict, and the Coming of the Civil War* (Urbana: University of Illinois Press, 1992), 150; Iver Bernstein, *The New York City Draft Riots and Their Significance for American Society and Politics in the Age of the Civil War* (New York: Oxford University Press, 1990), 96; *Voice of Industry*, July 27, 1848, cited in Lofton, "Abolition and Labor," 278–79.

66. John E. Cairnes, *The Slave Power: Its Character, Career, and Probable Designs* (repr. Columbia: University of South Carolina Press, 2003), 27–28; Laurie, *Beyond Garrison*, 3. A substantial literature has accumulated in recent years that calls into question the negative assessment of political antislavery on racial equality in the United States.

See especially Mark Lause's chapter on "Race and Solidarity: The Test of Rhetoric and Ideology" in Lause, *Young America: Land, Labor and the Republican Community* (Urbana: University of Illinois Press, 2005), 72. There he asserts that "the core of the [National Reform Association] challenged the assumptions of white supremacy [and] deliberately defied the color bar to solicit black involvement in a common movement." Similarly Eric Foner considers it an "oversimplification to equate Free Soil with an aversion to the presence of Negroes in the territories, as some historians have done. . . . In most of the states outside New York," he writes, "the Free Soilers came from a tradition of support for Negro rights, and the party, though by no means free from prejudice, sincerely strove to combat discrimination, [numbering] in its ranks the most vulgar racists and the most determined supporters of Negro rights, as well as all shades of opinion between these extremes" ("Abolitionism and the Labor Movement," 92–93). Mandel acknowledges that "many [Republicans] went out of their way to insist that theirs was the party of *white* labor" (149).

67. David Roediger, "White Slaves, Wage Slaves and Free White Labor," in Roediger, *The Wages of Whiteness: Race and the Making of the American Working Class* (repr. London: Verso Press, 1999), 87; Ignatiev, *How the Irish Became White,* 106. Although Frank Towers is right to credit Roediger's work with "bringing to the foreground . . . the negative, exclusionary side of the republican rhetoric that infused American political and social life in the century following independence," others have asserted a more mixed legacy. Roediger's "argument that whiteness was an essential element of free-labor ideology is unpersuasive," writes Peter Kolchin. "If some labor radicals took what amounted to the proslavery position that slaves in the south were better off than 'free' white workers in the north, others did not, and the argument in any case rested less on the degree of whiteness than on the degree of exploitation." Towers, "Projecting Whiteness: Race and the Unconscious in the History of Nineteenth-Century American Workers," *Journal of American Culture* 21, no. 2 (1998): 49; Peter Kolchin, "Whiteness Studies: The New History of Race in America," *Journal of American History* 89 (June 2002): 24.

68. Philip S. Foner, "Labor and the Copperheads," *Science and Society* 8 (1944): 223–42.

69. Laurie, *Beyond Garrison,* 140.

70. Lofton, "Abolition and Labor," 251, 266–67; Laurie, *Beyond Garrison.* Clearly, Schlüter overstates the case when he writes that "Garrison's

attack upon the labor movement was the sole cause of the estrangement existing between the two movements" (*Lincoln, Labor and Slavery*, 46).

71. In relation to these three scholars who have written extensively on the period discussed by Mandel, important distinctions can be made between Allen, who considers himself "with . . . but not altogether of" the "socio-economic historians," and Roediger, regarded by Allen as part of the "psycho-cultural" tendency. In a robust critique of Roediger's *Wages of Whiteness,* Allen contrasts his *Invention of the White Race,* "a socio-economic study that places ultimate responsibility for white supremacism on 'the rich and powerful,'" with Roediger's attempt to "[avoid] invidious references to the ruling class, while ascribing white supremacism to the 'creative' powers of the European-American workers." Allen, "On Roediger's *Wages of Whiteness," Cultural Logic: An Electronic Journal of Marxist Theory and Practice* 4 (Spring 2001) at eserver.org/clogic/4–2/allen.html. In a more recent but less rigorous article Noel Ignatiev distances himself somewhat from Roediger, whose work, he writes, "errs . . . [in offering] psychological and cultural explanations for [whites'] unproletarian behavior." Ignatiev, "Whiteness and Class Struggle," *Historical Materialism* 11, no. 4 (2003): 230.

Several general critiques of whiteness scholarship have appeared in print in recent years. They include Gregory Meyerson, "Marxism, Psychoanalysis and Labor Competition," *Cultural Logic: An Electronic Journal of Marxist Theory and Practice* 1 (Fall 1997) at eserver.org/clogic/1–1/meyerson.html; Frank Towers, "Projecting Whiteness: Race and the Unconscious in the History of Nineteenth-Century American Workers," *Journal of American Culture* 21:2 (1998): 47–57; Eric Arnesen, "Whiteness and the Historians' Imagination," *International Labor and Working-Class History* 60 (Fall 2001): 3–32; and Kolchin, "Whiteness Studies."

72. Laurie, *Beyond Garrison,* 2.

73. Kolchin, "Whiteness Studies," 15; Meyerson, "Marxism, Psychoanalysis and Labor Competition," 7.

74. Meyerson, "Marxism, Psychoanalysis and Labor Competition," 6; Ignatiev, *How the Irish Became White,* 3; Roediger, "Irish-American Workers and White Racial Formation," in *The Wages of Whiteness,* 140. Contrast Roediger's description of this relationship with Theodore Allen's argument about the active role of the Democratic Party and the Church in inculcating racism. "It was not the rank and file

of [New York] Irish immigrants . . . who framed the issues in pro-slavery terms," Allen asserts. "[Their] white supremacist and pro-slavery attitudes and behaviour . . . were driven first by the Demo-cratic Party's Tammany Hall, and then by the naturally conservative, 'merger' minded, Hughes-led American Catholic establishment" (Allen, *The Invention of the White Race,* 198). See also Albon P. Man Jr., "The Church and the New York Draft Riots of 1863," *Records of the American Catholic Historical Society of Philadelphia* 62 (March 1951): 33–50.

75. "Although they competed economically and lived closely together," Graham Hodges argues, "Irish and blacks coexisted far more peace-fully than historians have suggested. . . . Although disharmony and conflict abounded, there were also many points of cooperation." Hodges, "'Desirable Companions and Lovers': Irish and African Americans in the Sixth Ward, 1830–1870," in *The New York Irish,* edited by Ronald H. Bayor and Timothy J. Meagher (Baltimore: Johns Hopkins University Press, 1996), 124.

76. Ignatiev, *How the Irish Became White,* 35. A number of specialists, including David Brundage, have challenged the "one-dimensional picture of both Irish and Irish-American history" evident especially in Ignatiev's work, contending that its "discussion of eighteenth-century Ireland . . . misreads the patterns of social inequality that actually existed." Brundage, "'Green over Black' Revisited: Ireland and Irish-Americans in the New Histories of American Working-Class 'Whiteness,'" presented to the conference on Racializing Class, Classifying Race: Labour and Difference in Africa, USA and Britain, St. Antony's College, University of Oxford, July 11, 1997, 3, copy in author's possession.

77. Ignatiev, *How the Irish Became White,* 31. Roediger similarly asserts that "[t]he Garrisonians could claim a strong record of supporting Irish nationalism and rebuking American nativism" and makes no mention of their relative silence on northern inequality ("Irish-Amer-ican Workers and White Racial Formation"). Certainly, from the perspective of the immigrant working classes the abolitionist record on nativism was more uneven, a shortcoming that Democratic Party demagogues missed few opportunities to point out.

78. Precisely the same point is made by Philip S. Foner, who insists that although "the treasonable campaign of the Copperheads helped to incite bloody and destructive draft riots," it was "a tribute to labor's understanding of the deeper issues of the Civil War that so few per-

mitted themselves to fall prey to Copperhead propaganda, for there was truth in the assertion that the rich were getting richer and the poor poorer." The pro-slavery campaign failed among northern workers, he argues, because "the vast majority of them understood that their fate was being decided on the battlefields." Foner, "Labor and the Copperheads," 225, 228, 238.

79. Compare Mandel's argument, which acknowledges the *combination* of genuine grievances and orchestrated racial hostility fueling the riots, with Ignatiev's assertion that the riots demonstrated that "the Irish were rejecting not the rigors but the aims of the War" (*How the Irish Became White*, 88).

80. Roediger, "Irish-American Workers and White Racial Formation," 147; Roediger, "A New Life and Old Habits," in *The Wages of Sin*, 171–72; Allen, *The Invention of the White Race*, 194. Allen contradicts this flat denial of competition just four pages later when he argues (198) that "[t]here was indeed a real competition between African-American bond labor and Irish-American (and other white) workers . . . that if understood would have provided the basis for a joint struggle against slavery."

81. Allen provides no citation for either of these quotations.

82. Albon P. Man Jr., "Labor Competition and the New York Draft Riots of 1863," *Journal of Negro History* 36 (Oct. 1951): 376. Bruce S. Levine writes that "[t]he racism that pervaded the nation reinforced [the sentiment among northern white workers that they had no direct stake in the confrontation over chattel slavery] and undermined sympathy for the slaves as fellow human beings. So too did fears that emancipated bondmen would flee the south, surge into the north, and there compete with free white workers. . . . In the early 1830s, few abolitionists did much to challenge these perceptions or soften these antagonisms" (*The Spirit of 1848*, 157). In an early article, Roediger acknowledges the "vacillation, racism and opportunism of the Democratic Party" and contrasts it with "the achievement of [Boston's Reconstruction-era labor press, the *Daily Evening*] *Voice* in holding to principle in the face of opposition. . . . Job competition, real or imagined, appears to have fueled racial tension in Boston, where white fears caused the *Voice* to wage a protracted campaign to quell mounting hysteria over a rumored exodus of black labor from the South." David Roediger, "Racism, Reconstruction, and the Labor Press: The Rise and Fall of the *St. Louis Daily Press*, 1864–1866," *Science and Society* 42 (Summer 1978): 176.

83. Man, "Labor Competition and the New York Draft Riots," 381.
84. It is significant that rioting which occurred almost simultaneously elsewhere in the northeast did not involve racial attacks against African Americans. Brian Kelly, "Ambiguous Loyalties: The Boston Irish, Slavery and the American Civil War," *Historical Journal of Massachusetts* 24 (Summer 1996): 165–204. Man notes that strikes during the same period in Buffalo exhibited no overt racial aspect ("Labor Competition and the New York Draft Riots," 404–5 [emphasis added]; Man, "The Church and the New York Draft Riots," 34).
85. Bernstein, *The New York Draft Riots,* 120–23.
86. Matison, "The Labor Movement and the Negro during Reconstruction," 429. Ignatiev prefaces his extended treatment of the problem of labor competition with the curious argument that "[i]n the ideal situation . . . workers contracting for the sale of their labor power compete as individuals, not as groups," and that it was "true to some extent [that] no employer ever hired 'the Irish' or 'the Afro-Americans'" (*How the Irish Became White,* 98). Elsewhere he ponders why employers did not hire black workers, "who were hungry and desperate, willing to work for the lowest wage," to "undercut the wages of the Irish" (ibid., 111). The answer, of course, is that they did. Indeed, the hiring of black strikebreakers under police protection a month before was one of the elements historians have identified as precipitating the racial animosity evident in 1863 draft riots. See among others Emerson David Fite, *Social and Industrial Conditions in the North during the Civil War* (Williamstown: Corner House, 1976), 189–90.

    For compelling evidence that the calculated deployment of black strikebreakers had become common practice by the end of the War, see Matison, "Labor Movement and the Negro during Reconstruction," 430–32. On black strikebreaking after the Civil War, see especially Stephen H. Norwood, *Strikebreaking and Intimidation: Mercenaries and Masculinity in Twentieth-Century America* (Chapel Hill: University of North Carolina Press, 2002), 78–113. See also Eric Arnesen, "Specter of the Black Strikebreaker: Race, Employment, and Labor Activism in the Industrial Era," *Labor History* 44 (Aug 2003): 319–35, and Warren C. Whatley, "African-American Strikebreaking from the Civil War to the New Deal," *Social Science History* 17 (Winter 1993): 525–58. Arnesen suggests that although "white trade unionists exaggerated black strikebreakers' role," the "employers' deployment of black labor" had "weakened, at times decisively," a number of strikes in "many trades and industries" (320).

87. David R. Roediger, "On Autobiography and Theory: An Introduction," in Roediger, *The Wages of Whiteness,* 10.
88. Kevin Kenny, *The American Irish: A History* (Boston: Addison-Wesley Longman, 2000), 68.
89. Schlüter, *Lincoln, Labor and Slavery,* 225–26.
90. Christopher Phelps in the introduction to Max Shachtman, *Race and Revolution* (London: Verso Press, 2003), xxiii.

LABOR,
FREE AND SLAVE

CHAPTER I

THE LABOR AND
ABOLITION MOVEMENTS

_____

The Birth of the Labor Movement

In the first half of the nineteenth century, the United States and Europe took gigantic strides forward in the transition from an agrarian to an industrial economy. Getting a late start on England, the industrial revolution in America was faced with many handicaps. The agrarian tradition of Jeffersonian democracy had impressed upon the American people a deep repugnance for industrialism and urban concentration. These, it was feared, would bring in their wake the disruption of widespread land ownership and the substitution of a propertyless proletariat for the "sturdy yeomen" population, thus threatening the economic basis of Jeffersonian democracy, to say nothing of the rule of the Southern planters.

Furthermore, the owners of capital hesitated long before making the decision to divert their funds from the lucrative fields of commerce and land speculation to the less familiar and more doubtfully profitable domains of manufacturing. And who would man these enterprises? Skilled labor was scarce, and the vast virgin valleys and plains to the West appeared to many as a great magnet to draw much of the potential laboring class from the East, and to leave the remainder in a position to demand impossible rewards for their work. Then, the stupendous, sprawling spaces of the young country, with its scattered small-scale farm units unconnected except by long, arduous and expensive routes

on rivers, seas and primitive roads, presented a serious impedi-
ment to the development of a national market and an integrated
economic life. In any event, could an infant industry compete
against British manufactures, which more than once threatened
destruction to the early American factories? Finally, the development of industrial enterprise was thwarted by the institution of
slavery, which placed limits on the growth of a unified national
economy, kept its own section backward, and prevented the use
of the central government for the erection of tariff barriers, the
construction of internal improvements, the establishment of a
national banking system, and similar measures for the protection
and fostering of capital.

Gradually, however, and with accelerating tempo, most of these
obstructions were overcome. The Napoleonic wars, the Embargo
and the War of 1812 provided an opportunity for American businessmen to capture the home market and released a considerable
amount of capital from the depressed carrying trade. Even Jefferson agreed in 1816 that manufacturing must become a national
enterprise, for the sake of economic independence if nothing else.
A fecund population and a swelling tide of immigrants provided hands for new textile establishments, forges and foundries,
flour mills, shoe shops, paper mills and other enterprises, and
increased the market for their products.[1] The country was knit
together by a network of roads, canals and finally railroads, binding the Western and Southern markets to the manufacturing
areas and furnishing a means for the amazing growth of the
Middle West, inundated by floods of native and foreign immigrants.

Assisted by favorable corporation acts and internal improvements from state legislatures, industry was already exhibiting the
tendencies toward concentration and centralization that were to
be so marked after the Civil War. The total value of manufactures reached nearly two billion dollars on an investment of

one billion by 1860, and American manufacturing advanced to fourth place in the world by the time of the Civil War.

One of the most important factors in the fashioning of this economic structure was the army of workers—men, women and children—recruited from the fields and towns of three continents. In the ante-bellum period it was common to use such terms as laborers and workingmen quite loosely, and they were often meant to include independent farmers and small businessmen. But it is necessary to define and describe more precisely what is now understood as the working class, namely, those whose principal income is derived from wages.

The pre-war census reports, as well as other sources of statistical information on the economic structure and the laboring population, are quite inadequate and often inexact, but they permit a number of reasonably accurate observations, particularly when evaluated with the help of detailed studies of various industries and regions. A fairly reliable picture of the composition and characteristics of the working class emerges from these data.[2]

In 1850, there were 1,288,000 mechanics, artisans and skilled laborers in the United States. We are not told what percentage of these were wage-earners, how many were self-employed or engaged in domestic manufactures, and what number were employers, but a closer view of the various crafts included in this category supplies helpful information. By the nature of their trades, mariners and railroaders were almost exclusively wage-earners; the former held fourth place among this class of workers, numbering 71,000, but the latter occupation, still in its infancy, came sixteenth with 5,000. At the other extreme were the blacksmiths, the third largest group with 100,000 craftsmen. The average number of blacksmiths per establishment, throughout the ante-bellum period and in all parts of the country, was two, and it may be taken as virtually certain that this was not only the average but the actual number for the great majority of such shops. If account is taken of the many one-man smithies and family or partnership enterprises, it is clear that only a small percentage of the blacksmiths were wage earners. In the other crafts the proportion of wage-earners ranged variously between these two extremes. Most numerous were the 185,000 carpenters, and it would seem that some three-fourths of them were employees. In the next largest group, about 150,000 shoemakers, nearly 90% were employed either by merchant capitalists or by manufacturers. On the whole it would appear reasonable to estimate that at least half of the mechanics, artisans and skilled laborers were wage-earners.

The rest of the wage-earning population is easier to identify. In 1850 there were only 11,000 "factory hands" reported,[3] and farm laborers were not included in the census. But there were 910,000 unskilled workers, 77,000 miners, and several hundred thousand servants, apprentices and laundresses. In all, then, the working class in 1850, not counting the families of workers, constituted about 10% of the whole population, or nearly 12% of the free population. (See Table.)

THE WORKING CLASS, 1850-1870
(*All numbers given in thousands*)

	1840	1850	1860				1870
			Total	North	South	% in N.	
No. of wage-earners		1700	3533	2734	799	77	7000
% of free pop.		−12%	13%	15%	10%		20%
No. of factory hands		11	87	79	8	90	428
No. of mechanics &c.							
(wage-earners)		600	865	690	175	80	1400
% of working class		35%	24%	25%	22%		20%
No. empl. in manuf'g	790	945	1311	1120	191	85	2054
% of free pop.	+5%	−5%	+5%	6%	+2%		+5%
% of working class		56%	37%	41%	24%		29%

By 1860, the wage-earning class numbered some 3,500,000,[4] but its relative size in the population had not materially increased.

However, the decade 1850-60 marked a very striking increase in the number of factory operatives to 87,000, of railroaders from 5,000 to 36,000, and of miners to 147,000, which gives evidence of the rapidly growing industrial economy and the rise of the manufacturing class. The distribution of industry is indicated by the fact that the wage-earning class in the South constituted less than 10% of the free population, whereas it was 15% of the Northern population and over 21% of the population of Massachusetts. The stimulus of the Civil War on industry is apparent from the fact that by 1870 the wage-earning population had increased to nearly 20% of the total, numbering over 7,000,000 in a population of 38,000,000. The number of factory workers had reached 428,000, nearly a 500% increase in one decade; and railroading had become the fourth largest occupation among skilled laborers, with 154,000 employees, a gain of over 400% since 1860.

When we turn to an examination of the manufacturing population, we find a steady increase from 790,000 in 1840 to over 2,000,-000 in 1870, and an equal number were employed in mining, transportation and trade in the latter year. Of the number in manufacturing in these years, 76-85% were in the Northern states, and 15-25% in New England alone. However, in spite of the increasing numbers of persons employed, manufacturing no more than held its own with respect to the growth of other branches of the economy, for the percentage of the total population engaged in manufactures hovered about the 5% mark from 1840 to 1870. The proportion of the Northern population employed in manufacturing likewise remained static at 6%; but while the figure for the South declined from 4% to 2% of the free population, it increased in the New England states from 8% to 11%.

In 1840, New England and the Southern states had an equal number of persons employed in manufactures (186,000 in each section), but by 1870 the former had outdistanced the latter, 527,-000 to 316,000. During the same period about 2% of the Western population was engaged in manufactures, and 7% of the Middle

Eastern states. Naturally, manufacturing was more concentrated in the cities: in the 102 largest cities in the country, over 11% of the population was in manufacturing, and in some cities like Philadelphia and Cincinnati the percentage reached above 17%.

The various industries and regions were, of course, unequally affected by mechanization, concentration, and the trend toward factory organization.[5] For example, carpentering, which employed the largest number of workers of any trade, averaged five laborers per establishment in Ohio and ten in Mississippi in 1860, with little change in the ensuing decade, although there was a 42% increase in the number of persons employed in the craft. Nor was there any substantial increase in the annual average product per worker. Blacksmithing presented similar features: the average number of workers per establishment remained at 2, while the total number in the craft more than trebled between 1860 and 1870, and the average annual product per worker remained fairly steady at $600 to $700 in various parts of the country. In these two trades, then, there was little concentration, centralization, or mechanization.

In some of the other leading industries, however, there was not only growth but marked trends toward concentration and mechanization. The textile industry was the second largest with reference to size of the labor force, which increased from 96,000 in 1840 to 132,000 in 1850 to 156,000 in 1860. In the same years the average number of workers per establishment grew from 18 to 70 and the average annual product per worker from $600 to $1000. The cotton mills were the largest in the textile field, and in fact among all industries: in 1860 the Northern establishments averaged 140 workers, and in Massachusetts 250, while a few employed as many as 1000 operatives. The boot and shoe industry presented characteristics which were common to a number of other leading manufactures. The number of workers in the industry increased from 105,000 to 136,000 between 1850 and 1870, while the capital invested nearly quadrupled ($13 million to $49 million), the annual product was more than trebled ($54 million to $182 million), and the annual average product per worker rose from $500 to $1300. This rapid growth of productivity reflected the introduction of machinery and factory methods of organization, which began in the 1840's,[6] but the average number of workers per establishment actually decreased during these two decades from 10 to less than 6. This was a result of the large number of new enterprises which were started on a small scale even while others were growing in size, thus reducing the average. Similar phenomena are noted in the clothing, iron, carriage, and tobacco industries. The data for these industries, as well as for carpentering and blacksmithing, give some indication of the number of people, undoubtedly skilled laborers for the most part, who were establishing new enterprises and thus becoming small businessmen, even while the total size of the wage-earning class was increasing. In all branches of industry, 129,000 new establishments were begun between 1850 and 1870.

The conditions of labor in the first half of the nineteenth century impelled the workers to remedial action. One of the most persistent complaints of labor throughout this period, and one of the most common causes of strikes, was the length of the working day, which averaged twelve to fourteen hours for nearly all workers in the ante-bellum period. Many of those engaged in manufacturing performed their work in poorly lighted, unventilated buildings, under a regime of severe discipline. The wages for this work were often barely sufficient for survival, even when the entire family was employed, and even part of this pittance was sometimes filched by means of scrip payments and irregularities permitted by the absence of lien laws. In 1851, when wages were relatively high for the pre-war period, Horace Greeley published a weekly budget for a working-class family of five which, including only the most essential items, carefully planned and frugally expended, required $10.37. But in that same year Pennsylvania coal miners were getting $6.96 a week; New York carpenters $12.00; foremen in a Massachusetts cotton mill $12.00; and blacksmiths in a New York machine shop but $9.78.[7]

As a result, many workers were forced to crowd into wretched hovels, and the slum made its appearance as a regular part of the American city. Furthermore, the vicissitudes of illness, injury, age and business depressions imposed a tremendous burden of insecurity and destitution. Among the skilled laborers, these conditions were somewhat mitigated, but it was precisely among them that the early unions were formed. David J. Saposs has concluded that the only motive of this group for organizing was to protect their status and their standards as skilled mechanics. It was precisely those who had the best chance of becoming businessmen who formed the first unions: printers, shoemakers, tailors, carpenters and so forth. On the other hand there was little or no organization among the unskilled workers and factory operatives. This is explained by the general rise in their wages, while the wages of the skilled mechanics were kept down by the merchant capitalists, remaining stationary or even declining. "It was the desire to resist this pressure upon their standards of life that actuated the skilled workers to band themselves together."[8]

But the complaint was universal among all strata of the toiling population that low wages, long hours and irregularity of employment were reducing them to the edge of poverty. Factory workers and unskilled laborers, although they did not organize like the skilled craftsmen, did conduct strikes, and nearly all of them were on the issues of wages and hours.

As early as the last decade of the eighteenth century, skilled journeymen in various cities organized the first trade unions in this country, working mainly for higher wages, shorter hours and job security. In the 1820's a widespread movement for the ten-hour day sprang up, out of which arose the first city-wide federation of labor organizations, the Mechanics' Union of Trade Associations of Philadelphia, and later the New England Association of Farmers, Mechanics, and Other Workingmen. These organizations heralded the birth of the modern labor movement. Seth Luther, leader of the New England workers, animated the young labor movement with the spirit of struggle in defense of its rights which were, he said, "not only endangered, but some of them already wrested from us by the powerful and inhuman grasp of monopolized wealth."[9] By 1860 a number of crafts had organized nation-wide unions, and there had even been an effort to form a national federation of trade unions. Most of these organizations did not last very long, being swept away by recurring economic crises, crippled by the courts, and diverted by reformist leaders. But at times they reached dimensions that were not surpassed, proportionately, until nearly a century later. In the middle 1830's the *Workingmen's Advocate* estimated that at least two thirds of the workers in the largest cities were members of unions,[10] and *The National Laborer* estimated the total union membership in 1836 at 300,000.[11] If this figure was approximately accurate, it would mean that about 20% of the working class was organized, and about 60% of the mechanics and skilled laborers. In 1854, when unionism reached another peak, total membership was estimated at 200,000 which would have been 7% of all workers and 25% of skilled laborers.[12] These unions won many improvements for their members, and taught them the value, indeed the necessity, of cooperative action to raise their living standards.

At the same time, many working people were arriving at the conclusion that if the ideals of the American Revolution were to be achieved, they would have to organize for political action as well. Various political parties and associations were formed to work for the establishment of public schools, the abolition of imprisonment for debt, abolition of contract convict labor, opposition to monopolies, land reform and the extension of democracy. Many outstanding achievements were secured by these movements during their short life. For the most part, however, in the thirty years before the Civil War, American labor tried to achieve its redemption through the major political parties.

A large number of workers were also attracted to various reform

movements, the most important of which were the Utopian socialist schemes and the land reform movement. America had been a
fertile field for communitarian experiments since the seventeenth
century, but most of them had been of a religious character, and
usually their communal aspects were a result of expediency rather
than principle. But the early nineteenth century brought forth a
number of plans for the regeneration of society through the formation of cooperative societies which, by example and radiation,
should eventually encompass all of society. These experiments or-
iginated for the most part in Europe and were either brought to
America by their founders, like Robert Owen, Frances Wright,
Wilhelm Weitling, Etienne Cabet and Victor Considerant, or
propagated in this country by converts, as Horace Greeley proclaimed the virtues of Fourierism through the *Tribune*. In some
cases, they were native products, most notably the Transcendental
communities at Fruitlands and Brook Farm. While such utopias
never actually involved a significant number of workers, the
propagation of their ideas and the influence of their leaders played
an important part in developing an anti-capitalist orientation
among the workers.

Also, most of the Utopian programs were connected with land
reform, which won the support of large sections of the labor movement. The American people had always been dazzled by the
prospects of unlimited land, "with room enough for our descend-
ants to the thousandth and thousandth generation." When the
consequences of an encroaching industrialism revealed themselves,
it was natural for the workers, as well as the farmers and the
lower middle class, to look to unoccupied land for their salvation
from loss of status, degradation of living standards and depression
into the ranks of a permanent proletariat. But in spite of the
employers' fear that the West would drain off their working
force, and in spite of constant liberalization of the land laws from
1787 to 1841, it was apparent to those who actually proposed to
emigrate that the injunction to go West was not so easily accom-

plished. There were numerous difficulties, above all, the pro-
hibitive cost of the initial investment. The land reformers, led by
George Henry Evans, proclaimed that the workers were in thrall
to the capitalists who engrossed the land, and demanded that the
right to the soil be recognized by the free grant of inalienable
homesteads to all actual settlers. This movement, while achieving
partial victory only with the passage of the Homestead Act of
1862, was instrumental in molding the social philosophy of many
wage-earners, in determining their attitude toward the Southern
politicians who resisted land reform, and in helping to pave the
way for the Free Soil and Republican parties.

Finally, there was a small element in the late ante-bellum labor
movement, largely of German origin, which accepted the principles of scientific socialism as enunciated by Marx and Engels in
the *Communist Manifesto* of 1848. This group attempted to influence the working class to adopt a policy of militant, united struggle for economic improvements and to organize politically for
the achievement of a workers' government and a socialist system.

While the American labor movement in some respects developed along the same lines as in Europe, there were also some striking differences. Although class lines were well established by the
1850's, they had not yet become fixed, and the individuals within
each class were constantly changing. There was still considerable
opportunity to rise out of the laboring class and to become a small
farmer, shopkeeper or manufacturer, because of the rapid expansion of the American economy. Consequently, it can hardly
be said that the working class had achieved an independent position: class-conscious as it was in so far as economic struggles
were concerned, it still followed in the train of the middle class
politically and ideologically. The revolutionary working-class
movement of 1848 in Europe had no counterpart in the United
States.

Two other factors were also responsible for this circumstance.
The American laboring class was probably the most heterogene-

ous in the world, being separated into native and foreign-born constituents, and the latter sub-divided into a dozen or more nationalities. Language barriers, national and religious prejudices, and economic stratification along nationality lines, reinforced by the divisive policy of employers and politicians, were obstacles to mutual understanding and to united economic and political organization.

But the most decisive factor in disfiguring the American labor movement was the existence in the Southern states of the institution of chattel slavery.

The Anti-Slavery Movement

Not only the workers but all segments of the American people were profoundly affected by the existence and dynamics of the slave system, developing in juxtaposition to the emerging capitalist economy of the North. The overthrow of slavery was accomplished by certain of these groups against the resistance of others, and the role of each was determined by its position in the complex relationship of social and economic forces that operated in nineteenth century America. The anti-slavery movement, therefore, can be understood and evaluated only by analyzing these socioeconomic factors, their effect on the material conditions and ideology of the various classes, and the resulting actions of these people.

The only elements with a direct material stake in the preservation of slavery were the slaveholders themselves and their dependents and associates. This latter group consisted of Northern merchants, bankers and cotton manufacturers who had business ties with the South, and Democratic politicians with party connections; the Southern politicians, lawyers, ministers and teachers whose positions were dependent on the sufferance of the planters; overseers, police and others who constituted the apparatus of repression; and those who had aspirations to enter the slaveholding class. Every other stratum of the American population was at least a potential anti-slavery force.

Unquestionably the most persistent, thorough and effective anti-slavery force in the nation was the slaves themselves. For three hundred years they resisted bondage and exploitation by every means that ingenuity and courage could devise.[13] They frequently took advantage of their masters' concern for the "operating efficiency" of their human machines by feigning illness, and thousands of slaves assured their permanent incapacity by mutilating themselves, hacking off the fingers and hands that produced profit for their owners and unending drudgery for themselves. Many slaves took their own lives rather than doling them out piecemeal, and mothers destroyed their babies at birth rather than sacrificing them to the auction block and the lash. A common complaint of the slaveholders was the ceaseless, undetectable and varied forms of sabotage by which the slaves snatched precious minutes of their lives and silently registered their protest against bondage: an imperceptible slowing up of their work, the destruction of tools, implements and crops, the burning of barns and houses, the theft of property. Even the religion which was given to them by their masters in order to teach them humility, docility and obedience, was ingeniously turned into a means of expressing their yearning for freedom. Their religious songs were full of double meanings; they sang about the children of Israel in Egypt and their liberator Moses, but what thoughts and hopes must have filled their hearts as they chanted the pregnant refrain, "Let my people go"? In their silent prayers, they appealed to their Lord in Heaven to save them from the oppression of their lords on earth. Many, through hope and prayer, began their quest for a way of escape.

Perhaps the most effective form of resistance to slavery was flight. Tens of thousands of men, women and children made the dash for freedom, hiding in swamps and forests by day, moving by night toward the North Star, with patrols and bloodhounds on their heels. Many were aided by the engineers of the Underground Railroad—white and Negro men and women who guided the fugitives, harbored them and passed them from station to station. These conspirators against slavery rescued some seventy-five thousand slaves, and the boldest of them, like Harriet Tubman, herself a fugitive, went into the South to snatch the slaves from the plantations under the very nose of the masters and overseers. Thousands of other slaves fought for their liberation by rising in revolt. A few of the most extensive of these revolts and their leaders are well known—Nat Turner, Gabriel, Denmark Vesey—but there were hundreds of smaller risings and attempted rebellions, enough of them to require the conversion of the South into an armed camp and to cause slaveholders to sleep with revolvers under their pillows. In the 1850's the resistance of the slaves mounted, and during the Civil War many seized the opportunity to overthrow their oppressors as soldiers in the Union armies of liberation.

The vast majority of Southern nonslaveholding whites—farmers, mechanics and "poor whites"—also had a material interest in the demise of slavery, which subjected them to a crushing and demoralizing economic competition, saddled them with poverty and ignorance, and deprived them of their democratic rights. Although many of the most alert and ambitious of them emigrated from the South, and although the rest were restricted in the exercise of political rights and were confused, frightened and divided by a devastating torrent of racial prejudice, the slavocracy was nevertheless in constant fear of the "great upbearing of our masses."[14]

The Northern anti-slavery movement, on the other hand, was clearly capitalistic in its ideology and leadership. The ascendancy which that class had achieved in the American Revolution was not complete, being shared with the Southern planters. As long as there was a fairly equal balance between the sections, as long as there were no decisive points of conflict in national policy, as long as slavery appeared to be "in the course of ultimate extinction," and especially until the time when industrial capitalism had reached maturity and had drawn the entire economy of the North within its orbit, the capitalist class was willing to abide this marriage of convenience. But with the progress of industrialism, the domain of capital surpassed the slave states in size, population, wealth, energy and culture, and the capitalist class was no longer content with its role of partner. In fact, it had become virtually a junior partner, as the Northern allies of the planters had permitted the latter to fasten their control over the executive and judicial branches of the federal government. It was even in danger of becoming a silent partner when, in the face of threatening crisis, the South demanded additional security for its peculiar institution, including the suppression of free speech throughout the nation and in Congress, censorship of the mails, strict enforcement of the fugitive slave law, conquest of new lands for the expansion of slavery, and unlimited freedom for slavery in the national territories. Gaining one position after another by the threat of secession, the slavocracy had reached the point where the North must either abdicate or make a stand against the "aggressions of the slave power." The contest for control of the national goverment began with the struggle for the territories.

People do not often speak publicly of ambition for mastery, particularly when the support of others is needed to gain it, and it was easy to place the moral issues in the foreground—and moral issues were certainly involved. So the air and the press were filled with talk about the conflict between free labor and bondage, humanity and barbarism, democracy and aristocracy, progress and decadence, virtue and sin. To many people these seemed to be the main points of contention, and to some they were everything. The abolitionists appealed to the conscience of the world, reminding it of the Sermon on the Mount and the

Declaration of Independence. They won many converts, and made many more uneasy with their embarrassing demands on the application of Christian principles and democratic professions to the solution of the irrepressible conflict. But many merchants and politicians did not like this kind of talk, or the freeing of fugitive slaves by mass action. That was not the way to do things. Southern customers would cancel their orders, party associates would withdraw their support, the South might even secede; besides, this unhealthy disrespect for property rights and legality could become a dangerous business. Freedom must be defended, they agreed, but defended legally and peacefully.

The farmers, the large majority of the Northern population, had no organization of their own, nor did they have an independent position on the major political and social questions of the day, being dominated by the lower middle class viewpoint and bound to the industrial East by economic ties. But their strong attachment to democracy, and their special concern for the exclusion of slavery from the territories—which they looked upon as a domain reserved for their enjoyment and a guarantee of their future prosperity—gave a tremendous fillip to the anti-slavery movement, the struggle for non-extension, and the organization of the Free Soil and Republican parties. The agrarian Northwest, in fact, was a decisive force in the electoral victory of 1860 and the successful conclusion of the war.

Finally, we return to the special subject of our study, the laboring class, whose interests demanded the abolition of slavery and the overthrow of the slave power as a condition for its future advancement. The growth of a vigorous labor movement in the North was impeded by the restrictions placed on industrial progress by the slave system; the formation of a united national movement was virtually impossible while the Southern workers were few in number and unable to organize effectively; and the "labor question" could never be resolved so long as the nation was torn by the slavery controversy and part of the republic was deformed by an antiquated social system. Furthermore, the advancement of labor was jeopardized by the slaveholders' attack on civil liberties and the threat to extend slavery to the territories. It was plain to many that "American slavery . . . must be uprooted and overthrown before that elevation sought by the laboring classes, can be effected."[15] The majority of the workers, however, probably did not attain such a clear understanding of the issue at least until the time of the Civil War. Still in its infancy and tied to the leading strings of the middle class, the labor movement was unable to play a decisive independent role in the political life of the nation. But it did exercise some influence on the course of events, getting a good education in the process, and emerging from the Civil War in a better position to work for the advancement of labor, which then included four million ex-slaves. This is the story that is told in the following pages.

CHAPTER II

IN THE LION'S DEN

Slavery and the Southern Workers

The blighting effects of slavery were much greater on the
Southern workers than on wage-earners in the North. If the
Northern labor movement was in its infancy, that of the South
was hardly more than an embryo. The bulk of the labor force was
the slaves, who in 1850 numbered three and a half million, more
than four times the number of white workers in the Southern
states. The number of factory workers was infinitesimal before
the Civil War, and only 24 per cent of the free laborers were
employed in manufacturing in 1860, as compared with 41 per
cent in the North. Because the available wealth was invested in
land and slaves rather than in industry, a relatively high percentage of the Southern workers were farm laborers. Among the
mechanics and artisans, only a handful of trade unions was formed
because of the small number of such workers (175,000 in 1860),
their dispersion, and the opposition of employers and slaveholders. Furthermore, many could find no steady employment at all;
they were occupied seasonally or when they could pick up a job,
or grubbed out a meager existence in the wastelands. A Southern
political economist had observed as early as 1820 that the propertyless white class in the South was in "a deplorable state of
degradation" because of slavery. The workingmen, he stated, were
reduced to the level of the slaves and regarded as an inferior order
of beings.[1]

Cassius M. Clay, cousin of Senator Henry Clay and one of the
leading Southern abolitionists, constantly drove home the lesson

that a mechanic in the South could not make a go of it because
the local market was continually evaporating through the process
of engrossing the land, driving out the small farmers, and replac-
ing them with slaves, who were not very good customers. The
mechanic could not sell his products in the open market because
of the undeveloped transportation facilities and his inability to
compete with Northern manufacturers; nor could he find employment elsewhere, for all trades were in the same condition. There
was nothing left for him and his children but to move away or
die. The tendency of slavery, Clay concluded, was "to destroy
every free white laborer, or reduce him to the physical necessity
and mental subservience of the black slave! The state loses all
her middle class; effeminate aristocracy ensues on the one hand,
and abject slavery on the other. *This is barbarism!*"² Repeatedly
the complaint was made that slavery was reducing the working
population to a state of physical debility, moral decay and hopeless
idleness, which must inevitably lead them to complete degradation or desperate revolt.³ A policy of industrialization as the only
means to avoid these results was often urged by manufacturers
like William Gregg and political leaders like Governor Hammond of South Carolina, but their pleas met with slight response.⁴

It was generally recognized that the economic backwardness of
the area was inherent in the slave system, and one of the most
frequently recurring themes in the literature was the lament over
Southern stagnation as compared with Northern progress. During
the Virginia convention of 1831-32, Thomas Marshall made a
speech on the abolition of slavery which was frequently quoted
by anti-slavery men in both the North and South for many years
to come. Stating that he had no objection to slavery on moral
grounds or because it was bad for the slaves, he averred that it
was ruinous to the whites, drove out the yeomen and craftsmen,
deprived the workmen of employment, made labor disreputable,
and crushed incentive. He noted the impoverishment of Virginia,
a state which, if cultivated by free labor, would sustain a dense

population of honorable laborers, and the " 'busy hum of men' would tell that all were happy, and that all were free."[5]

This was the dream of the Southern middle-class farmers and manufacturers and those who aspired to that station: to develop an industrial society with "busy men" working for them. The complaint was often expressed that white workers, under the influence of slavery, adopted the careless habits of the slaves and were even more indifferent than the slaves to the interests of their employers,[6] whereas the laboring class of the free states was "incomparably more industrious, more thriving, more orderly. . . . "[7] There was a still greater advantage to free labor for employers: it did more work, with greater skill and less waste, and some thought that it was cheaper than slave labor because it received the same subsistence as slave labor and did not have to be maintained in illness and old age.[8] Many slaveholders recognized these facts but were unwilling to encourage a policy that would strengthen the industrial classes, especially if that could be done only by abolishing slavery. But the incipient Southern capitalist class was restless over the "stand-still" policy of slavery, which "dampened the spirit of enterprise"; it desired to emulate the motto of the rising Northern bourgeoisie: "Forward, always forward."[9]

The institution of slavery was an instrument for the oppression not only of the bondsmen, but also of the wage-earners. The Newport, Kentucky, *Watchman* perceived this fact when it observed, although with some exaggeration, that the "wealthy men encourage slavery more for the purpose of making profits out of the white men, who work hard to be decent livers, than they do for the profits received from the black slave."[10]

The most frequent and direct contact between the Southern workers and the slaves was in the labor market, where they met as competitors, if a situation in which one party had all the disadvantages might fairly be called competition. Since the number of white laborers was generally small outside a few towns, the price of wage labor was determined by the price of slave labor, which was less than the minimum necessary to maintain the worker and his family (for the slave did not have that responsibility). Consequently, the wages of the workmen constantly tended to fall to the level of the price commanded for the hire of slaves, and probably reached that point most of the time.[11] C. M. Clay aptly compared this situation with the competition offered by convict labor, against which the mechanics had petitioned the legislature of Kentucky, and concluded that only emancipation of the slaves would prevent them from continuing to underbid the free workingmen.[12]

Not only did the laborers have to meet the price of slave labor, but they also had to produce as much as slaves to hold their own in the struggle for existence, and consequently had to deliver a long day's labor. The ten-hour movement never achieved the dimensions that it did in the North, and had little possibility of success in those circumstances. When the journeymen bricklayers of Louisville were struggling for the ten-hour system, they met an insuperable obstacle in the fact that they were replaceable by slaves, so they had to work as many hours as the slaves or abandon their trade. The stonecutters were able to win the ten-hour day because no slaves were employed in that occupation. But when the carpenters and painters called a strike for shorter hours, it was broken by the employment of slaves on their jobs; some strikers went back to work on the old terms, and others, disgusted and demoralized, emigrated from the state. Thus "slavery triumphed over freemen."[13]

Even when they reduced their standards to those of the slaves, the mechanics of "Egyptland" could not always win jobs from them, and found it increasingly difficult to do so as the years wore on, for there were many reasons why the slave was given preferential employment. In the self-sufficient economy of the plantations there was no place for hired labor. The master had to find employment for his slaves throughout the year, for an idle slave was an unprofitable and a dangerous one, and there were generally some who were physically incapable of the gruelling field tasks. Such men were often trained as skilled craftsmen: carpenters, blacksmiths, wheelwrights, bricklayers. General Marion had called attention to this situation long before when he noted that "the people of Carolina form two classes—the rich and the poor. The poor are generally very poor, because, *not being necessary to the rich, who have slaves to do all their work,* they get no employment from them."[14]

This situation was not confined to the plantation but overflowed into the neighboring towns. It was quite common for the masters to hire out their mechanic chattels when they were not needed "at home," and they could afford to do so at very low rates. In some cases they were almost exclusively employed elsewhere, even being allowed to contract for their own hire, as young Frederick Douglass did on the Baltimore waterfront, to the peril of the white men's jobs and his own skin. The "wages," of course, went to the owner of the laborer, not to the laborer. This practice became a specialized business, as some men with capital bought up gangs of slaves, qualified them as craftsmen, and let them out to farmers, inn-keepers, and others who found it cheaper to job than to buy slaves.[15] Another device by which slave artisans were acquired at the expense of free labor was illustrated by the story of a Long Island carpenter who had moved to the South and was asked for an estimate on a job. His prospective employer demurred at the price, "and remarked that *he could do better to buy a carpenter, let him do the work* and sell him again when it was done. The free carpenter, being a man of sense, packed up his tools and returned to New York, where a rich man cannot *buy* a carpenter and sell him again. . . . "[16]

Even the State of Louisiana, not content with being the instrument for the rule of the slavocracy, became a slaveholder itself and engaged in the business of displacing day laborers with slaves. The planters in the legislature concluded that the latter were cheaper than the former for relatively skilled labor as well as for field work, and the Senate Committee made the following estimate of their relative cost for the construction of levees, canals and roads:

FREE LABOR

300 whites, at $30 per month	$108,000
Provisions	18,000
6 superintendents, at $1,000	6,000
	132,000

SLAVE LABOR

300 slaves, valued at $1,000 each ($300,000)	
Interest on investment, at 5%	15,000
Provisions and clothes	16,500
Loss by death	15,000
6 superintendents	6,000
Food for superintendents	360
	52,860
Balance in favor of slave labor	79,140

Consequently, in 1853, Louisiana abandoned the system of hiring free labor and purchased one hundred slaves. When they were sold in 1860 (those not included in "loss by death"), the state had made a considerable profit, the planters had benefited by the improvements, the slaves were richer by so many worn bodies and broken bones, and an equivalent number of workers had to search elsewhere for employment at slave-labor standards.[17]

The employment of the white workers in factories was considered by some to be the last refuge of hope for their salvation, but even that possibility was threatened by the same curse of crushing competition that drove them from other fields. One writer referred to slave labor as "the best and cheapest factory labor in the world,"[18] and his judgment was vindicated by the calculations and experiences of numerous practical businessmen. At the Saluda cotton mills near Columbia, South Carolina, the superintendent employed 128 slave operatives, most of whom were discarded from the fields as not sufficiently strong to work there. After two years of experimentation, he concluded that the difference in labor costs was over 30 per cent in favor of slave labor. In some cases, the rising cost of slaves in the 1850's forced employers to give up slave labor in their factories in favor of free white labor,[19] but the most common experience throughout the South was that slave labor was considerably cheaper than free labor.[20] One planter observed that a slave could be supported for $20 a year, whereas a free laborer required $100 for food and clothing alone, besides the "irregularities" incident to all labor, such as illness, rent, "useless mouths" of children to be fed, occasional relaxation, and dissipations. Laborers living in such "style," he said, could not hope to compete with slaves for employment.[21]

Throughout the 1840's and '50's there was a growing tendency to replace white workers with slave labor in many branches of employment. The principal reason for this was, as has been indicated, the cheaper cost of the latter. Slaves were also commonly preferred because their employment assured a steady labor force without the hazards of "fluctuations," for they could neither quit nor strike nor organize unions. As the London *Times* expressed it, "The real foundation of slavery in the Southern states lies in the power of obtaining labor at will at a rate which cannot be controlled by any combination of labourers." When a sugar planter experimented with the employment of a hundred Irish and German laborers who went on strike in the middle of the grinding season at a loss to him of $10,000, the lesson was not lost upon his confreres. The New Orleans *Crescent* commented succinctly that "'the dragon of democracy,' the productive laboring element, having its teeth drawn, [is] robbed of its ability to do harm by being in a state of bondage."[22] Moreover, slaves could be subjected to a degree of control and discipline that free men would not tolerate. A number of people expressed to Olmsted the thought that, as a Virginia planter put it, "You never could depend on white men, and you couldn't *drive* them any; they wouldn't stand it. Slaves were the only reliable laborers—you could command them and make them do what was right." He believed that for this reason white workers could never compete with the slaves.[23]

There were several other inducements to the preferential employment of slaves. It seems to have gradually become more fashionable and respectable in Southern society to prefer slaves as a badge of "belonging" to the upper crust. It was also felt that the employment of white men in duties that were ordinarily performed by the slaves was humiliating not only to the employee but to his employer as well.[24] Besides, the slaveowner was able to use the weight of prestige, social influence and political power to get jobs for his "hands," and could make it easier by offering accommodating terms for their hire.[25] There was one exception to the rule: on dangerous jobs, the slaveholder wanted protection from the premature liquidation of his investment. One planter explained the employment of Irishmen on a dangerous job with the remark that "It's dangerous work, and a negro's life is too valuable to be risked at it. If a negro dies, it's a considerable loss, you know." And in unloading cotton bales, the slaves often worked on deck while Irishmen stopped the bales as they slid onto the wharf. "The n—s are worth too much to be risked here; if the Paddies are knocked overboard, or get their backs broke, nobody loses anything."[26] These Irish workmen were literally "fall guys" for the slaveowners!

Little wonder that complaints were increasingly voiced against the encroachment of slave labor upon domains that had formerly been reserved by wage-earners. A Virginian wrote despairingly that, whereas young men could once find ready employment on the farms, they could no longer secure it at half the wages, because "Slavery is doing the labor on the rich lands of the Valley, and the sturdy young free white man must now learn a trade . . . or leave the country and his friends." And in Mississippi it was observed that white mechanics, unable to provide their families with the necessities of life, had to stand by while the available jobs were given to slaves.[27] A Montgomery, Alabama, mechanic commented bitterly on the competition of slave labor, which, "like the encroachments of Pharaoh's plagues, . . . has extended its conquest throughout the land, and consumes all the sources of the poor man's living. It has hunted the ingenious mechanic from town to town and from shop to shop. . . . " He asserted that the mechanics had often held secret meetings to discuss the problem. Some of them even suggested incendiarism and open rebellion, which betrayed the "extreme opposition that is now rising in every sensible mechanic's mind against the damnable pest which brings poverty to each of their homes."[28]

White laborers also came into competition with free Negro mechanics, whose wages were lower than the average and who were victims of a vicious fear and prejudice. While the oppressed status of the free Negroes increased the difficulties of the white workers, they themselves were sufferers from a triple band of exploitation which made their condition little better than that of the slaves, if any. They were subjected not only to the usual exploitation of the working men, increased by the competition with slave labor, but in addition were victimized by the hatred which fell to them as belonging to an oppressed race. When the wages of white carpenters were $1.56 a day, Negroes received no more than $1.25, because of the determination of the employers to mark the distinction between the status of the white and Negro artisan.[29] Furthermore, the free Negroes were discriminated against in the granting of employment, and in the 1840's and '50's they were virtually driven from many of the fields they had occupied previously.[30]

In addition to economic exploitation and social pressures, the free Negroes were also feared as a constant source of disturbance to the slaves, and their very presence, especially if they prospered in their trades, was considered a dangerous influence on the slaves. As a result of these circumstances, the free Negro population was subjected to a campaign designed to drive them out of the South, by restrictions on their movement and employment, heavy taxes, and prohibitions on their immigration. Thus the Negro working men were placed in a status between that of the white workers and the slaves, suffering from the competition of both, while the division between the three groups made it possible to increase the exploitation of all of them.[31]

The unequal competition between slavery and free labor not only tended to reduce the material standards of the latter to the level of the former, but, as a result, inevitably degraded it to the same social level. Performing work that was associated with slavery, on virtually the same terms as the slave, the free man suffered a loss of dignity and respect even in his own eyes. Manual labor in itself became a badge of servility, branding its executor with the stain of the auction block and stigmatizing him with the loss of caste. This was the unanimous observation both of the enemies of slavery who viewed it as one of the most damning accusations against the system, and of upholders of the institution who recoiled from its contaminating influence on the "master race." Scarcely one of the hundreds of Northern and European travelers in the South failed to take note of this phenomenon, like the Englishman who remarked:

When a person is accustomed from early youth to see every description of work performed by slaves, and by slaves of a different color from himself, he imbibes an opinion which is not to be wondered at, that labor is derogatory to a free white man. When he is taught in addition to this, to consider the blacks as an inferior race to the whites, he acquires not only the greatest reluctance to work, but habits of indolence from which he seldom recovers.[32]

Many slaveholders corroborated this assertion, William Byrd having stated as early as 1736 that slavery made the whites proud and disdainful of work because doing work that was usually performed by slaves made them look like slaves.[33] It was a constant complaint of the poor whites themselves,[34] and received a sharp indictment from Helper. He stated that in the South no kind of labor was either free or respectable, and that every workingman was treated like a "loathsome beast, and shunned with the utmost disdain." Any man who owned no slaves was a slave himself, and "would be deemed intolerably presumptuous, if he dared to open his mouth, even so wide as to give faint utterance to a three-lettered monosyllable, like yea or nay, in the presence of an august knight of the whip and the lash."[35]

As a result of this contempt for labor, the workers lost self-respect, immigrants shunned the Southern states, and Northern workers were repelled, quickly returning to their homes.[36] The employers, too, tended to look upon the wage-earners as their thralls, entitled to no more rights or consideration than their Negro co-workers, and tried to quell their protests as they would those of the slaves. When the white deck hands on the Mississippi steamboats, who were exploited worse than "the lowest African on the plantation of the most cruel master," resorted to a strike, the owners got the legislature to outlaw stoppages on the ships and wharves, and the strike leaders were arrested for "tampering" with the crew. Roger Shugg points out that labor, both free and slave, suffered from the feudal outlook of the slaveholders and could not easily organize for self-defense. Consequently, the free worker was in danger of losing his freedom and being pulled into the orbit of slavery.[37]

That the slaveholders, born to command and trained to ride

their saddled underlings, assumed the usual aristocratic disdain for the "lower order," whether Negro or white, was the most natural thing in the world. And there was no mistaking it. While it was often thinly disguised by a patronizing attitude, especially around election time, people felt it, and saw it, and heard it. And, from time to time, it came straight from the horse's mouth, proclaimed boldly by the masters themselves or their political and journalistic spokesmen. These professions of the master-class ideology were broadcast through the country by the enemies of slavery, reprinted in a hundred newspapers, publicized in pamphlets, repeated a thousand times over by politicians and abolitionists, so that no one could be unaware of them. Some of the favorites were these:

Free Society! we sicken of the name. What is it but a conglomeration of *greasy mechanics, filthy operatives, small fisted farmers* and moon struck *theorists?* All the Northern, and especially the New England States are devoid of society fitted for well-bred gentlemen. The prevailing class one meets with is that of mechanics struggling to be genteel, and small farmers who do their own drudgery; and yet who are hardly fit for association with a gentleman's body servant. This is your free society which the Northern hordes are endeavoring to extend into Kansas.[38]

We have got to hating everything with the prefix *free*—from free negroes down and up, through the whole category of abominations, demagogueries, lusts, philosophies, fanaticisms, and follies, free farms, free labor, free n——s, free society, free will, free thinking, free love, free wives, free children, and free schools, all belonging to the same breed of damnable isms whose mother is Sin and whose daddy is the Devil. . . . [39]

On the murder of an Irish hotel waiter by a Southern Congressman:

Any provocation that may have been given for the assault upon him [the Southerner] . . . was at the most a provocation of words, and such a provocation as a servant should not have a right to resent; and, if white men accept the offices of menials, it should be expected that they will do so with an apprehension of their relation to society, and the disposition quietly to encounter both the responsibilities and the liabilities which the relation imposes.[40]

The ruling oligarchy of the Southern states, according to its view, governed by divine right, for "nature puts the ruling elements uppermost, and the masses below and subject to those elements."[41] B. Watkins Leigh asked his colleagues in the Virginia state convention "whether they believe that those who depend on their daily labor for their daily subsistence, can, or do enter into political affairs?" and supplied the answer which was on all their lips: "They never do, never will, never can."[42] Why this must be so was explained by F. W. Pickens of South Carolina in the House of Representatives. He asserted that an elect and chosen few were made the "peculiar receptacles of the favors and blessings of an all-wise and all-pervading Providence." All societies were divided into capitalists and laborers, and the former must own the latter, either collectively through the government, as in the North, or individually in a state of servitude, as in the South. "If laborers ever obtain the political power of a country," he concluded, "it is in fact in a state of revolution, which must end in substantially transferring property to themselves . . . unless those who have it shall appeal to the sword and a standing army to protect it."[43] Calhoun recognized with equal clarity that the prevalence of democracy "would destroy our system and destroy the South."[44] Edmund Ruffin described the character of the Southern governments even more frankly, stating that they excluded from the suffrage "all of the lowest and most degraded classes, who, *whether slaves or free, white or black* . . . are and must be incapable of understanding or caring to preserve the principle or the benefits of free government." He predicted that if the propertyless classes were given the ballot, they would use it to plunder the property of the rich.[45]

Plainly the landed aristocracy intended to keep a tight control over their government in order to preserve their privileged position against the rising tide of slave revolts as well as the popular resistance of those they deigned to call the "mean whites." The methods by which they strove to hold power were many and varied in the different states, but commonly consisted of property qualifications for voting and office-holding, unequal representation, *viva voce* voting, demagogy, the prestige of wealth and social standing, the ignorance and division of the people, control of the churches, restriction of freedom of speech and the press, and terrorism. The working men of all the Southern states, in alliance with the backcountry farmers, waged a long and difficult struggle for democratic constitutional reforms and won a number of significant victories.[46] While these gains were of considerable aid in the fight for economic improvement, they did not seriously threaten the reign of the slavocracy. The ruling class of the South learned from experience that it could maintain the substance of despotism while yielding the forms of democracy. As General Downs, a leader of the Louisiana Democratic party, commented, there was no danger from the poor classes because property and money would always exercise an efficient control over them, and it was not necessary to deny them the suffrage.[47]

One of the major victories of the Northern labor movement in the ante-bellum years was the establishment of free public schools. In the South also this was a recurrent demand of the workers, but here it met the fierce resistance of the governing class. Many Southern leaders could see little value, and possibly much danger, in universal education. Chancellor Harper of South Carolina thought that a man destined to a life of labor would better be reared in ignorance and apathy and trained to endure his station in life. "If there are sordid, servile, and laborious offices to be performed," he asked, "is it not better that there should be sordid, servile, and laborious beings to fill them?"[48] The Richmond *Examiner* likewise feared that an educated people would not long remain servile, but would be a danger to "all conservatism of thought and all stability in general affairs." Free education, it stated, was "charged to the brim with incendiarisms, heresies, and all the explosive elements which uproot and rend and desolate society."[49] The nature of the plantation system, the scattered population, and the poverty of the South were forbidding obstacles in the way of public education, but an important reason for the failure to achieve this reform was the intransigence of the oligarchy and the weakness of the working class.[50]

On the issue of unequal taxation, however, significant successes were achieved, particularly in North Carolina. The complaint of the workers was that, whereas their tools and implements were taxed ten dollars per thousand, the tax on slaves was only fifty cents, and that was imposed only on those between the ages of twelve and fifty. A Raleigh worker voiced the grievance of his class in a letter to the Greensborough *Patriot,* complaining that his wages were subject to taxation, but the income of the employers and slaveowners escaped.[51]

In 1858 Moses A. Bledsoe, a Democratic state senator, introduced a bill into the legislature to equalize the tax burden by imposing an ad valorem tax on all property, including land and slaves. Defeated and read out of the party, he found support in the newly organized Raleigh Workingmen's Association, which declared its purpose to be "to insist upon that political equality and that participation in public affairs to which they as free men are entitled." The slaveholders took alarm, not only because of the increased cost to them of the proposed tax, but because they saw an impending split in the Democratic party based on a division between themselves and the non-slaveholders and involving indirectly the slavery question, a division which could become a serious challenge to the political supremacy of the aristocracy and to their Institution. Although the immediate issue was lost in the crisis of 1860-61, the organization of the workers politically had produced deep repercussions. Kenneth Rayner wrote in December

1860 that he had found great support in favor of "Union at any and all hazards," and that the non-slaveowners did not care to fight to protect rich men's slaves. He ascribed this sentiment partly to the recent agitation on ad valorem taxation, which had infused among the people the idea that there was an antagonism between poor people and slaveowners. "We shall, I fear, have to reap a harvest of trouble from the seeds of mischief then sown."[52] These struggles, which were echoed in other states as well, were harbingers of a maturing class conflict and served to strengthen and expand the consciousness and organization of the workers.

Anti-Slavery and the Southern Workers

In the face of the economic, social and political oppression described in the preceding section, a large number of Southern workers gave up the unequal struggle for survival in the slave states where, as one emigrant said, "there is no chance for the poor white man among slaves—he can not get work, and he is treated like a dog."[53] The furtive flight of fugitives on the Underground Railroad was paralleled by a denser traffic of thousands of white workers likewise seeking freedom from an unbearable burden of exploitation and tyranny. The *Kentucky News* gave a vivid description of this exodus and its effects, stating that society was divided into classes, with embittered prejudices and opposing interests. "The slaveholder despises the slave, the slave despises the poor white man, (except where each sees that the system makes them both slaves alike to the same master,) the poor white man regards both as his natural enemies." As a consequence, reported the writer, all parts of Kentucky held deserted farm houses falling into decay. He saw long processions of white farmers emigrating to the Northwest, alongside processions of slaves, "handcuffed and fettered, with tearful eyes and sorrowful countenances." Meanwhile, the schools and mechanical arts were neglected, and labor was falling into contempt. "Our country towns languish and decay. Enterprise is checked, manufactures perish. The young man of energy and enterprise finds nothing to do."[54]

* * *

In the summer of 1830, a group of workers in Wheeling were discussing their problems. They were hard pressed to earn a decent living for their families and provide an education for their children. They agreed that the country was in the hands of a gang of degenerate aristocrats bent only on its own pleasures, and giving no thought to the heartaches and misery of the workers. Something ought to be done about it, and since they couldn't expect anything from the politicians they would have to figure something out for themselves. Probably the only way out is to leave this God-forsaken place—get some land in the West—start over again. Why not go together, get some farmers in on it to raise the crops, while we'll take care of the building and manufacturing. Ideas sprang from unknown sources, a plan began to take shape. It sounds good. Come over to my place tonight, and we can work this out.

A dense smog hung in the heat of the crowded little room, but it was not the weather that produced the flush on the men's faces; it was the fevered visions of the promised land, the agitated excitement of planning a new life. They had been thinking this over all day, and now they shot out their schemes without restraint. Some of the women folk had a few ideas too. It was getting a little complicated now, too many different plans, too many people talking at once. Somebody better write these things down—the printer had a gift for fancy words, let him do it. Provided with a sheet of paper and a pencil, he began to write, and the words came easily: " . . . for bettering our condition and circumstance: not only in providing for the Temporal wants of ourselves and families; but for the moral and intellectual cultivation of the rising generation; and handing down to our posterity, the fair inheritance bequeathed to us, and purchased by the blood and toil of our fathers unimpaired by the cunning, intrigue and sophistry of aristocrats. . . . tyranny . . . oppression . . . misrule. . . ." All farmers and laborers are invited to join us.

He put down some of the ideas they had mentioned. These were discussed, refined and elaborated; some of the men were carried away by self-intoxication; a little grandiosity might be forgiven— it was not every day that a constitution for a new society was created. Then it was all written down for the world to see. A company would be formed, and shares would be sold for $50—no more than two per adult, one for a child. Land would be purchased from the government, a whole county in Illinois, at $1.25 an acre, one-fifth down. A city would be built for 10,000 families— on the plan of Philadelphia, thought one man who had been there —and the farms would be all around it. Everything would be owned in common, and the profits used for the benefit of all. They could sell the surplus products of the farms, workshops and forests at 25 per cent profit, which would be deposited in a cooperative bank and used to pay off the land, build schools, libraries, lyceums and reading rooms. There would be a cooperative warehouse and a mutual insurance company. There would have to be a few rules too: no liquor, gambling, whorehouses, lotteries, banks, horse-racing, cock-fighting or bear-baiting. Everything was figured out; the age-old dreams of mankind for freedom, security and opportunity were finally bearing fruit—"a splendid undertaking to emancipate ourselves and our fellow-workingmen, from the slavery, the bondage and thralldom of oppression and misrule, of narrow-minded aristocrats, and short-sighted politicians." The meeting was over, work would begin tomorrow.

In the cool light of morning the constitution-makers wondered if the plan would really work. People were wary about buying in; ten thousand families didn't want to leave, nor one thousand, nor a hundred. Things will get better, they were told; you can't change human nature; smarter people have tried to remake the world and failed; that's life; what's the use? The plan was gradually forgotten, and the working men's utopia did not dawn. Nobody knew just what happened to the sheet of brown wrapping paper on which the plan had been drafted, or to the men and women who designed it; but many understood the thoughts that poured through their minds and the feelings that pulsed through their hearts on that hot summer night.[55]

* * *

For those who were unable or unwilling to choose exile, there was no effective alternative but resistance to exploitation and oppression. Not understanding the true cause of their problem, they at first directed their force not against their rulers or the slave system, but against the slaves themselves, much as the English workers earlier had vented their wrath against the invasions of capital by smashing the machines that seemed to be the root of their poverty and unemployment. It was natural for the workers to turn their attention first to the competition they suffered from slave labor, and attempt to exclude it by economic or political action.

One of the outstanding examples of the former method was the strike at the Tredegar iron works at Richmond, Virginia, an event which received wide publicity in both the North and South. After 1843 most of the unskilled jobs at the rolling mill were filled by slaves supervised by skilled white mechanics, the manager having made a successful experiment along those lines because of the relatively high wages of white labor. In 1847 the plant was expanded, necessitating a sudden doubling of the number of operatives. Consequently, some of the slaves were placed in more responsible positions and a number of white puddlers and rollers assigned to teach newly hired slaves. Fearing that their jobs would be usurped once the training period was completed, the workers held a meeting and pledged "not to go to work unless the negroes be removed from the Puddling Furnaces at the new mill—likewise from the squeezer and Rolls at the old mill." The president of the iron works, Joseph Anderson, refused to bargain or to recognize the right to strike. Accepting the strike action as "quitting my employment," he advertised for Negro operatives and broke the strike.[56] In this action he had the complete support of the propertied classes, for they recognized that in spite of its limited objectives, the strike was, as Anderson said, "a direct attack on slave property." The Richmond *Times and Compiler* seconded this view: "The principle is advocated for the first time, we believe, in a slaveholding state, that the employer may be prevented from making use of slave labor. This principle strikes at the root of all the rights and privileges of the master and, if acknowledged, or permitted to gain a foothold, will soon wholly destroy the value of slave property."[57]

The *National Anti-Slavery Standard* correctly defined the issue as "a struggle between Slave-labor, and Free-Labor—between the slaveholder, who lives upon the toil of others, and the laboring man, who only asks a fair field and no favors; and the latter, of course, went to the wall."[58]

As the intensity of competition with slave labor grew, more and more workers came to agree with the artisan who said he was "only better than the slave because he is entitled to vote and must give that sometimes for promise of a job," and in some cases they resorted to desperate action.[59] A mechanics' association was formed in Wilmington, North Carolina, as early as 1795, and among other things discussed ways of protecting the skilled trades from encroachment by slave labor.[60] In 1857 the framework of a new building that had been erected by slaves was burned to the ground, and a placard was left threatening similar action against other buildings so constructed.[61] This house-warming party received applause and the flattery of imitation elsewhere, but the local authorities were horrified, denouncing the perpetrators as abolitionists, plug uglies and dead rabbits. The mechanics held a meeting in which they repelled these accusations but repeated their indignation that the laws prohibiting the hiring and contracting of slave labor were flouted by the slaveowners with impunity.[62]

While these demonstrations had the merit of dramatically calling attention to the problem, they could not have much more than a nuisance value, and the workers turned to political action for redress of their grievances. Throughout the Southern states, and for many years, laborers held meetings at which they endorsed resolutions and drew up petitions addressed to the city councils, state legislatures, and even the Navy Department. In one case at least the slaveholders themselves were moved to join in the campaign because of the unprecedented emigration of laborers from their vicinity, and one pro-slavery newspaper supported it because it feared that the continuation of this situation would place a severe strain on the loyalty of the laborers to the "institution."[63] These memorials described the ruinous effects of the competition and demanded laws prohibiting the apprenticing of Negroes to the skilled trades, restricting the movement of slaves and free Negroes looking for jobs, forbidding free Negroes from teaching their trades to any but their own sons, excluding slaves and free Negroes from any mechanical occupations, and placing a poll tax on free Negroes.[64]

Once again the workers had to face a storm of reaction from the intransigent autocracy. This movement was feared, and justly, as the first blow in the struggle for democracy. L. W. Spratt of Charleston wrote that if this campaign succeeded the workers would question the right of masters to employ their slaves as they wished, and would use their votes to that end. " . . . they may acquire the power to determine municipal elections; they will inexorably use it; and thus the town of Charleston, at the very heart of slavery, may become a fortress of democratic power against it."[65] When the mechanics of Concord, North Carolina, held a meeting to protest against the underbidding of their contracts by the owners of slave mechanics, the leader was driven out of town.[66] A laborer in Columbia, South Carolina, was tarred and feathered and expelled from the city for suggesting that slaves be confined to the plantations.[67] In 1860 Robert Tharin, an Alabama lawyer, set up a paper called the *Non-Slaveholder*, which he hoped to make an organ of the workingmen in the campaign against competitive slave employment in industry and the handicrafts; he was run out of the state before the appearance of the first issue.[68]

Consequently, this movement also failed to achieve any significant success. With the solitary exception of a Georgia law passed in 1845, which included slaves in its provisions, every law relating to the employment of Negroes was confined in its application to free Negroes: restrictions on their movement and employment, poll taxes, prohibition of manumission, exclusion of immigration of free Negroes. The kind of law the workers wanted most was defeated by the objection that they interfered with the rights of slaveholders. And the legislation that was passed was designed more from fear of the abolitionist and revolutionary activities of the Negro freemen and to deflect the discontent of the workers than from any desire to protect them. Furthermore, whenever these laws conflicted with the interests of the slaveholders and employers, the influence of the latter was great enough to have them ignored.[69] Nevertheless, these economic and political activities by wage-earners for the protection of their living standards and their jobs were bound, as the slaveholders realized, to clarify the workers' comprehension of their problems and tasks and to build the organizations by which they would advance further. The violent reaction of the slaveholders provided an important lesson in this educational process. The working class was ineluctably forced toward opposition to the slavocracy and the whole system of chattel slavery.

John Palfrey wrote in 1846: "So long as the black working man is held in bondage, just so long will and must the white working man be held in miserable darkness and bondage of mind. The momentous issue will soon be seen to be, continued and increased *depression of the non-slaveholding freeman,* or manumission for the Slave."[70] The oppression of the Southern workers and their struggles against it—for the right to work without competition of slave labor, for democratic reforms, for public schools, for equal taxation—gradually led an increasing number of them to a comprehension of the truth of Palfrey's statement. In their education, an important role was played by the Southern abolitionists.

It is significant that, whereas most of the Northern abolitionists ignored the possibility of an alliance with labor, practically all of the Southern members of that fraternity of agitators directed their appeals and their propaganda primarily to the working men and farmers. Although they did not neglect the moral issues, they had a much more realistic perception of the economic effects of slavery, and recognized that, apart from the slaves, the workers and farmers were the only force capable of overthrowing the institution. While the Northerners spoke for the rights of the slaves alone, the Southerners preferred to represent the non-slaveholding whites as well. One of these was William S. Bailey, a machinist of Newport, Kentucky, "with a large family, and a hatred of slavery such as only an experience of its unspeakable oppressions on the white mechanics as well as the negro can engender. . . . "[71] During the last ten years preceding the Civil War, intermittently interrupted by mob attacks on his presses and himself, he edited an anti-slavery newspaper in Kentucky in which he said, "We plead the cause of WHITE MEN and WHITE WOMEN in the South—we ask for their sake, a patient and candid hearing."[72]

Likewise, *The True American,* published in Lexington by Cassius Marcellus Clay, a former slaveowner, was devoted "to

Universal Liberty; Gradual Emancipation . . . the Elevation of Labor Morally and Politically." Deciding to give up his opportunities for a political career, he cut himself off from his own class, emancipated his slaves, and entered his life-long occupation of explaining to the working men that their only path to freedom lay in the overthrow of slavery. Here is a typical example of his vigorous editorial style:

> When a journeyman printer *underworks* the usual rates he is considered an enemy to the balance of the fraternity, and is called a *"rat."* Now the slaveholders have RATTED us with the 180,000 slaves till forbearance longer on our part has become criminal. They have *ratted* us till we are unable to support ourselves with the ordinary comfort of a laborer's life. They have *ratted* us out of the social circle. They have *ratted* us out of the means of making our own schools. . . . They have *ratted* us out of the press. They have *ratted* us out of the legislature. . . . What words can we use to arouse you to a sense of our deep and damning degradation! Men, we have one remedy, untried, omnipotent, power of *freemen* left—the ballot box: yes, thank God, we can yet *vote*! Our wives, our sisters, our children, raise their imploring eyes to us; save us from this overwhelming ignominy —this insufferable woe; place us upon that equality for which our fathers bled and died. Come, if we are not worse than brutish beasts, let us but speak the word, and slavery *shall die!*[73]

It is, of course, impossible to measure the effect of this propaganda or the extent of anti-slavery sentiment among Southern workers. It can be said with certainty that the majority of them never attained to such a level of political consciousness, but there can also be no doubt that there was a strong and growing undercurrent of hostility to the system. This is attested to by the observations of a number of American and European travelers, contemporary journalists, and residents of the South,[74] by the hysterical alarm of the slaveholders and their repressive measures, and by occasional public expressions such as the resolution adopted by a mass meeting of the mechanics and working men of Lexington, Kentucky, in 1849. This resolution asserted that slavery degraded labor, enervated industry, interfered with the occupations of free laborers, created a gulf between the rich and the poor, deprived the working classes of education, and tended to drive them out of the state. While recognizing the right of property in slaves under existing laws, the statement concluded that, "as slavery tends to the monopoly as well as the degradation of labor, public and private right requires its ultimate extinction."[75]

The febrile apprehensions of the ruling class mounted to unprecedented heights in the late 1850's, particularly in connection with two events. One was the growing restlessness of the slaves, whose real and fancied preparations for revolt produced a panic in the South in 1856, with the press complaining that the "low down poor whites" were inciting the slaves to rebellion and joining in their conspiracy to overthrow the government by force and violence.[76] The other event was the appearance in 1857 of *The Impending Crisis of the South: How to Meet It,* by Hinton Rowan Helper, a small farmer of North Carolina. Helper expressed a strong antipathy to the Negroes, a sentiment shared by many of his class, but he presented a documented damnation of the depressing consequences of the Institution on the poor whites and a ringing challenge to them to rise up against it.

He warned the farmers, mechanics, and workingmen that the slaveholders who controlled the government had hoodwinked them and used them as tools to maintain their power and their "peculiar institution." By subterfuge and misrepresentation, by keeping the people in ignorance and inflaming their prejudices, they taught the people to hate the abolitionists, and thus temporarily averted the vengeance which was bound to overtake them. Helper urged the non-slaveholders to join the abolition movement and rescue the South from "the usurped and desolating control of these political vampires." He concluded that if the people of the South allowed the slavocrats to fasten slavery on Kansas, the entire nation would soon fall prey to their designs; "if you do not voluntarily oppose the usurpations and outrages of the slavocrats, they will force you into involuntary compliance with their infamous measures."[77] This book struck at a vulnerable point in the armor of slavery, and the heavy artillery of calumny and "refutations" was turned against it and its author.[78]

Two sections of the working class were thoroughly and actively anti-slavery: the free Negro mechanics and the German-American laborers. It required no agitators to convince the former that their salvation depended on the uprooting of slavery, which branded them both as workers and as Negroes. They were correctly regarded by the slave power as a "disturbing element," for they furnished a strong core of participants and leaders in every phase of the anti-slavery movement, and played a prominent part in aiding the slaves to escape, in distributing abolitionist literature in the South, in organizing and leading slave revolts, in the Northern abolition movement, and in assisting the Union armies as servants, scouts, spies and soldiers.[79]

The Germans were recognized as another "danger to the community." The Morehouse, Louisiana, *Advocate* noted that "The great mass of foreigners who come to our shores are laborers, and consequently come in competition with slave labor. It is to their interest to abolish Slavery; and we know full well the disposition of man to promote all things which advance his own interests. These men come from nations where Slavery is not allowed, and they drink in abolition sentiment from their mothers' breasts."[80]

When a group of Turners resolved to secede from the National Association because of its anti-slavery position, they received a spirited reply from the Wheeling society, which said: ". . . it is plain that the Turners must oppose the extension of slavery into the free territories, because they are all free laborers and must seek to preserve the soil for free labor, and because it is only through the emigration of free laborers into the territories that the future great States can be kept free from the institution of slavery, while to make these territories into slave States would be to consign their soil to the monopoly of a few rich planters and close them against free laborers." The proposition to form a separate Southern branch of the Turner-Bund was therefore regarded "as a miserable business, and as a treason to the principles of our fraternity."[81] The Free Germans of Louisville, led by Karl Heinzen, adopted a platform in a mass meeting in 1854 calling for the organization of a reform party embracing all "who want that liberty now so much endangered." In addition to its demands for land reform, labor legislation, free schools and free justice, the platform referred to slavery as a "moral cancer, that will by and by undermine all republicanism," and demanded the prohibition of slavery from the territories, repeal of the fugitive slave law, gradual abolition, and equality of rights for the Negro people.[82]

Even more sweeping in their abolitionism were the German-American communists, who organized opposition to slavery in several Southern states. Several anti-slavery papers were published in Texas by German communist workers, the most significant of which was the *San Antonio Zeitung,* a weekly abolition paper published from 1853 to 1856 by Adolph Douai, a leading American socialist.[83] The Social Democratic Society of Working Men, consisting of German-Americans in Richmond and calling itself "the party of the future," put forward a platform which stated: "Both political parties of our land have proved their incapacity to develop and build up the true democratic principles of the Constitution. Their fate is inevitable—already the process of dissolution has commenced." The Society's program included universal suffrage, direct election of officials, abolition of the Senate and Presidency, the recall, a foreign policy in aid of all people struggling for liberty, complete freedom of religion and separation of church and state, abolition of land monopoly, tax on property, public education, an eight-hour law, state ownership of the railroads, and "the supporting of the slave emancipation exertions of C. M. Clay by congressional laws."[84]

If the Southern working class as a whole was not "abolition-

ized" by the time of the war, it nevertheless had mature spokesmen, and had itself, in the course of many guerilla battles against
the aristocracy, advanced along the path of self-conscious development. This was to prove a matter of considerable significance
during the crisis of 1860-65.[85]

Divide and Rule

The ruling class understood much more clearly than the workers that the interests of the latter were in opposition to slavery and
that, to maintain their subjection (and that of the slaves), it was
necessary to keep them down, keep them ignorant, keep them
weak, and keep them divided from their natural allies. A few
suggested that it might be safer to keep them satisfied, but they
were quickly ruled out of order.

So long as the laboring class was small, scattered and unorganized, there was little possibility of its becoming a serious threat.
But let it grow to a large, concentrated, industrial proletariat, and
it would be time for the slaveowners to book passage for Brazil.
This problem presented the South with one of its great dilemmas.
On the one hand, industrialization seemed to be the only means
of providing decent employment for the poor whites and allaying
discontent. A writer in *De Bow's Review* noted that the poor,
having the vote, might overbalance the rich. They had been content to endure their degraded conditions in plantation labor
because they were satisfied that they were above the slave, socially
if not economically. But the mass of the poor whites were beginning to understand their rights and to learn that there was a world
of industry opening before them by which they could elevate
themselves from wretchedness and ignorance to competence and
intelligence. *"It is this great upbearing of our masses that we are
to fear, so far as our institutions are concerned."*[86]

On the other hand, it was generally accepted that the creation of a free laboring class was an even greater danger. C. G. Memminger, a prominent South Carolina statesman, wrote to Governor Hammond in connection with this problem, that those who were "agog about manufactures," like William Gregg, were unwittingly lending aid to the abolitionists. If Negro mechanics and operatives were driven from the cities, he feared, their places would be taken by the "same men who make the cry in the Northern cities against the tyranny of Capital—and there as here would drive before them all who interfere with them—and would soon raise here the cry against the Negro, and be hot Abolitionists. And every one of these men would have a vote."[87] The Richmond *Enquirer* expressed the same idea somewhat more crudely when it stated that the South could have industry, but would not have "your brutal, ignorant and insubordinate factory hands in our midst, for all the wealth of 'Ormus and of Ind,'" nor exchange its situation "for the countless millions of paupers and criminals, who lift up and sustain the cowardly, selfish, sensual, licentious, infidel, agrarian, and revolutionary edifice of free society."[88]

Furthermore, the establishment of manufacturing in the South would undoubtedly draw immigrants from Europe and the North, who were considered by the Charleston *Standard* a curse instead of a blessing because they were generally opposed to slavery. Unlike the merchants, who were intelligent and trustworthy and able to discern their true interests, the paper bemoaned that the mechanics were *"continually carping about slave competition* ... most of them are pests to society, dangerous among the slave population, and ever ready to form combinations against the interests of the slaveholders."[89] Nor was it believed prudent by many to employ slaves in manufacturing, for the instruction which they would have to receive, their concentration in large numbers, and their contact with free labor would "foment discontent."

There were many factors which hindered the industrialization of the South, particularly the lack of investment capital, competition from Northern producers, and the relatively greater returns from agriculture. But the social consequences of the introduction of manufacturing was a question that received considerable attention from the leaders of the South. The preponderance of opinion on the subject was that a slave in industry was already half free, and a free laborer already half an abolitionist, and that it would therefore be better to keep the South agrarian, backward and enslaved than industrialized, prosperous and free.[90]

The guiding principle of the slavocracy was *divide et impera.* Its basic policy followed two lines, the first of which was to convince the white laborers that they had a material interest in the preservation of the chattel system. They were constantly told that, by consigning the hard, menial and low-paid tasks to slaves, the white workers were enabled to constitute a labor aristocracy which held the best and most dignified jobs, and that the latter were lucrative only because they were supported by the super-profits wrung from the unpaid labor of slaves. Unless abolitionism was "met and repelled as becomes a proud spirited people," the whites would have to take over the menial jobs and the emancipated slaves would be able to compete with them in every branch of industry.[91] Furthermore, since the South was not blighted by the curse of industry and urbanization, the workers did not have to compete with the "remorseless and untiring machine" or with "foreign pauper labor," they did not suffer unemployment from periodic business depressions, they did not have to work in crowded cities and in "close and sickly workshops," and, best of all, they were not subject to contact with "all the absurd and degrading isms which have sprung up in the rank soil of infidelity. . . . They are not for breaking down all the forms of society and of religion and of reconstructing them; but prefer law, order and existing institutions to the chaos which radicalism involves."[92] Finally, just as Northern workers were taught that they could, by application and thrift, become employers themselves, the slogan was advanced in the South: "Every laborer a slaveholder." It was

argued in the Southern commercial conventions, for example, that
the slave trade should be revived so that every worker and farmer
could own at least one slave, thereby preventing "an antagonism
between slavery and labor, like that between capital and labor in
the North."[93]

No less important as an ideological weapon against labor
militancy was the use of a technique in which the Southern Bour-
bon has become a world authority: race prejudice. Every effort
was bent to prove that there was no conflict between rich and
poor in Southern society, and that, in fact, there were no class
distinctions at all, the only gradations being those of color. The
meanest of the "mean whites" was placed, by virtue of his skin,
on a "perfect spirit of equality" with the gentlest of the gentlemen
planters. Southern society was said by Robert Toombs of Georgia
to exemplify the principles of the Declaration of Independence,
for, since that document obviously did not refer to Negroes when
it said that all men were created equal, "the perfect equality of
the superior race, and the legal subordination of the inferior race,
are the foundations on which we have erected our republican
society."[94] The workers were beguiled by a spurious pride of caste
and social status, and in addition frightened by the specter of race
war, Negro supremacy and miscegenation. The "purity" of the
races had to be maintained by a strict observance of prescribed relations, and any worker who showed signs of treating a Negro
fellow-worker as a human being was likely to be chastised by
expulsion or violence.[95] And it was the very degradation to which
slavery consigned him that made the deluded worker susceptible
to the ideology of race supremacy. Because he was himself reduced
virtually to the status of the slave, he could preserve a modicum
of self-respect only by identifying himself in some way with a
master class, with whom he could share the "privilege" of lording
it over a helpless class of pariahs.[96]

Thus, the workers were blinded in order that their conflict with
the slaveholder might be diverted and directed against the slaves,

while at the same time the slaves were used to keep them in subjugation. (Did not William Gregg assure his fellow slaveholders and capitalists that there could never be any conflict between labor and capital in the South, since ". . . capital will be able to control labor, even in manufactures with whites, for blacks can always be resorted to in case of need.")[97] Frederick Douglass exposed the significance of this racial prejudice:

The slaveholders, with a craftiness peculiar to themselves, by encouraging the enmity of the poor, laboring white man against the blacks, succeed in making the said white man almost as much a slave as the black man himself. The difference between the white slave, and the black slave, is this: the latter belongs to *one* slaveholder, and the former belongs to *all* the slaveholders, collectively. The white slave has taken from him, by indirection, what the black slave has taken from him, directly, and without ceremony. Both are plundered, and by the same plunderers. The slave is robbed, by his master, of all his earnings, above what is required for his bare physical necessities; and the white man is robbed by the slave system, of the just results of his labor, because he is flung into competition with a class of laborers who work without wages. . . . At present, the slaveholders blind them to this competition, by keeping alive their prejudices against the slaves, *as men*—not against them *as slaves.* They appeal to their pride, often denounce emancipation, as tending to place the white working man, on an equality with negroes, and, by this means, they succeed in drawing off the minds of the poor whites from the real fact, that, by the rich slave-master, they are already regarded as but a single remove from equality with the slave.[98]

As a delegation of Negroes explained to President Johnson many years later:

The hostility between the whites and blacks of the South is easily explained. It has its root and sap in the relation of slavery, and was incited on both sides by the cunning of the slave masters. Those masters secured their ascendancy over both the poor whites and the blacks by putting enmity between them.
They divided both to conquer each. . . .[99]

The Southern obligarchy attempted to smother the development of the working class and to keep it in blinkers, but it had another means of maintaining its power: dictatorship. Every form of legal and extra-legal repression was employed to prevent the enlightenment of the people and to crush resistance. Freedom of speech, press and assembly was infringed upon, the mails were censored, personal liberty was violated, and the entire apparatus of the state, civil and military, was utilized to maintain slavery.[100] The fact that such methods had to be resorted to more frequently as the crisis in the South deepened justified the expectations of Douglass that "The crafty appeals to the prejudices of the white laborer, against the black laborer, will lose their power to deceive in due time, and that prejudice, so long existing and augmenting, will one day find a new object upon which to discharge its terrors."[101] This hope was not sufficiently realized by the time of the war to enable the workers to play a decisive role in the overthrow of slavery, but emancipation created the conditions under which both Negro and white workers could more readily learn that lesson which was indispensable for the advancement of both.

CHAPTER III

NORTHERN LABOR CONSIDERS SLAVERY

Slavery and the Northern Workers, 1830–1845

During the first decade and a half after the inauguration of the "new" abolition movement in 1830, the attitude of Northern labor to slavery differed from that of its Southern counterpart as a result of three circumstances. First, the Northern working class was much larger, stronger, and more concentrated, and had developed a higher degree of class-consciousness. Consequently, it was necessarily concerned for the most part with its own immediate struggles for economic improvement and with building up and defending its own organizations. Its energies were engaged in the establishment of a labor movement as such.

Secondly, the workers had little direct contact with slavery and its consequences, at least until the expansionist program of the slaveholders became a national problem. The problem of slavery and the oppressions of the slavocracy did not have for them the immediacy and urgency that they had for the workers in Dixie, and their position on the slavery question was determined by different considerations and took a different course.

Finally, the character of the Northern abolition movement itself had a considerable effect in defining the role of labor. Because the abolition leadership was predominantly of the middle class and its attitude to labor generally cool if not hostile, many workers were repelled from the anti-slavery cause or tended to take an independent position which would enable them to put

61

forward their own demands as well. One of the most difficult problems of the labor movement in the struggle against slavery, like that of the European workers in the democratic revolutions of the nineteenth century, was to find a way to cooperate with the middle class against a common enemy without losing its identity and its independent program.

Although the workers did not satisfactorily solve this problem in the ante-bellum period, they did contribute greatly to the movement which finally brought about the destruction of chattel slavery. In fact, the backbone of the abolitionist movement in the 1830's was made up of farmers and artisans in whom the spirit of liberty was strong, and who, "when the great principles of freedom are jeoparded can neither be intimidated by Slaveholding bluster, nor bribed by the factorage of Cotton-bales, nor sugarhogsheads however numerous they may be."[1] It was, said Thomas Wentworth Higginson, "predominantly a people's movement, . . . and far stronger for a time in the factories and shoeshops than in the pulpits or colleges."[2] It was the support of farmers and artisans that sustained the movement in those days of mob violence and persecution. But the abolitionists constituted a small sect, and the majority of the workers, like the rest of the people, were not deeply influenced by them. Politically immature, the workers' consideration of slavery was determined largely by its real or supposed effects on their economic conditions, those things that trade unionists call bread-and-butter issues.

Bread and Butter

When slavery had existed in the North, not long since, the workers had the same problem of competing with slave labor as had the Southern workers, and their opposition to this competition was a factor in the abolition of slavery in the Northern states. As a result of petitions from mechanics, the legislature of Pennsylvania passed a resolution condemning the hiring out of slaves by their masters, and later embodied this in law. This was a blow to the slave system, because it virtually confined the use of the slaves' labor to the personal needs of their owners and made it prohibitively expensive.³ In Massachusetts, John Adams asserted that the real cause of the abolition of slavery was the increase of white workers, who would no longer permit the rich to employ slaves because of their injurious rivalry. "If the gentlemen had been permitted by law to hold slaves," he admitted, "the common white people would have put the negroes to death, and their masters too, perhaps. . . . The common white people, or rather the labouring people, were the cause of rendering negroes unprofitable servants."⁴

Economic rivalry did not cease when slavery was confined below Mason's and Dixon's line, for the institution cast its shadow over the entire nation. As early as 1834 the attention of the Northern operatives was directed to the appearance in the Philadelphia market of cotton yarn manufactured in Virginia by slave labor, and selling at a price which could not be met by Northern industry, and they were warned that this was the beginning of an enterprise that would result in reducing the condition of workingmen to one "but little better than that of the slave."⁵ By the next decade the warning was becoming a reality, and when the Southern conventions began to talk of a systematic development of industry, the situation began to cause considerable alarm. A political economist pointed out in 1847 that slave labor in Virginia, at a cost of $120 a year, would soon destroy the Pennsylvania iron industry, which paid $300 for labor.⁶ During the depression of 1858 it was said that while a thousand operatives in the factories and rolling mills were unemployed, many thousands of dollars worth of the products of Tennessee iron establishments, worked exclusively by slaves, were being sold in the Northern markets.⁷

The anti-slavery papers began to report on the progress of

industrialism in the Southern states, explaining that their products would undersell those of Northern factories and either drive their employees out of work or force them to lower their standards to those of the slaves, and the Philadelphia *Daily Republic* cautioned the striking workers in that city that if they did not yield their demands for increased wages and shorter hours the manufacturers would move to the South and employ slave labor.[8] The Fall River *Mechanic* noted that the demand for a ten-hour day was being opposed on the ground that competition with slave labor made it impracticable, and called upon the workers to assemble and express their views on the subject of "white slavery and Negro slavery."[9]

Nor did state boundaries provide protection against the stigma with which slavery branded labor and laborers. The abolitionists repeatedly pointed out that "Slavery blights the industry of the nation by making labor disreputable. It degrades the laboring population assimilating them to slaves. It leads our statesmen to imagine, and sometimes say, that the laboring people are incompetent to self-government, and thus it emboldens them to treat them as slaves."[10] Thomas Morris of Ohio charged in the Senate that the demeaning of labor had gone so far as to inspire attacks on the principle of universal suffrage and warned the workers to take heed of what was happening before it was too late.[11]

Political economists who sympathized with the labor movement likewise noted this phenomenon. Theodore Sedgwick said that the taint of slavery was poisoning the blood of the people in the free states. "Slavery had given to the common people those mean names of reproach which have been attached to all who profess the common man's labours. . . . In our own country, the poorest class in the free states, have been sometimes called 'white slaves.'" Thus, he noted, the slavery question was one which concerned the white working men of the entire country.[12]

Nor were the workers unaware of the degradation with which slavery marked labor. *The Boston Reformer* believed that the association of labor with slavery caused labor to be looked down upon, and that the attitude of the slaveholder was imparted to the Northerners. "He looks upon the free laborer here very much as he does on the slave in his own section of the country, and the first we know, all those with whom he has intercourse here, also become unable to distinguish any essential difference between the free white, and the enslaved black laborer."[13] A. H. Wood, another labor editor, seconded this remark. He added that the Northern capitalists were inflamed and captivated by the example of the slaveholding aristocrats who had "no *Saturday nights* in their financial calendars, no *Januarries* with the laboring herd. No Trade Unions are there, no combinations to raise wages, no levelers are there, but one eternal harvest of productive industry prevails," and that they "have racked their ingenuity to find out *ways and means* to bring the laboring classes of the North, into the same state of subjugation." The workingmen of the North, therefore, had a direct interest in the overthrow of slavery.[14]

If this problem seemed somewhat remote both in time and space to many workers, they were faced with another immediate and present form of competition that was no less clearly a result of the continuing existence of slavery in one section of the country, namely, the competition with the labor of free Negroes. These people, branded with the stigma of the auction block and the victims of discrimination, persecution and a double measure of oppression, occupied a status only a degree higher than that of the slaves themselves. The prejudice against them was so intense that it became increasingly difficult for them to get employment, particularly after the heavy influx of immigration began in the early 1840's, and a demand arose for new kinds of skills which the Negroes did not have and were not permitted to acquire. Frederick Douglass referred to this situation in his paper in 1853. It was becoming increasingly evident, he stated, that the free

Negroes must learn trades or perish. The old avocations of the Negroes were rapidly and unceasingly passing into the hands of whites, whose color and hunger were thought to give them a better title to employment. White men were becoming house-servants, cooks, stewards, porters, stevedores, wood-sawyers, hod-carriers, brick-makers, white-washers, and barbers, so that the Negroes could scarcely find the means of subsistence. This would continue, Douglass believed, until slavery and the prejudices nurtured by slavery were abolished.[15]

This was the case throughout the North. The Negroes were forced to abandon one trade after another, in one city after another, were even driven out of the menial offices of which they once held a virtual monopoly, and were finally forced to emigrate from the cities in large numbers.[16]

This policy was the result not only of the prejudices of employers but of the workers also, who found themselves pitted against the Negro workers and taught that their own prosperity depended on the adversity of others. Many workers refused to work with Negroes, and trade unions proscribed the employment of Negro mechanics and forbade their members to teach them trades.[17] The Negroes, a disfranchised and unprotected minority, were the chief sufferers from this suicidal division, but the white workers were exploited by it as well, and especially the Irish laborers who filled the unskilled and low-paid jobs. By failing to unite with the Negroes in a common struggle to improve their conditions, they were forced into a mad strife for jobs, and the whites were able to come out on top only at the cost of meeting or underbidding the depressed wages of their rivals, and even then the losers in the skirmish were held as a club over their heads to keep them in place.[18]

It is not to be wondered that in this brutish contest, the weapons of the brute were employed. In many Northern cities passion and hunger exploded into fierce riots, most often involving attacks by Irish against Negroes, as when Negroes were employed

to fill the places of striking stevedores in New York; and sometimes the warfare spread from the waterfront to the town, and a
helpless population were expelled from their homes.[19] Finally,
demands were heard for the complete exclusion of free Negroes.
In practically every Northern legislature laws were introduced
prohibiting their immigration into the state or imposing restrictions on them, and some of them were enacted. So the pattern
of second-class citizenship spread from the South and engulfed
the nation, and Negro and white workers alike were caught in
the trap.[20]

Few white workers understood that this difficulty was a product
of the slave system; instead of seeking a solution in the abolition
of slavery, many were frightened by the specter of an emancipated people swelling the ranks of the job-hunters and became
ardent opponents of abolition. Some of them even believed that
abolitionism was inspired by the capitalists for this purpose, like
the one who wrote in the *Voice of Industry* that the "selfish
capitalists, and those who are disgustingly subservient" to their
system "seem quite anxious to bring labor of the black slave into
competition with that of the whites, by reducing its compensation one quarter. This would be fun to the capitalists, but death
to us, who are their slaves."[21] The *Working Man's Advocate*
asserted that emancipation would bring the freedmen into direct
competition with the white workers, and concluded: "It is not
difficult, therefore, to foresee in whose favor the competition,
between three millions of blacks and a yet greater number of
whites, would terminate; and who would first suffer from want
of employment and the reduction of wages consequent on competition." The editor favored gradual emancipation and colonization of the ex-slaves in a special state set aside for them in the
West.[22]

Southern politicians and pro-slavery publicists were assiduous
in propagating this idea among the workers, and Henry Clay
wrote to the Rev. Calvin Colton urging him to write a popular

tract whose purpose should be to arouse the working classes of
the North against abolition. He suggested that Colton argue that
the free Negroes would come North, enter into competition
with the free laborer, reduce his wage standards, undermine his
social standing and his "racial purity," and reduce him to the
"despised and degraded condition of the black man."[23] The
abolitionists worked just as hard to convince the workers that
emancipation would not produce these consequences. They
pointed out that Negroes only came to the North to escape from
slavery, and that emancipation would remove the motive for
their emigration; that the majority of free Negroes stayed in
the South unless they were driven out; and that their associations
and family ties, their familiarity with conditions and suitability
to the climate, and the high price which their labor would command if slavery were abolished, would not only keep the freed
slaves in the South but would induce most of those in the
North to return, thus redounding to the advantage of the white
laborer.[24]

Special efforts were made to wean the Irish laborers from
their hostility to abolition. Since they had nearly all been peasants
in the old world they came to this country with little industrial
skill and consequently were consigned to the most menial jobs.
They therefore felt the competition of free Negro labor more
acutely than any other group and were more sensitive to the
propaganda that emancipation would endanger their standards by
deluging the North with a flood of low-paid workers. They were
even more susceptible to this propaganda because of the sources
from which much of it emanated: the Democratic party and the
Catholic Church.

The Irish-Americans had always been strongly attached to the
Democratic party, whose very name attracted them, while they
were repelled by Federalists and Whigs because of the well
founded suspicion that those parties represented the money
power and harbored the nativist elements who wanted to estab-

lish second-class citizenship for the immigrants. The Democrats, opposing nativism and posing as the friends of the workingmen, were able to gather the Irish into their fold. While the Irish workers were less concerned with national than local political affairs, their loyalty to the party made it possible to keep them in line on all major issues, including the slavery question.[25]

The Catholic Church was officially neutral in the slavery controversy, avoiding any dogmatic position which would result in the kind of schism that had rent several of the Protestant churches. In the South it was unanimously pro-slavery, like every other religion except that practiced by the slaves. In the North the Church embraced every gradation of sentiment except outright abolitionism, which was identified with radicalism and strong government—both were feared as encouraging anti-clericalism. Such a large number of the spokesmen for the Church held pro-slavery views that they were generally regarded as reflecting the policy of the Church itself.[26] The Irish Catholic press was, with scarcely an exception, vigorously opposed to abolition, branding it as a British agency whose sole object was to destroy the Union, and even defending mob violence against the abolitionists. These papers also toed the Democratic party line on all issues and supported its candidates in every campaign.[27]

To overcome these handicaps was no small task, but the abolitionists attempted to enlist the Irish love of liberty and deep hatred of oppression in the anti-slavery cause. In this endeavor they had the assistance of Daniel O'Connell, the great leader of the struggle for Catholic emancipation and Irish independence, and many other Irish democrats. In 1841 O'Connell, Father Mathew, the famous temperance reformer, and sixty thousand other Irishmen addressed an appeal to the Irish residents of the United States calling upon them to espouse the anti-slavery cause as part of the fight against oppression everywhere. Mass meetings were held in several cities, at which this address was read and resolutions voted upon. A meeting in Faneuil Hall resolved:

That we rejoice that the voice of O'Connell, which now shakes the three kingdoms, has poured across the waters a thunderpeal for the cause of liberty in our own land; and that Father Mathew, having lifted with one hand five millions of his own countrymen into moral life, has stretched forth the other—which may Heaven make equally potent—to smite off the fetters of the American slave.

. . . That we receive with the deepest gratitude the names of the sixty thousand Irishmen, who, in the trial-hour of their own struggle for liberty, have not forgotten the slave on this side of the water; that we accept with triumphant exultation the address they have forwarded to us, and pledge ourselves to circulate it through the length and breadth of our land, till the pulse of every man who claims Irish parentage beats true to the claims of patriotism and humanity.

Wendell Phillips made the keynote speech, which he concluded by asking, "Will you ever return to his master the slave who once sets foot on the soil of Massachusetts? [No, no, no!] Will you ever raise to office or power the man who will not pledge his utmost effort against slavery? [No, No, no!]"[28] While many Irish-American workers were persuaded by such appeals, the majority probably retained their hostility to abolition throughout the ante-bellum period.[29]

Our Fair Escutcheon

> May the foul stain of slavery be blotted out of our fair
> escutcheon; and our fellow men, not only declared to
> be free and equal, but actually enjoy that freedom and
> equality to which they are entitled by nature.

—"Workingmen's prayer" submitted in 1830 by the trade unions of Massachusetts to the state legislature.[30]

In 1836 the Working Men's Association of England addressed an appeal to the American working class, inquiring why "the last and blackest remnant of kingly dominion has not been uprooted from Republican America?"

Why, when she has afforded a home and an asylum for the destitute and oppressed among all nations, should oppression in her own land be legalized, and bondage tolerated? Did nature, when she cast her sunshine o'er the earth, and adapted her children to its influence, intend that her varied taints of skin should be the criterion of liberty? And shall men whose illustrious ancestors proclaimed mankind to be brothers by nature, make an exception, to degrade to the condition of slaves, human beings a shade darker than themselves?

Surely it cannot be for the interest of the working class that these prejudices should be fostered—this degrading traffic be maintained. No, no; it must be for those who shrink from honest industry, and who would equally sacrifice to their love of gain and mischievous ambition, the happiness of either black or white. We entertain the opinion, friends, that all those who seek to consign you to unremitting toil, to fraudulently monopolize your lands, to cheat you in the legislature, to swell their territory by injustice, and to keep you ignorant and divided, are the same who are the perpetrators and advocates of slavery.[31]

Lewis Gunn, a Philadelphia labor leader, transmitted this address to the workers of America with the admonition that "Our Voice should *thunder* from Maine to Georgia, and from the Atlantic to the Mississippi—the voice of a nation of *Republicans and Christians* demanding with all the authority of moral power, *demanding* the immediate liberation of the bondsmen."[32]

The majority of the workers were not yet ready to respond to this appeal, but a growing number began to discern a menace to labor in the oligarchic pretensions of the slaveholders.[33] The labor leader and land reformer, George Henry Evans, was no great admirer of the abolitionists, whom he considered honest but fanatic, but as early as 1831 he had become convinced that the interests of labor demanded that they should exert themselves in the cause of emancipation. Free men could never enjoy equal rights, he maintained, in a nation in which two million human beings were held in bondage. It was therefore the duty of every freeman and every friend of equal rights to save the country from the evils which threatened it by lending their aid to the fight for the total eradication of slavery.[34]

Probably there was no stronger concentration of anti-slavery sentiment anywhere in the United States than among the "factory girls" of New England, whose humanitarianism and devotion to democracy and the rights of labor gave them an ardent hatred of the slavocracy. They were very active in the abolition movement, in spite of intimidation both for their views and for their impudence in transgressing the bounds of female decency by expressing them.[35] The love of freedom and the plebeian virtue of these girls were enshrined by Whittier in one of his more youthful efforts, "The Yankee Girl," written for the *National Enquirer*:

> She sits by her wheel at that low cottage door,
> Which the long evening shadow is stretching before,
> With a music as sweet as the music which seems
> Breathed softly and faint in the ear of her dreams.
>
> . . . .
>
> Who comes in his pride to that low cottage door?
> 'Tis the haughty and proud to the humble and poor,
> 'Tis the great Southern planter, the master who waves
> His whip of dominion o'er hundreds of slaves!
>
> "Nay, Ellen for shame, let those Yankee fools spin,
> Who would pass for our slaves with a change of their skin,
> Let them work as they will at the loom or the wheel,
> Too haughty for shame and too vulgar to feel.
>
> "But thou art too lovely and precious a gem
> To be bound to their burdens or sullied by them.
> For shame Ellen, shame, cast thy bondage aside,
> And away to the South as my blessing and pride.
>
> "Oh come to my home where my servants shall all
> Depart at thy bidding and come at thy call;
> They shall heed thee as mistress with trembling and awe
> And each wish of thy heart be felt as a law."

Oh could you have seen her, that pride of our girls,
Arise and cast back the dark wealth of her curls,
With a scorn in her eye which the gazer could feel,
And a glance like the sunshine that flashes on steel.

"Go back haughty Southron, thy treasures of gold
Are dimmed by the blood of the hearts thou hast sold.
Thy home may be lovely, but round it I hear
The crack of the whip and the footsteps of fear.

. . . .

"Full low at thy bidding thy negroes may kneel,
With the iron of bondage on spirit and heel,
Yet know that the Yankee girl sooner would be
In fetters with them than in freedom with thee."[36]

The anti-slavery press, and particularly the *National Anti-Slavery Standard,* which was first edited by Nathaniel P. Rogers, one of the few abolitionist leaders who actively championed the cause of labor, began to harp on this theme. In his first issue Rogers stated his aim to be to convince the "hard-handed workingmen" that their fate was indissolubly linked to that of the slave and that their progress was dependent on the broadening and deepening of democracy, of which the workers were the greatest beneficiaries and the stoutest defenders. Time after time the abolitionists quoted from the anti-democratic and anti-labor speeches of Harper, Leigh, McDuffie and other Southern spokesmen, and hammered home the precept that slaveholding was the natural enemy of the working class.[37]

That this viewpoint was taking hold in the labor movement was indicated when in 1842 a cargo of slaves revolted on the *Creole,* seized the vessel and took it into a British port where they gained their freedom. The *New York State Mechanic* lauded this blow for liberty and denounced "our Chivalrous southern neighbors—those men who sneeringly call the mechanics and laborers

of the free North *slaves*—these men would rush into war with
England, and then, as they have done before, leave the 'northern
slave' to bear the brunt, and pay the cost with their treasure and
their blood."[38] The workers were not prepared to fight
England in order to maintain the "property" of the slaveholders,
nor were they willing to defend the institution against a rising of
the slaves at home. The New England Workingmen's Convention
in 1846 declared that *all* men were entitled to the rights for which
the workers were contending, and that if the "three millions of
our brethren and sisters, groaning in chains on the Southern
plantations," should follow the example of the revolutionists who
resisted British oppression, "we will never take up arms to
sustain the Southern slaveholders in robbing one-fifth of our
countrymen of their liberty."[39]

In 1848 a mass meeting of workers assembled in Faneuil Hall
to hail the revolution in Europe and passed a resolution declaring
"That while we rejoice in the organization of free institutions in
the Old World, we are not indifferent to their support at home,
and that we regard the despotic attitude of the slave power at the
South, and the domineering ascendency of a Monied Oligarchy
in the North, as equally hostile to the interests of Labor, and
incompatible with the preservation of popular rights."[40] The
German communist workers of Cleveland resolved to "use all
means which are adapted to abolishing slavery, an institution
which is so wholly repugnant to the principles of true Democracy."[41]

The attack on the civil liberties of the abolitionists aroused
many more workers to an awareness of the danger from that
quarter. A meeting was called in Lowell in 1835, at which resolutions were presented to muzzle the anti-slavery press, close
all halls and churches to the abolitionists, and to "prevent all
over whom they have any control, from attending meetings of
such discussions." The workers in the hall created such a com-
motion that the speaker was unable to continue and a vote on

the resolutions was impossible. The Southern press was in a rage over this, bitterly lamenting that abolitionism had gained such inroads into the working class, and proposing a boycott of their manufactures that would cause Lowell to "wither or be forced to expel the abolitionists."[42]

When the Southern congressmen attempted to put a gag on the right of petition, the *National Laborer* noted that the petitions of the abolitionists and those of the trade unions in behalf of the ten-hour day received the same treatment, and the significance of their common plight was plain.[43] Especially alarming to labor was the mob violence against abolition meetings and newspapers and against the Negro people. Even Evans, who did not see eye to eye with the abolitionists on their program and tactics, denounced attacks on Negro abolitionists as calculated to create prejudice between Negroes and whites, "which *might,* in the end, produce much bloodshed, and which *must,* at any rate be highly injurious to both."[44] The lynching of Lovejoy, the assaults on anti-slavery meetings, and the destruction of C. M. Clay's press likewise drew vigorous protests from the labor press, which asserted that "when we see the craven tyrants of the South . . . warring with the freedom of the press and the liberties of the white man, in order to rivet more securely the chains of black slavery, we will denounce them as the cowardly enemies of all rational liberty, who dare not tolerate the liberty of the press, because they know that the unrighteousness of their system would cause it to be abolished, if exposed to the light of free discussion."[45]

Some of the abolitionists tried to show the workers that the slaveholders had designs not only on their civil rights but even on their personal freedom. Liberally quoting the apologists of slavery who stated that servitude was the normal condition of the laboring classes, that the slaves were better off than the Northern workers, and that the free states would have to introduce the institution within a few years, the abolitionists proclaimed that

a plot was brewing to actually enslave the entire working class
of the United States. They charged that in this enterprise the
slaveholders had the willing cooperation of the Northern capitalists, who had a "peculiar affinity" with them and were "in love
with the beauties of that system." The struggle was on, they
declared, between the antagonistic principles of free and slave
labor. The two could not much longer co-exist; one must prevail
to the destruction of the other. Either the laborers in the South
would be free or the laborers in the North would lose their
freedom. "The laboring population of the North have it *now*
in their power to turn the scale which way they please. On which
side will they place themselves?"[46] The workers would one day
take this matter seriously, but at the time most of them were
less concerned with the possibility of their future enslavement
to the "man-stealers" than with the actuality of what they considered their present slavery to the capitalist class.

"Chattel Slaves and Wage Slaves"

> Remember, too, that wrong is here,
> And give the North one pitying tear;
> Oh! the fruits of love go forth,
> To free the South and bless the North!
> *The Voice of Industry*[47]

The young American labor movement very quickly developed
a high degree of class-consciousness. Subjected to a galling yoke
of long hours, low wages, and insecurity, the workers naturally
compared their conditions with those of the Southern slaves,
and discovered a startling similarity. Of course, the conditions
of the Northern working class as a whole were not as bad as
those of the slaves, especially during prosperous business periods,
and besides the free workers had the opportunity of advancing
or of rising out of the working class which the slaves did not

have. Many of the statements were merely fanciful fictions, designed by labor spokesmen to emphasize the deplorable conditions of the workers and by defenders of slavery to apologize for the conditions of the slaves. But the fact that such comparisons could be seriously made indicates what laborers thought about their status, and greatly affected their attitude toward the slavery problem, because it strengthened their tendency to place the abolition of "wage slavery" before that of chattel slavery.

Seth Luther, the outstanding labor leader in New England in the 1830's, doubted if the mill workers were better off than the slaves, and thought that children born in slavery did not work half as long, nor perform one-quarter of the labor that the white children did in the cotton mills, and had many advantages which the latter did not possess.[48] The *Mechanics' Free Press* described the circumstances of the laborer who, working more than the slave, "can not secure to himself and children the necessaries of life; he commences in the morning of his life his daily task, and so long as his breath continues he *may* supply himself and children with food; but when sickness, the oft consequence of over exertion, overtakes him, he is stretched on his bed, his wife can not leave him to obtain work; he has no master interested in prolonging his life, therefore none to send him food or medicine; his children want bread, he has none to give them; and the sons of freedom are oft compelled to go forth and solicit from the cold hand of charity, the crumbs that fall from the rich man's table." The writer concluded that John Adams was right when he considered the difference between the working class and the slaves to be principally a "custom of speech."[49]

Referring to the alarming increase in pauperism the *Voice of Industry* declared that wages were steadily sinking until thousands were reduced to the starvation point, and the workers were subject to "a subtle, indirect slavery rarely acknowledged, but everywhere felt." In this respect, observed the writer, the slaves were better off than the free laborers of the North, for at least their conditions remained pretty much the same from year to year.[50] If the workers were exploited as much as the slaves, they suffered even more in one respect, for they had no means of support during sickness, old age and unemployment other than the meager and uncertain bounties of charity, whereas the slaves were maintained by their masters at all times.[51]

Not only were their conditions as bad or worse than those of the slaves, in the opinion of many laborers, but even the forms of oppression sometimes exhibited a remarkable similarity. The Cabotsville *Chronicle* charged that the mill owners were recruiting labor by "forcing poor girls from their quiet homes, to become their tools, and like the Southern slaves, to give up her life and liberty to the heartless tyrants and taskmasters." They sent a long black wagon, known as a "slaver," cruising about the countryside of Vermont and New Hampshire, with a "commander" who was paid a dollar a head for each operative he brought back, often enticing them under false pretenses.[52] A much more comprehensive analogy between the two forms of slavery was drawn by some. One writer noted that while slave families were sometimes separated by force, the families of workingmen were likewise often compelled to separate to find employment, and their children were frequently sent into the factories, to the detriment or destruction of their health and morals. The black slave could not choose his own master, but it was frequently the same with the white worker, who was indeed thankful to have any master at all. Both the female slaves and the working women were sometimes compelled to submit to the licentious desires of their masters. The slaves could not vote; neither could the white women. Besides, "the black slave is free from the care, responsibility, and perplexity which is the lot of the poor white . . . , nor does he fear that he will be compelled to go to the almshouse for want of employment, or in consequence of old age, sickness, or misfortune."[53]

It seemed to many workers that in the systems of chattel slavery and "wage slavery" there was a difference without a distinction, for "The poor negro must work or be whipped,—the poor white laborer must work or be starved." While the Southern slave's labor was bought for a certain sum during his life, the Northern slave's labor was bought yearly.[54]

When some labor spokesmen looked beyond the legal sanctions of slavery and defined its essence, they discerned a basic identity between chattel slavery and the wages system. William Cobbett construed a slave as a man who had no property. ". . . any man who is compelled to give up the fruit of his labor to another, at the arbitrary will of that other, has no property in his labor, and is, therefore a slave, whether the fruit of his labor be taken from him directly or indirectly," by force or by fear of starvation. Did this fit the wage-earner?[55] "In what does slavery consist?" asked the *Mechanic's Free Press*. "In being compelled to work for others, so that they may reap the advantage." Did this fit the wage-earner?[56] Mike Walsh summed the matter up in a speech in Congress:

The only difference between the negro slave of the South, and the white wages slave of the North, is, that the one has a master without asking for him, and the other has to beg for the privilege of becoming a slave. . . . The one is the slave of an individual; the other is the slave of an inexorable class. . . . If a dozen of us own a horse in common, we want to ride him as much as possible, and feed him as little as possible. But if you or I own a horse exclusively, we will take good care to feed him well, and not drive him too much to endanger his health, but just enough to keep him in good traveling order.[57]

These conclusions, widely held among the working classes, were drawn primarily from their own experiences and observations rather than from any understanding or investigation of economic theory. This explains why they almost completely overlooked one of the glaring inconsistencies of the abolition argument. The latter pointed out over and over again that one of the chief advantages of free labor over slavery was that the wage-earner, working under the incentive of reward (that is, the necessity of supporting himself and his family) produced twenty-five per cent more than the slave working under the compulsion of the lash. In other words, the slaveholders were virtually told that they could exploit their workers more if they emancipated them and could increase their profits by twenty-five per cent.[58] Some of the political economists who defended the interests of labor made a more searching analysis of the economic basis of the wages system and nearly approached the doctrine of surplus labor as a measure of exploitation, which was later expounded by Marx.

John Francis Bray, in *Labor's Wrong and Labor's Remedy,* stated that labor was the only measure and true title of property, and that since wages contained less labor than that incorporated in the product, the surplus went to the owner; whether a capitalist or slaveholder, the process and the result were the same.[59] Stephen Simpson, the author of *The Working Man's Manual,* believed that wages generally amounted to the smallest pittance compatible with the preservation of life. Employers fixed the wages of their workers as absolutely as did the slaveholders those of their chattels, and were no more disposed to dole out more than enough to keep them alive and working. And what was it, he asked, but the principle of slavery that made it a felony for workingmen to ask for just wages, that punished them as conspirators, and that sentenced them to jail as it did the robber?[60]

More important than these works was *The Working Man's Political Economy* by John Pickering, a land reformer.[61] The book opens with the words: "Every where we see toiling millions the slaves of the capitalists; consequently we find unconsumable wealth in the possession of a few, while poverty, discomfort and wretchedness is the lot of the great mass of the people." He found evidence in the entire history of the world for the fact that in civilized countries the rich became richer and the poor became poorer. The greater the wealth of a country, and the greater the riches, power, and splendor of the capitalists, the less was the poor man's share and the harder he had to work for a bare subsistence, until he finally sank into poverty, want, and wretchedness. When the country became completely overstocked with wealth, the workingman could find no work at all. Capitalists would not employ him, being unable to realize a profit from his labor, and he was turned into the street to starve, beg, or steal. But the slaveholder could not do this, said Pickering, for his interest prompted him to keep his slave in a healthy working condition until the surplus wealth was disposed of and he could again be profitably employed.[62] The wages of laborers and slaves were both the same, he argued, namely "such as to enable them to continue the race of journeymen and servants, as the demands of society may happen, from time to time, to require." He cited the authority of Adam Smith for the fact that an employer can realize more profit from the use of free labor than from a chattel slave, and with less risk of capital, and went on to give a detailed analysis of the comparative costs in both cases, the results of which seemed to confirm the theory of Smith.[63] Pickering concluded that the exploitation of slaves and wage-workers was at best identical, and probably greater in the case of the latter. "In neither case would the victims consent to part with the product of their own labor, if they could help it, except for an equivalent; but the masters, having virtually made the laws, have taken good care to protect themselves from violence, while they commit the injustice."[64]

The conditions and status of the workers, and their conception of the nature of that status, were of crucial importance in molding their position on the question of slavery and abolition. An insignificant element in the labor movement came perilously close to defending slavery, like the *American's Own and Fireman's Journal,* which published "A Plea for Slavery" by Las Casas,[65] or the drunken congressman Mike Walsh, whom Frederick Douglass aptly dubbed "that living embodiment of *Subterranean filth and fury*."[66] A much larger number simply paid no attention to the slavery question until about 1845, considering it as a matter of little concern to them, who had their own problems. Their attitude was expressed by a meeting of workers in Massachusetts who said that the slaves were taken care of by their masters—let the workers take care of themselves.[67]

Among those who did take a stand on the slavery question, the great preponderance of opinion was on the side of emancipation, although most labor leaders were not willing to subordinate themselves to the narrow policy of the "pure abolitionists" or subscribe to their philosophy and tactics.[68] The workingmen, believing that their condition was as bad as that of the slaves, were naturally in favor of abolishing "wage slavery" as well as chattel slavery. The most important and the most difficult problem they faced was a matter of strategy: which issue should be given primacy, which was most likely to be accomplished first, and how could they best work for the emancipation of slavery without sacrificing their own cause and retarding its victory? It was a rare labor leader who had the insight to comprehend that the labor movement could not achieve a really independent position until the field had first been cleared by the final overthrow of the slave system and the power of the landed aristocracy—and, as we shall see, the abolitionists hindered their approach to such an understanding. Consequently, the dominant view in the labor movement at this time was that they had to strive for the emancipation of *all* workers, white and Negro, with the immediate and pressing issue being the abolition of wage slavery.

It should be understood that when they spoke of the abolition of wage slavery, most workingmen and their spokesmen did not have in mind the abolition of capitalism. There were some socialists, Utopian and Marxian, in the ante-bellum American labor movement who believed that wage slavery could be ended only by the establishment of a cooperative commonwealth. More commonly, wage slavery was equated not with capitalism but with the worst aspects of it, such as extreme exploitation, narrowing of opportunities for the workers, and disregard for their rights and feelings. To bring these conditions to an end, they proposed such reforms as easy and equal access to the land, public education, a shorter work-day, abolition of monopolies and national banks, and the abolition of slavery. These reforms were intended more to give the workingmen equal opportunity to rise out of the working class than to abolish class society. But in either case the concept of wage slavery was based on a recognition of the existence of classes with different if not opposing interests. This is the essence of class consciousness.

Representative of this viewpoint was the *New England Artisan,* published by the New England Association of Mechanics and Working Men, whose object was to secure the realization of the principles of freedom and equality. The *Artisan* commented on the great exertions made by philanthropists to arouse the sympathy of the white people for the suffering and wretchedness of the slaves. While endorsing these efforts, the paper also called on the philanthropists not to overlook the wrongs inflicted on the white workers every day. The slaves were not the only oppressed and degraded portion of the population, it asserted. "We see oppression all around us; and what is still worse, we see it often inflicted by those very persons who profess to have the most pity for the slaves of the South." The *Artisan* asked the reformers to fight against injustice everywhere and to labor for the destruction of oppression at home as well as for the abolition of slavery in the South.[69] It proposed that slavery, being a "national curse," should be immediately abolished by national means, and suggested that the workingmen petition Congress to accomplish this, possibly by the proceeds from the sale of public land or the surplus revenue of the imposts.[70] A decade later a meeting of 25,000 workers in New York adopted a resolution expressing the same idea: "To slavery in the abstract, slavery in the concrete, to slavery absolute, slavery feudal, and the slavery of wages; to slavery where it is, and where it is not . . . to slavery we are opposed under every phase and modification, and so with firm and solemn purpose will remain until our lives end."[71] The German-American workers generally held the same position, strongly opposing slavery but giving priority to the struggle for the overthrow of wage slavery.[72]

During the 1840's a position of considerable influence in the labor movement was gained by the land reformers, and their attitude toward slavery and abolition strengthened that which was already dominant among the workers. The outstanding leader of the land reformers was George Henry Evans, an English-born associate of Robert Owen, a printer by trade, and a leading figure in the American labor movement from the time of the New York Working Men's Party organized in 1829.[73] During the 1830's he edited *The Man* and the *Working Man's Advocate*, the latter being the foremost labor paper of the decade. In the early 1840's he began to express his views on land reform in *The Radical* and the revived *Advocate*, whose name was later changed to *Young America*. The basis of Evans' program was the belief that labor was enslaved by industrial capitalism and that its only hope of escape lay in breaking the monopoly in land and assuring to every man his share—a quarter-section inalienable homestead. This panacea was to be achieved by political action: "Vote yourself a farm."

Evans had long been an advocate of the abolition of chattel slavery, and he now made this issue a part of his general program for the eradication of all slavery. He believed that it was impractical to attempt to abolish chattel slavery before abolishing "that form of slavery that is nearest home. Having accomplished this, we could with much more effect, it seems to me, turn our attention to that at a distance."[74] Furthermore, he thought it would be foolish to try to "persuade the overworked *white* slaves (supposing they had the power) to vote the *personal* freedom only of the *black,* thereby enabling their former masters, by the lash of want, to get as much labor of two-thirds of them as they formerly got of the whole, throwing the labor of the other third on the already overstocked labor market. Evident, it seems to us, is it the *first* duty of Democracy to decree the freedom of the soil."[75]

Nor would it be of any advantage to the Negroes to substitute wage slavery for chattel slavery, contended Evans. The abolitionists had employed bad arguments, based on false principles, because they failed to recognize man's right to the use of the earth as an essential freedom. They said to the slaveowners, "Free your slaves (retaining your land), and you will compel them to compete with each other for wages, and get more work from them at less cost. . . ."[76] What benefit would be derived, asked another "Agarian," by granting legal freedom to a man who was denied the means by which he must live? "What profiteth the starving operative, who is *free,* indeed, but is only *free to starve?*"[77]

John Pickering went further than most land reformers in denying that the slavery question was of any practical concern to the workers at all. He believed that the whole slavery controversy was nothing more than "the jealousy and contention of Northern and Southern capitalists—the Northern white slave driver and the Southern black slave driver." The Northern capitalist begrudged the slaveholders the political power they derived from their right to vote in lieu of their slaves; while the slaveholder was similarly aggrieved that the Northern employers were able to cajole or compel their workers to vote as they were directed. The entire question was simply a matter of which was "the best and most certain scheme, by which the wealth producers of all colors, may be plundered of the greatest amount of the product of labor in a given time?"[78]

The Utopian socialists, who also influenced the labor movement in the 1840's, took a similar position on the slavery question,
although they had a different panacea for the regeneration of
mankind. The most important of these schemes in America was
Fourierism, or Association, propagated by Albert Brisbane. Believing that the great evil of modern society was industrialism,
which enthralled the workers in disreputable labor to the profit
of a handful of capitalists, Fourier proposed that society be
reorganized into phalanxes, cooperative agrarian communities
which would gradually spread until they encompassed all of
society. The text-book of the American Fourierists was Brisbane's
Social Destiny of Man, published in 1840.[79] In it he attacked
slavery as an infringement of both "Divine law which proclaims
the equality of human nature before God, and of Human law,
which declares an equality of political rights." But slavery was
only one of the defects of the social mechanism, and was rooted
in the same system of industrial servitude which made labor the
serf of capital. It was merely a symptom of a vast social malady
which must be cured in order to eradicate the numberless evils,
including slavery, which were the disgrace and scourge of humanity. That malady was "repugnant industry." "If labor be
repulsive, degrading and but poorly rewarded," Brisbane asked,
"how are the mass to be forced to it otherwise than by *Con-
straint?*" Therefore, concluded Brisbane, chattel slavery should
not be attacked first, and above all not separately, but as part
of a complete social reformation.[80]

The Fourierist brief against the abolitionists was that the
latter attacked slavery violently, endangering both property
rights and the Union, and strove for the most meager results—a
mere dabbling in effects. The Associationists, on the other hand,
would proceed gradually and peacefully, with compensation
for the slaveholders, and the underlying cause of slavery would
be extirpated rather than simply changing one form of servitude
for another and more aggravated form.[81] In 1845, Horace Greeley,

a prominent convert to Fourierism, was invited to attend the anti-slavery convention at Cincinnati. His declination, together with the letter explaining his action, threw the abolitionists into a furious rage.

I understand by Slavery [wrote Greeley] that condition in which one human being exists mainly as a convenience for other human beings—in which the time, the exertions, the faculties of a part of the Human Family are made to subserve, not their own development physically, intellectually and morally, but the comfort, advantage or caprices of others. In short, wherever service is rendered from one human being to another, on a footing of one-sided and not of mutual obligation—when the relation between the servant and the served is not one of affection and reciprocal good offices, but of authority, social ascendency and power over subsistence on the one hand, and of necessity, servility and degradation on the other—there, in my view, is Slavery.

You will readily understand, therefore, that, if I regard your enterprise with less absolute interest than you do, it is not that I deem Slavery a less but a greater evil. If I am less troubled concerning Slavery in Charleston and New Orleans, it is because I see so much Slavery in New-York, which appears to claim my first effort. . . . In esteeming it my duty to preach Reform first to my own neighbors and kind, I would by no means attempt to censure those whose consciences prescribe a different course. Still less would I undertake to say that the Slavery of the South is not more hideous in kind and degree than that which prevails at the North. The fact that it is more flagrant and palpable renders opposition to it comparatively easy and its speedy downfall certain. But how can I devote myself to a crusade against distant servitude, when I discern its essence pervading my immediate community and neighborhood?[82]

Another group of Utopians and labor reformers, led by Robert Dale Owen and Frances Wright, had a peculiar solution for the problem of slavery, combining communitarianism and colonization. Fanny Wright had early formed the conviction that slavery was a moral sin and a social cancer, but believed that any plan for its removal must take into consideration the pecuniary interests of the slaveholders and the existing laws of the states, and that the slaves must first be prepared for freedom by education, and, when emancipated, colonized in Africa or some unsettled part of this country. In 1825 she became a convert to Robert Dale Owen's socialist theories and immediately conceived of applying them to the slavery question. Her plan was to persuade the slave-holders to turn their bondsmen over to a cooperative community, where they would be employed in common for five years, thus learning independent industry and at the same time earning enough to buy their freedom (with interest!). Then they would be manumitted and colonized, enabling the poor whites to find a place in Southern agriculture and manufacturing. She established an experimental plantation at Nashoba, near Memphis, but it was a miserable failure, both in the number of slaves involved and in the results achieved. Ten years later, Miss Wright was saying that the problem must be left to time and the growth of public opinion.[83]

Owen also opposed slavery chiefly on moral and philosophical grounds, and supported Wright's emancipation scheme. He believed that the slaveholders could be persuaded to adopt it, just as he supposed the capitalists would accept his plan for the reconstruction of society. He constantly attacked prejudice and encouraged the education of the Negroes, but in his own colony at New Harmony Negroes were excluded, except as helpers "if necessary" or "if it be found useful, to prepare and enable them to become associated in Communities in Africa. . . ."[84] He was an anti-slavery advocate all his life, but his views were always tempered by constitutional reservations and his ties with the Democratic party, as a member of which he served two terms in Congress. He remained a gradualist and a colonizationist long after the latter had been exposed as a pro-slavery device. His greatest service to the cause came only during the war, when he helped to push Lincoln along the path to emancipation.[85]

Orestes A. Brownson was another radical labor reformer (in the late 1830's and early 1840's) who insisted that the wages system was a worse form of oppression than chattel slavery; he called it "a cunning device of the devil, for the benefit of tender consciences, who would retain all the advantages of the slave system, without the expense, trouble, and odium of being slaveholders." Therefore it would do no good to emancipate the slave, for he would be "a slave still, although with the title and cares of a freeman." The best way to hasten abolition, he argued, was not by direct efforts in behalf of the slaves, but by the development and realization of democratic freedom in the non-slaveholding states. "Let us correct the evils at our own doors, elevate the free white laborer, and prove by our own practice, and by the state of our own society, that the doctrine of equal rights is not a visionary dream. O we have much to do here at home."[86]

The abolitionists could simply not understand this language. They were a heroic band of martyred men, defying poverty, social ostracism, the venom of the press and the priesthood, and the violence of lynch mobs to do battle for the downtrodden slaves. Some of them believed they should keep their nose to the abolition grindstone, while others eagerly embraced the multitude of reforms that engaged the "frantic 'forties": women's rights, temperance, world peace, spiritualism, vegetarianism, and the cold-water cure. But whether "one idea men" or "universal reformers," they had, almost without exception, a blind spot for the ills that beset the working men, except as the abolition of slavery would benefit them. The abolitionists of course denied resolutely that wage-earners could be compared with the slaves, and devoted much space in their literature to prove it. Scarcely an issue of any of their papers lacked an article or poem demonstrating the nobility of free labor, refuting the arguments of labor leaders and reformers that the wages system was a disguised form of slavery, and presenting evidence of the constant improvement in the condition of the proletariat. Every time they heard some

one say a laborer was a slave they saw red, and occasionally their
indignation stirred them to a literary explosion such as this:

> And is *this* the man, thou vaunting knave!
> Thou hast dared to compare with the weeping slave?
> Away! find *one* slave in the world to cope
> With him, in his heart, his home, his hope!
>
> He is not on thy lands of sin and pain,
> Seared, scarred with the lash—cramped with the chain;
> In thy burning clime where the heart is cold,
> And man, like the beast, is bought and sold!
>
> But O, thou slanderer, false and vile!
> Dare but to harm his garden-stile;
> Dare but to outrage his lowly thatch;
> Dare but to force that poor man's latch;
>
> And thy craven soul shall wildly quake
> At the thunder peal the dead shall wake;
> . . . [87]

Not content with proving the superiority of free labor over
slavery, the abolitionists often went further and denied that there
was any real labor problem at all, at least in this country. Garrison received the shock of his life when he visited London for
the World's Anti-Slavery Convention in 1838 and was handed a
leaflet reading: "Have we no white slaves?" and signed by "A
White Slave." Reading this to his audience, he answered emphatically "No." But he admitted that the British operatives were
"grievously oppressed" and dying of starvation, and when he
asked his listeners if the abolitionists did not show their friendship for all humanity by their sympathy with the laborers, he was
nearly knocked off the platform by a resounding "No!" Feebly
recovering his composure, he said he was sorry to hear it, but
assured the audience that "it is not true of the abolitionists in the

United States, for they are sympathetic with the oppressed, as well as the enslaved throughout the world." This incident gave him food for thought on the voyage home, but after an intense soul searching he concluded that his words "throughout the world" were somewhat hasty—he really meant throughout the British Empire. He told his welcoming committee when he disembarked: "In England I have seen dukes, marquises, and earls, and royalty itself, in all the hereditary splendor of an ancient monarchy, surrounded with luxury and pomp, and the people impoverished and oppressed to sustain it all; but here, in New England, one looks for such inequality in vain. . . ."[88]

Garrison had always been hostile toward the labor movement. In the very first issue of the *Liberator* he wrote:

An attempt has been made—it is still making—we regret to say, with considerable success—to inflame the minds of our working classes against the more opulent, and to persuade them that they are contemned and oppressed by a wealthy aristocracy. That public grievances exist, is undoubtedly true; but they are not confined to any one class of society. Every profession is interested in their removal—the rich as well as the poor. It is in the highest degree criminal, therefore, to exasperate our mechanics to deeds of violence, or to array them under a party banner; for it is not true, that, at any time, they have been the objects of reproach. . . . We are the friends of reform; but that is not reform, which, in curing one evil, threatens to inflict a thousand others.[89]

A few weeks later he returned to the subject to deny that wealth and aristocracy were allied and that they were the natural enemies of the "poor and vulgar." There was no evidence, he asserted, that the wealthy were hostile to the interests of the working classes, and those who inculcated that "pernicious doctrine" were the worst enemies of the people. "It is a miserable characteristic of human nature to look with an envious eye upon those who are more fortunate in their pursuits, or more exalted in their station."[90]

Garrison finally had to admit that there was poverty and suffering in the United States, and he brought forward a solution for the difficulties of the poor: "They must be sought out by personal effort, and their want be made known, and then enough ready hands and willing hearts can be found to give relief." Rich women especially should "forsake, awhile, the gaieties and follies of your parties of pleasure, to enjoy the bliss of relieving distress. . . . 'GO ABOUT DOING GOOD.' "[91]

Wendell Phillips, after the war to become an outstanding labor reformer, was embarrassed when mistaken for one in 1847. He was misquoted (and still is) as having said that "the great question of Labor, when it shall fully come up, will be found paramount to all others, and that the rights of the peasant of Ireland, the operative of New England, and the laborer of South America, will not be lost sight of in sympathy for the Southern slave." *The Harbinger* hastened to hail him for taking "the high road to the principle of social reform," but Phillips shortly corrected the misapprehension. He had spoken of the workers in *England,* not *New England;* the latter he did not regard as wage slaves. In fact he denied that they were wronged or oppressed, and if they were they could remedy it by voting and by practicing economy, self-denial, temperance, morality and religion, eventually becoming capitalists themselves.[92]

C. M. Clay also had an "impartial word" on the subject of the "elevation of labor." He was quite sure that society would never be organized differently than it was then or ever had been. As for trade unions and strikes, while he would not outlaw them, he was convinced that they rarely, if ever, did the workers any good, and often did "infinite evil." And the practice of strikers hindering other workers from taking their jobs by force he regarded as "the most infamous despotism—another name for lynch or mob law, which is at war with all order and human society. . . ." The solution: "Repeal all laws which obstruct man in the use of all the powers which God has given him; and then render those powers as perfect as possible!"[93] Other abolitionists had occasion to give their views on the labor question from time to time. Ebenezer Hunt, an abolition candidate for office in Lowell, replied to a questionnaire: "I am in favor of limiting Labor to such hours, as are mutually agreed upon by the laborer and his employer. . . . As a general rule salaries should be low."[94]

When they were face to face with the workers, the abolitionists were willing to hold their tongues on the issue of labor reform and tried instead to persuade them that the abolition of slavery must precede any improvement in the status of labor. In 1847 the Labor Reform League of New England held its convention in Boston, the headquarters of Garrisonianism. Among the resolutions to be voted on was one advocating the abolition of *all* slavery. But the abolitionists packed the meeting, took over the leadership, and introduced a substitute resolution stating "That American Slavery is an evil of such gigantic magnitude, that it must be uprooted and overthrown, before that elevation sought for by the laboring classes, can be effected." There was some discussion, but the resolution never came to a vote—the workingmen had all gone home.[95]

The abolitionists pointed the finger of shame at the workers for their selfishness in striving for their own salvation and failing to join in the crusade for emancipation,[96] and the working men in turn accused them of sheer hypocrisy for ignoring the merits of the labor question. "What say, friend Garrison?" asked the *Voice of Industry*.

Are we not more liberal than you had supposed? Affinities find each other, you say, and we shall understand each other in due time. Till then let us exercise charity for each other, and not claim for ourselves more of the genuine spirit of reform, than we are willing to award others, who are laboring as sincerely as ourselves, if not in the same department, in some other, to bring about the glorious era, when wrong and injustice shall cease, and universal rights shall be recognized from East to West, from North to South.[97]

The Boston *Pilot* attacked the false philosophy of the abolitionists whose "hearts were as soft as butter towards the oppressed laborers in the South, but as hard as flint towards a large portion of the white laborers,"[98] and many labor papers admonished the abolitionists that "charity begins at home."[99]

Many working men believed that the abolitionists not only overlooked the labor question but that they were the bitterest opponents of labor reform and were themselves exploiters of labor in their kitchens and in their factories. The Fall River *Weekly News,* commenting on the thirteen-hour day at Lowell, said: "The owners of the factories hand round the paper for the girls to sign against black slavery in the South, while at the same time they are over-working the free white laborers, of the North, that they may swell their gains and revel in aristocratic pride."[100] George Henry Evans observed that if the alleviation of human suffering were the real object of the philanthropists, they could find ample room for their work close at home. "When they shall have ceased to oppress and grind in the dust the widows and orphans whom Providence has placed at their mercy—when they convince us that the laborers in their factories are better clothed and fed, and in truth enjoy the boasted rights of freemen in a greater degree than the slaves of the South, we will give them that credit for sincerity, and honesty of purpose which we cannot now award to them."[101]

A poem widely printed in the labor press told of the death of a factory girl from overwork and ended:

> That night a chariot passed her,
> While on the ground she lay;
> The daughters of her master
> An evening visit pay—
> Their tender hearts were sighing
> As negroes' woes were told;
> While the white slave was dying
> Who gained their father's gold.[102]

Suspicion of the abolitionists' sincerity was not alleviated when a group of Negroes applied for employment at their places of business, and were either rejected or given menial jobs.[103] Some workers went so far as to charge that the abolitionists were motivated by a desire to "divert you from the protection of your rights and interests, by occupying your attention upon the condition of the colored men while they are enslaving the whites."[104] Others accused them of wanting to emancipate the slaves in order to reduce the wages of their employees.[105]

In this atmosphere of mutual recrimination, in which exaggeration and needless vituperation were employed on both sides, and in view of the opposing philosophies of the two groups, the possibility of cooperation was remote. The Associationists urged unity among all reformers,[106] and the Lynn *Pioneer* suggested that the Massachusetts Anti-Slavery Society and the New England Workingmen's Association should be composed of the same persons, for until they united to work for their common objectives, neither could expect to accomplish much.[107] Some of the abolitionists likewise urged that they should take up the laboring men's cause and thus enlist them in the anti-slavery movement.[108] But the abolitionists were only willing to unite on the condition that the workers abandon their own struggle, and this they would not do.[109] A rapprochement could not be effected until the workers became convinced that the slavery question was of immediate and vital concern to them and the abolitionists learned that they could not go it alone. Talk was useless—only the events of the next decade could bring this about.

Lords of the Lash and Lords of the Loom

Just as the slaveholders feared the revolutionizing effects of industry in their midst, they also took alarm at the growth of capitalism in the Northern states. The conflicting interests and needs of the Southern planters and Northern middle class had furnished the dominant theme in American history since the founding of the Republic, and while they had been able to work out a *modus vivendi,* however uncomfortable at times for one or the other, a showdown was clearly approaching in the not too distant future. "The truth is," admitted Pickens of South Carolina, "the moral power of the world is against us. It is idle to disguise it. We must, sooner or later, meet the great issue that is to be made up on this subject."[110] Both sides began polishing their weapons, including the ideological weapons aimed at rallying the support of the people. One of the sharpest in the armory of the slaveholders was the propaganda assault against the "failure of free society."

This campaign had three principal components, the first of which was an attempt to demonstrate that the conditions of the slaves were superior to those of the Northern workers. James Hammond exposed the absurdity of the view that slavery was "unpaid labor," and repelled the accusation that the slaveowners were robbers because they did not pay wages to their slaves. In fact, he said, slaves received more in return for their labor than did the wage-earners. Men labored only to support themselves and their families, he contended, and the reward of manual labor was seldom sufficient to provide more than a bare subsistence. As evidence he pointed to the factory workers of England, most of whom "drag out a miserable existence, and sink at last under absolute want." What is the value, he asked, of going through the form of paying wages when they amounted to only a pittance which was not enough to feed, clothe, and lodge them in reasonable comfort? Though the slaves were not paid their wages in money, Hammond insisted that they were actually better rewarded with the necessaries and comforts of life, in sickness and in health, than the wage earners.[111] In proof of this the statistics of the Northern states were borrowed liberally and paid back with interest.[112] The figures on pauperism and crime were reported avidly, and they exhibited a shocking incidence and an even more alarming tendency to increase rapidly.[113] Wide publicity was given to exposures of starvation wages paid to Northern laborers, the extreme poverty and destitution that were suffered by large numbers of workers in the cities, the breakup of families, the prevalence of prostitution, and the abominable conditions in the factories—". . . overheated rooms, containing a hundred persons each, confined to spaces of five feet square, for thirteen hours a day. . . ."[114] During the hard winter of 1855, the slaveholders of Alabama infuriated the Northern press by raising a subscription among their slaves for the relief of destitute workers in Northern cities.[115]

One of the most telling indictments against Northern society was its complete failure to provide insurance against the vicissitudes of unemployment, sickness and old age, which left the laborer at the mercy of meager and uncertain charity, in contrast to the paternalistic chattel system which allegedly provided the necessities of its wards throughout life. The defenders of slavery claimed this as among the greatest boons it conferred upon the slaves. Chancellor Harper thought that wage-earners would appreciate it if some superior power imposed upon them the necessity to be temperate and to perform regular and healthful labor, in return for which they would be saved from the torturing anxiety of their future support, be amply provided with their natural wants, become parents without fear of being unable to support their children, be relieved in sickness, and in old age "wear out the remains of existence among familiar scenes and accustomed associates, without being driven to beg, or to resort to the hard and miserable charity of a work-house. . . ." And this, he boasted, was the actual condition of the Southern slaves![116]

The literary masterpiece of this pro-slavery argument was William J. Grayson's long poem, *The Hireling and the Slave*.[117] The object of the poem he stated in the preface: ". . . I have merely desired to show that there is a poor and suffering class in all countries, the richest and most civilized not excepted—laborers who get their daily bread by daily work, and that the slave is as well provided for as any other. The poor we shall have with us always. . . ." The poem begins with an assertion of the divine injunction on man to earn bread by the sweat of his brow:

> Fallen from primeval innocence and ease,
> When thornless fields employed him but to please,
> The laborer toils; and from his dripping brow
> Moistens the length'ning furrows of the plow;
> In vain he scorns or spurns his altered state,
> Tries each poor shift, and strives to cheat his fate;
> In vain new-shapes his name to shun the ill—
> Slave, hireling, help—the curse pursues him still;
> Changeless the doom remains, the mincing phrase
> May mock high Heaven, but not reverse its ways.
> How small the choice, from cradle to the grave,
> Between the lot of hireling, help, or slave![118]

After describing the poverty and misery of the English laboring class, Grayson mocks the Pharasaism of the British philanthropists for their attack against slavery, which is the best agency discovered for "civilizing" the Negroes in accordance with God's command. A diatribe against the abolitionists follows, and then he gets down to his main object of showing the slave to be better off than the hireling.

> If bound to daily labor while he lives,
> His is the daily bread that labor gives;
> Guarded from want, from beggary secure,
> He never feels what hireling crowds endure,
> Nor knows, like them, in hopeless want to crave,
> For wife and child, the comforts of the slave,
> Or the sad thought that, when about to die,
> He leaves them to the cold world's charity,
> And sees them slowly seek the poor-house door—
> The last, vile, hated refuge of the poor.[119]

Idle dreamers like Fourier and Owen seek a scheme for elevating the workers, but much more useful would be an angel descending from heaven and offering them the answer to their prayers—

> Food, clothing, free from the wants, the cares
> The pauper hireling ever feels or fears;

which can be provided only by chattel slavery.

> How freely would the hungry list'ners give
> A life-long labor thus secure to live!

The poem ends with a lengthy panegyric on the happy life of the slave, with all his needs provided, working happily in the fields by day, enjoying the warm society of his family in the cabin at night, idling through life in "the summer shade, the winter sun," and without fear of the poor-house at its close. The description grows more rapturous line by line until we finally find the slave "luxuriating" in a "lotus-bearing paradise."[120]

These arguments were misleading because they were based on the conditions of the most exploited workers, often used statistics of conditions during depression years, and frequently employed illustrations of English factory workers but gave the impression that they were typical of all American workers. However, there was just enough truth in them to make a plausible argument that the status of the working class was as bad as that of the slaves.

It was but a short step from this proposition to the next, that the so-called free laborers were actually slaves in all but name, and the socialists (St. Simon and Fourier) were given credit for having discovered the true character of capitalist exploitation. In fact, the slaveholders' argument on that score diverged very little from that of the workingmen, except in the conclusions they drew from it: the former thought it would be just as well to reduce all workers to chattel slavery, while the latter proposed to abolish all forms of slavery. James Hammond said in the Senate that in all social systems there must be a class to perform the mean duties, the drudgery of life. That class required vigor, docility, fidelity, little skill, and a low order of intellect. Its exertions made possible the existence of a leisure class which provided progress, refinement, and civilization. "It constitutes the very *mud-sills* of society and of political government; and you might as well attempt to build a house in the air, as to build either the one or the other, except on the *mud-sills*." Fortunately for the South, he stated, the Negro race had been found at hand, well adapted to fill that role. "We use them for that purpose, and call them slaves. We are old-fashioned at the South yet; it is a word discarded now by ears polite; but I will not characterize that class at the North with that term; but you have it; it is true; it is everywhere; it is eternal." All the powers on earth could not abolish slavery until God repealed the fiat that "the poor ye always have with you." The man who lived by daily labor, and had to sell it in the market for the best price he could get, was truly a slave. The only difference was that the Negro slaves were hired for life and well paid, while the white slaves were hired by the day, not cared for, and scantily compensated.[121]

Calhoun, Edmund Ruffin and Chancellor Harper defined slavery in much the same way, that is, as the latter put it, a system whereby "a man is compelled to labor at the will of another, and to give him much the greater portion of the product of his labor . . . and it is immaterial by what sort of compulsion the will of the labor is subdued," whether by force or by starvation. They also agreed that in all cases the laborer received for his labor only enough to maintain existence.[122] All "good and respectable people," said Fitzhugh, "who do not labor, or who are successfully trying to live without labor, on the unrequited labor of other people," are cannibals, and the capitalists were the greatest cannibals of them all, for they did not even allow their slaves to retain enough of the proceeds of their labor to maintain themselves when they could no longer work—the wage-earners were slaves without masters. All were striving to obtain "property in man," he asserted, and why should they not be obliged to take care of men, their property, as they did their horses and their cattle? "Now, under the delusive name of liberty, you work him, 'from morn to dewy eve'—from infancy to old age—then turn him out to starve. You treat your horses and hounds better. Capital is a cruel master. The free slave trade, the commonest, yet the cruellest of trades."[123]

The final argument in the Southern gravamen against capitalism was that it bred an irrepressible conflict of classes that threatened to destroy the property relations of both the capitalist and the slaveholding systems. This was what they really meant when they spoke of the "failure of free society"—its failure to control the "mudsills." And this was what the slaveholders regarded as the real difference between slavery and free labor: while both might be exploited in the same degree, and while both might be virtually slaves, the former had no legal or political rights, but the latter were able to conduct an economic and political struggle for the improvement of their conditions. The propagandists pointed to the working class revolutions in Europe and were "haunted by the specter," for they saw signs of the same development in the United States. They noted the growing concentration of capital in a few hands, the steady deterioration in the conditions of the workers, and the increasing difficulty of their rising from the ranks of the working class. In the rise of the labor movement, the spread of socialist doctrines, the outbreak of strikes, and the growing class- and political-consciousness of the workers they saw visions of an impending social upheaval.[124]

The slaveholders held to the stake-in-society doctrine of the Federalists, that the government must in effect be controlled by one class or group of property interests and that its principal function was to protect those interests against the "jealousy and licentiousness" of the "lower orders." In an agrarian society such as existed at the time of the founding of the Republic, it might be possible to maintain republican forms of government, for the majority of the people were property-holders. But with the development of capitalism and the creation of a large and growing class of propertyless workers a "dangerous element" was introduced into society, a "reckless and unenlightened" population which would use its unbridled liberty and its votes to plunder the rich. There were two possible solutions to this menace of a "rampant and combative spirit of discontent," and in the last analysis they were really the same. One was to abandon the pretense of democracy and establish an undisguised dictatorship of the "rich and the educated," excluding the "poor and the ignorant" from all participation in the management of public affairs, and maintain order by a standing army.[125] The second solution, most effective if applied along with the first, was to abandon the pretense of freedom and establish an undisguised slavery for the laboring classes. The advantages seemed almost too obvious to name: it cured the workers of their habit of contracting "deep and inveterate hatred against society; at least, against the prosperous portion of it . . . ;"[126] it established "order" in society; it restored the "true relations between capital and labor," that is, the capitalist owned the laborers, and "the problem is solved; there is no further contest; all that is conflicting gives way, and there is harmony between them. . . ."[127] As Grayson wrote:

> No mobs of factious workmen gather here,
> No strikes we dread, no lawless riots fear;
> . . . not where slaves their easy labors ply,
> Safe from the snare, beneath a master's eyes;
> In useful tasks engaged, employed their time,
> Untempted by the demagog to crime,
> Secure they toil, uncursed their peaceful life,
> With labor's hungry broils and wasteful strife.
> No want to goad, no faction to deplore,
> The slave escapes the perils of the poor.[128]

The slaveholders did not quite have things in such perfect "order" in their own domain as they pretended, but they enjoyed taunting the capitalists with this picture of an employers' heaven, and gave them something to think about. And the workers also gave it more than passing thought.

This pattern of anti-capitalist propaganda was no mere philosophical excursion or intellectual exercise, although it was no doubt inspired partly by a sensitive compulsion to rationalize an institution against which the moral power of the world was turned. It was a planned campaign designed to assist the slavocrats in their losing battle to maintain political supremacy in the national government.[129] What was their game?

There was some loose talk about an alliance between the Southern planters and the Northern working class directed against the "swindling bankers," the speculators, and the "mushroom aristocracy," and the words of the Sage of Monticello that the Northern democracy was the natural ally of the South were frequently recalled. But few responsible Southern statesmen had really taken this seriously since John Taylor, the die-hard exponent of pure Jeffersonianism. Of course, they had to maintain a base of popular support in the North, and they appealed to it for aid in the fight against the national bank, the sub-treasury, protective tariffs, abolition and slavery restriction, and against centralized government.[130] In this policy they were highly successful, chiefly through the instrumentality of the Northern wing of the Democratic party. The Federalists and their successors, the Whigs, had always been considered the representatives of the commercial and monied interests, while the Democrats, tracing their ancestry from Jefferson and Jackson, had taken the popular side on the great political issues of the early nineteenth century and won a reputation as the friends of the common people, gaining additional support from the immigrant workers by opposing the nativist trends of the other parties. Many workers responded with interest to the Southern attack on wage slavery and considered the Southern wing of the party as a strong bulwark against the aggressive designs of the capitalists.[131] They hoped to turn to account the division in the ruling classes in the same way that the English workers did to win the ten-hour law. And many demagogues and ambitious labor leaders and politicians exploited the possibilities for securing "offices of honor and profit" by turning the anti-capitalist sentiments of the workers to the service of the slaveholders.[132]

Brownson, although disapproving of slavery, believed that the factory operatives had more to fear from their employers than from the planters and considered their greatest menace to be the consolidation of the federal government under the hegemony of the capitalist class. Since he did not have confidence in the ability of the workers to emancipate themselves, he proposed, as a policy of expediency, the formation of a political party which would unite the working people and the South under the banner of constitutionalism and state rights. In return he offered to resist the efforts of the abolitionists; but he warned the slaveholders that if they chose to unite with the capitalists instead, the workers would "go *en masse* against slavery."[133] Ely Moore, the first president of the New York Trades' Union, chairman of the National Trades' Union, and the first representative of labor in the United States Congress, agreed with this point of view. The consolidating tendencies of the Federalist school, he said, were calculated to "impoverish, depreciate, and degrade the Democracy; especially that portion who, in obedience to the command of Heaven, eat their bread in the sweat of their face." Successful resistance to these tendencies depended on the maintenance of state rights and on the thwarting of the abolitionist effort to destroy the federal system by employing the powers of the national government to achieve their ends. He therefore joined with the slaveholders in pushing through the gag on abolition petitions and voted for the resolution declaring that the government had no jurisdiction over slavery.[134] Mike Walsh, a Tammany opportunist representing the Irish working class wards of New York fifteen years later, followed in his footsteps by endorsing every policy put forward by the politicians of Dixie.[135]

But while the slavery party made political capital by taking advantage of the antagonism between Northern labor and capital, they had no idea of forming an alliance with the former in the sense that they should jointly run the government. John Randolph had long before revealed the meaning of this strategy: "Northern gentlemen think to govern us by our *black* slaves; but let me tell them we intend to govern them by their *white* slaves."[136] They had no intention that the "white slaves" should govern, either alone or jointly, as they made abundantly clear, although they strove for Northern votes to sustain their own supremacy. When they spoke of an alliance with the workers, they were engaging in a game of semantics. Representative Bayly of Virginia, for example, stated that the interests of the two classes were identical because "the greater part of the capital of the Southern planter, as the whole of the capital of the indigent white man, is labor." Therefore the protection of the rights of labor and of the property of the slaveholders were one and the same problem![137] Pickens and Calhoun are sometimes represented as being among the chief advocates of an alliance with Northern labor. But the former defined the meaning of this "community of interests" in much the same way as Bayly: "When we contend for the undivided profits and proceeds of our labor, do you not see that we stand precisely in the same situation as the laborer of the North?" He went on to affirm that, while the slave owners were identified with the laborers, "at the same time, we shall ever form a barrier against breaking up the laws and foundations of society."[138] Calhoun's line was the same. There is no conflict between labor and capital in the South because "Every plantation is a little community, with the master at its head, who concentrates in himself the united interests of capital and labor, of which he is the common representative." In the Union as a whole, the South forms "the balance of the system; the great conservative power, which prevents other portions, less fortunately constituted, from rushing into conflict. In this tendency to conflict in the North between labor and capital, which is constantly on the increase, the weight of the South is and ever will be on the Conservative side; against the aggression of one or the other side, which ever may tend to disturb the equilibrium of our political system."[139]

Furthermore, cooperation with Northern democracy was not only galling to the planters but recognized as very tenuous and unreliable, as Chancellor Harper said in his oration in support of Van Buren in 1840: "Is there anything in the principles and opinions of the other party, the great *democratic rabble,* as it has been justly called, which should induce *us* to identify ourselves with that? Here you may find every possible grade and hue of opinion which has ever existed in the country. Here you may find loafer, and locofoco, and agrarian, and all the rabble of the city of New-York, the most corrupt and depraved of rabbles. . . ." The essential principles of democracy, he stated, were the natural equality and unalienable right to liberty of every human being and the divine right of majorities. These doctrines were not only false but portentous to the future of the slaveholding system. While the Northern democracy might be willing for the present to modify those doctrines in favor of the planters, the spirit of democracy made no such exceptions, and the alliance with the Northern democracy could not be expected to last longer than the latter found it necessary or expedient.[140]

When Harper wrote these words he very likely had in mind the statement made by the *Loco-Foco* not long before. It had repudiated the "dough-faced democrats" who compromised the principles of universal liberty in order to please their Southern brethren, but had succeeded only in gaining their scorn and contempt. Neither Washington, Jefferson, Madison, Monroe, nor Jackson had dared to sacrifice the interests of one part of the Union to the policy of the other, and no true democrat would do so now. The Loco-Focos pledged themselves to use all legal means to eradicate the curse of slavery from the land. Democracy, they declared, might tolerate slavery in deference to Constitutional rights, but it could not brook a union with slavery.[141]

In the days of Jefferson, when the country was largely agrarian, there had been a basis for an alliance between planters and Northern democracy against the incipient capitalist class. John Taylor had said, "The question is, whether the landed interest . . . had not better unite with the other popular interest, to strangle in its cradle any infant visibly resembling this terrible giant."[142] But by 1840 the infant who resembled the giant had grown to a gangling youth who was the spitting image of the monster, and quite plainly it could not be easily strangled. But it could be cajoled, threatened, bribed and bullied, and this the slaveholders set out to do.

An essential part of the strategy was to convince the capitalists that abolitionism was a menace to their property as well as that of the slaveholders. The slaveholders' indictment of wage slavery had shown how easily the assault against the slave system could be directed against the property interest of the North, and slavery apologists repeatedly emphasized that the attack on slavery was inculcating a disregard for property rights that created fertile ground for socialist doctrines. Indeed, screamed Fitzhugh, the abolitionists were only socialists in disguise, stirring up the muddy waters of reform in order to rouse the "Oi Polloi rats" against the very edifice of society.[143] And if the "kindred spirits" of abolitionism and radicalism should ever unite, as McDuffie predicted they would, "no human institution will be regarded as a guarantee of any human right, and the property holders of the North, so far from being able to do anything to secure our property from these fanatics and plunderers, will tremble for the safety of their own."[144] In 1830 Thomas Cooper had warned that "the wealth of the wealthy is in danger," and a generation later Fitzhugh was sounding the alarm "that the North has as much to apprehend from abolition as the South, and that it is time for conservatives everywhere to unite in efforts to suppress and extinguish it."[145]

This was the proposition of the slaveholders: the "gentlemen of property," North and South, should hold the reins of government as an instrument for maintaining order and stability, against slave revolts and fugitive slaves on the one hand and against abolitionism and radicalism on the other; the "conservatism of slavery" would save Northern capital "from the thousand destructive isms infecting the social organization" of the North[146] and the capitalists would suppress the "fanatics" who wanted to destroy the social organization of the South. But within this alliance the South was to be "first among equals," and to insure its supremacy it had a few aces in the hole. The ace of spades was the threat of secession, which, it was avowed, would ruin the business of the North and leave it helpless before the wrath of the masses.[147] Or either of those results might be brought about even without secession: the first by the cancellation of business with those suspected of "heresy," and the second by stirring up class strife. Pickens warned that he might "preach up insurrection to the laborers of the North" and Hammond repeated the threat twenty years later: "You have been making war upon us to our very hearth-stones. How would you like for us to send lecturers or agitators North . . .?"[148]

The strategy of the slaveholders was eminently successful. The bulk of the Northern capitalist class was, throughout the antebellum years, opposed in principle to slavery, the domination of the slave-power in the federal government, and the policies which it carried out. But it was even more perturbed by the tumult aroused by the slavery controversy, by the disturbing ferment of radical ideas, by the possibility that the Union might be disrupted and the Southern market lost.[149] Under the influence of these fears and ambitions, and under the pressure of Southern promises and threats, the merchants relinquished one position after another, made concession after concession and compromise after compromise until, by the 1850's, they had become a reliable support of the slave-power in its projects of supremacy and aggrandizement. One of the essential terms of the bargain, it will be recalled, was that the Northern partners should suppress abolitionism. This proviso was faithfully carried out. In 1837 a "Committee of Fifty" New York merchants, rebuffed by Van Buren in their demand for repeal of the Specie Circular, decided to issue an appeal to "the intelligence and virtue of the people." They would report that Van Buren had acted on the principle that the poor naturally hate the rich rather than on the belief that the possession of property was the proof of merit. They would also appeal to their "brethren of the South" for their generous cooperation, promising that the property owners of the North would be the last to interfere with the rights of property of any kind, and that they would "discourage every effort to awaken an excitement, the bare idea of which should make every husband and father shudder with horror. . . ."[150]

What they meant by "discouraging every effort to awaken an excitement" was revealed in the wave of violence that swept through the North during that decade. In the destruction of the press of *The Philanthropist* at Cincinnati, the lynching of Lovejoy at Alton, the mob attacks against abolition meetings in Boston, Philadelphia, Utica, Haverhill and other cities, it was the universal observation that the inspiration, organization and often the perpetration of the attacks were the work of the "respectable gentlemen of property and understanding" intent on putting down disquieting innovations and propitiating the slaveholders.[151]

The consummation of the marriage between the "slave power of the South and the banking power of the North" was announced by Senator Morris of Ohio in 1839. "The cotton bale and the bank note have formed an alliance, . . ." he declared. "These two congenial spirits have at last met and embraced each other, both looking to the same object—to live upon the unrequited labor of others—and have now erected for themselves a common platform . . . on which they can meet, and bid defiance, as they hope, to free principles and free labor."[152] Of course, part of the business class did not enter into or approve of this alliance, choosing rather to challenge the slave owners for control of the government, and even those who did put on the harness chafed under the restraints. But it required the events of 1845-1860 to disrupt the coalition and throw the two groups into an unreserved contest for hegemony. The same events forced the working class also to re-evaluate its role in the unfolding conflict and its position on the issue that was swallowing up all others—the issue of slavery in the western territories.

CHAPTER IV

THE SLAVE-POWER AND
THE MUDSILLS

Land of the Free

The economy of the United States was bifurcated: in the North a young, vigorous capitalistic order, and in the South an old, decadent slave system. Both were aggressive and expansive —the one because it was young and vigorous, with a rapidly increasing population, stretching forth to reach new markets, trade routes and raw materials, grasping for land to satisfy the yearning hunger of the multitudes of native and immigrant farmers and would-be farmers and the avid appetites of speculators; the other because it was old and decadent, grasping for new lands to replenish the worn-out soil of the seaboard; both because they had to maintain the imperative balance of sections which would assure parity at least in the Senate. For three centuries the white men had been pressing onward, despoiling the Indians of their inheritance and their lives, with scarcely a voice to recall St. Luke 6:31. The new nation by 1840 passed beyond the Mississippi, its cupidity fed by the vision of endless space and blessed with a new name: Manifest Destiny.

But after 1800 it was not enough to seize more land—the division of the booty had to be arranged in advance. While one covetous eye swept the prospective pickings, the other was fixed on the rest of the pack to see that it didn't swallow a larger bite. New England Federalism saw a vision of its tombstone on the plains of Louisiana and fought the Purchase tooth and

111

nail. The campaigns of 1812 to 1815 were shackled by mutual suspicions, and both North and South were baffled in their hopes for Canada and Florida. In 1820 a line was drawn across the map—the Missouri Compromise; and the two sections settled down to enjoy the peaceful repast of new states—one for you and one for me.

For a generation the fearful issue was forgotten as each section developed in its own way within the new limits. But they did not develop at the same rate; the "balance" was becoming lopsided on the Northern end. As Seward noted, the political equilibrium was being upset by the growing physical disequilibrium. Over two million immigrants came to the United States in the two decades after 1830, most of them staying in the North, and by 1850 the Northern population exceeded that of the South by the order of four to three, with every prospect that the numerator would quickly grow larger. In wealth, industry and railroads the disparity was even greater, and as the Western regions were filled, 36° 30′ came to appear to the South less like a dividing line than a restraining rope. The moral balance was turning against her as well, for all the world regarded the chattel system as an anachronism that could not be long for this world. Most Northerners were willing to let it run its course slowly and peacefully out of regard for constitutional guaranties, compromises and property rights, but only because they were satisfied that it was "in the course of ultimate extinction." The assurance of such an eventuality lay in the confinement of the slave area to its then limits, for, as both North and South understood, the law of slavery was Expand or die. But the slaveholders were not prepared for ultimate, let alone imminent, extinction, and in 1845 they got a new lease on life with the annexation of Texas. The irrepressible conflict was under way.

At once the wonted patterns of American life were transfigured. While the dominant section of the Northern business class fulfilled its obligations to the alliance, another business group, represented by the Northern Whigs, rose up in wrath as it saw the probability of unlimited postponement of its expectations of "ultimate extinction" for slavery and ultimate ascendancy for itself. The appeasement of the slave-power must give way to a firm stand; the contest for control of the Union must be decided in the territories. And the common people recoiled from the perversion of a traditionally democratic foreign policy to one of aggression in the interest of the planter autocracy. For fifteen years the abolitionists had represented the conscience of an apathetic people, but now the still small voice within swelled to a roaring shout of indignation and alarm, and Hosea Biglow took over the job of William Lloyd Garrison. Political parties began to crumble and re-form, as Conscience Whigs and Barn-burning Democrats stood up against the new dispensation, and anti-slavery men experimented with new parties.

The labor movement was no less deeply stirred by these events. Since the time of the Missouri Compromise the American public had shown little interest in the slavery question, and many working people shared this indifference. One can turn the pages of a large number of the workingmen's newspapers, issue after issue and year after year during the 1830's and early 1840's, and scarcely be aware of the existence of slavery. Besides, since the disappearance of the first labor parties shortly after 1830, the working class passed through a period in which political activity was definitely subordinated to economic struggles. In spite of the victories won by those early organizations, it was the opinion of many that the working class was not yet strong enough to maintain an effective independent party, although political action as such was not eschewed. In most of the trade unions of those days the discussion of political questions was not tolerated, for fear of diverting them from their immediate tasks and introducing divisions that would impede a united effort.[1] But the annexation of Texas and the subsequent unfolding of the expansionist program of the slavocracy roused them to a sense of danger and propelled them into the vortex of the political struggles.

Shortly after the establishment of Texan independence in 1836, the Boston *Weekly Reformer* sounded an alarm, warning that by receiving Texas into the Union, "we recognize deliberately and solemnly the right of conquest," and that this would be the signal for the dissolution of the Union. "Much as we love the Union, we love honor, justice, liberty more, and when we are forced to choose between a dissolution of the Union and slavery and national disgrace, we shall not be long in making up our choice."[2] The Loco-Foco legislature of Massachusetts echoed these sentiments, and stated that annexation "will furnish new calumnies against republican governments, by exposing the gross contradiction of a people professing to be free, and yet seeking to extend and perpetuate the subjection of their slaves."[3] The Manchester *Operative* called annexation a base action, "because it would be giving men that live upon the blood of others, an opportunity of dipping their hands still deeper in the sin of slavery. . . . Have we not enough slaves now?"[4] When the act had been consummated, *The Harbinger* branded it as a conspiracy of the slave-power, but added that the slave-power would never have won the day had not the capitalists of the North been willing. "The commercial, manufacturing, industrial, speculating interest of the North fought faintly, trimmed, compromised, conceded; and the instant they could do so with grace, went over with flags flying to the enemy." Northern and Southern capital linked hands against labor under the common war cry: Money before Men.[5]

It is notable that all these expressions came from groups which had until then been indifferent to the slavery issue or decidedly opposed to giving it a prominent place in the consideration of the workers. But now they had their eyes opened to the fact that slavery, particularly in its aggressive phase, constituted a menace to the democratic institutions and principles necessary for the growth of the labor movement. All labor spokesmen, of course, did not react so soon or so fast to the new state of affairs; Robert Dale Owen, now a congressman from Indiana, believed that the benefits accruing to the Union by admitting Texas outweighed the benefits conferred upon slavery,[6] and the land reformers shrugged it off as only another phase of the "contest between rich and avaricious planters, and rich and avaricious manufacturers, for exclusive privileges."[7] But the rank and file, not being wedded to the utopian philosophies of these reformers, could not view it so lightly, and from 1844-1845 they demonstrated in the Northern cities against the absorption of the Lone Star Republic unless provisions were made for the extinction of slavery in her borders.[8]

When the inevitable invasion of Mexico was launched in the following year, the protests became more vociferous and more numerous, as workers throughout the North condemned slavery, the war and its perpetrators, and demanded the withdrawal of American troops "to some undisputed land belonging to the United States."[9] The New England Workingmen's Association, meeting in Boston in 1846, resolved that it deeply deprecated the "unhallowed war now being waged with such inhuman results" and entered its protest against having any part in the matter, "having no lives to lose, or money to squander in such an unholy and unprofitable cause, to enhance the price of 'Texas Script,' and plunder Mexican soil for the United States officers, slaveholders, and speculators to convert into a mart for traffic in human blood and human rights."[10]

At the conclusion of the Mexican War—fought, according to President Polk, to protect Texas and "to vindicate with decision the honor, the rights, and the interests of our country"—it was found necessary, apparently as an object lesson to other would-be bullies, to despoil the Mexican people of an immense chunk of their nation and bring it safely under the wing of the spread-eagle. The Texas question thus became the much broader issue of the expansion of slavery into the territories of the United States, the control of those territories and, ultimately, the control of the federal government. This was the dominant political issue of the next dozen years. The anti-slavery-extension politicians were quick to note and to grasp the significance of labor's changing orientation on the slavery question which resulted from the Southern policy of aggrandizement and its implications for the workers; and in the Congressional debates they sedulously cultivated this development. For the first time since Jackson's bank war, a major national issue was fought out largely on the basis of the rights and interests of the wage-earners and farmers.

When David Wilmot of Pennsylvania launched the campaign to exclude slavery from the territories by the introduction of his famous Proviso, he remarked, "I would preserve for free white labor a fair country, a rich inheritance, where the sons of toil, of my own race and color, can live without the disgrace which association with negro slavery brings upon free labor." Preston King later reintroduced the Wilmot Proviso with the observation, "If slavery is not excluded by law, the presence of the slave will exclude the laboring white man."[11]

Apart from the Constitutional debate over the right of Congress to exclude slavery, much of the discussion followed these lines. It was asserted that if slavery were permitted to enter the territories, free labor would be virtually excluded from them, "for it is folly to think that our Northern men would emigrate to the most inviting territory in the world where they know they will be compelled to labor side by side with the slave." In proof of this, speakers cited the degraded condition of the workers in the South, the "lamentable lack of skill in every department of industry, in agriculture, and the most common branches of mechanical pursuits," and the mass exodus of Southern workingmen to the free states and territories; in contrast they pointed to the honor and respect in which labor was held in the North and the prosperity of the free laborers. Since the territories must be either all free or all slave, it was demanded that they be reserved for the benefit of the Southern workers who required them as a refuge and for Northern workers who, if confined to the already free states, would become so populous that their wages would sink to the starvation level. The North, proclaimed Congressman Tappan, must unite "to preserve the Territories of the nation, yet unmoistened by the sweat of the slave, to the *free labor* of the country, which constitutes the greatest element of its prosperity, its strength, and its future glory!"[12]

David Wilmot warned that if the free laborer did go into the territories, along with slaves, the ensuing competition would soon reduce him to the status of the Southern workers, his dignity destroyed, his wages depressed and his means of employment snatched from him. In the shadow of the planting aristocracy, the white worker would be forced into the pattern of a fixed social stratification of lords and vassals, and "if he can not rise to the condition of the former, he must sink to a level with the latter."[13] The contest, then, was but a new form of the old fight of popular rights against privilege and monopoly, of labor against capital, but this time not the money-power of the North but the "money-power in the South, more potent and more dangerous than all other enemies of labor combined." If freedom was overcome in this contest, Wilmot predicted, it would be the last struggle ever made against the advancement of the slave power, which would then overshadow the country and bear down all opposition to its will. "Holding in its iron grasp by far the larger and better portion of the soil of the Republic, the great resource of the laboring man, it will trample at pleasure upon the rights of the masses, and in the end deprive them of their just influence and control in the government."[14]

Few Southerners had the hardihood to meet these arguments on their own ground. The congressmen from Virginia, rising to the full height of their chivalrous posture, repudiated with indignation the argument that free labor could not thrive along with slave labor as a "vile imposture" and a libel against the "industrious and energetic" laboring people of the South.[15] But for the most part the Southerners shunned this phase of the controversy, preferring to stick to Constitutional and legal questions and the rights of the Southern states. While they were expounding their doctrine of slavery as the best condition for the working class they undoubtedly felt that, on the score of labor's rights in the territories or elsewhere, the less said the better.

The anti-slavery forces were not yet strong enough to stop the slave-power and its Northern allies, and the Wilmot Proviso was defeated. By the admission of Texas and the Compromise of 1850 the slave territory was doubled, and one of the most infamous laws ever enacted by the United States Congress was wrapped up in the package. The Fugitive Slave Law dedicated the full power of the federal government to the noisome task of hunting down men and women seeking freedom and clamping their shackles tighter than ever—all without trial and without the right of the victim to testify in his defense The slave-power demonstrated that it had secured a firm grip on the government and that it intended to destroy whatever stood in its way, including the democratic traditions and the plain sense of decency of the American people.

But it reckoned without its host. Every victory had its price —the increasing alarm, disgust and hostility of the people. The working people were thoroughly aroused over the bargain of 1850. Even the land reformers, who had only a few years earlier washed their hands of the slavery controversy as of no concern to them, now became among the most vociferous opponents of the slave-power's aggrandizement. They could hardly be otherwise, for the policy of handing the territories over to slavery was certainly the greatest blow that could be delivered to their plan for destroying land monopoly and leading the working class to salvation by dividing among it the treasury of merits stored up in the unsettled lands of the West. The National Industrial

Congress, meeting in the summer of 1850, condemned slavery as a moral, social and political evil and resolved to oppose the further extension of slavery. It repelled the notion that the slave area must be extended in order to satisfy the South and secure the perpetuation of the Union. "Slavery can never be a bond of union and of freedom," it declared.[16] A land reform journal demanded that the slaves as well as the workers be free and the territories dedicated to their use, "without reference to sex, color, or condition."[17] The Fugitive Slave Law gagged them, as it did every person who was not bound hand and foot to the slave-power. The New York Convention of the Industrial Reformers condemned the law "which converts the citizens of the free states into man-catchers for the slave owners of the South" as a "gross violation of the Constitution, an infamous usurpation, and a despotic enactment, not binding in law or conscience on the people, and ought to be resisted, if necessary, to death, by every friend to our country, to humanity, and to justice."[18] *The Monthly Jubilee* declared that this act did "more to stimulate the Northern mind against slavery than all the abolition speeches and excitement that have been made these last ten years," and that it would "be the cause of the overthrow of the 'peculiar institution.' " Then, "another question, of still more importance, will take the field, namely, the Rights of free Labor."[19] The workers, as a result of stern reality, were arriving at a recognition of the fact that their own elevation could be achieved only after the slavery question had been settled by the abolition of chattel slavery.

The nation swallowed the Compromise of 1850, though it stuck in the throats of many. The Compromise was sold as a measure of finality, putting an end to the vexatious problem and preserving the integrity of the Union. After all, the free states had gained California and Oregon, and the slaveholders would never go into the Southwest anyhow—they had fought only for the principle, but really meant no harm. The two sections could go their own ways, and no one would be the worse for it, except the slaves. But what were three and a half million slaves compared with the maintenance of the Constitution and the Union? The people dozed, restlessly and fitfully to be sure, under the sedative of these illusions, until 1854, when finality, banality and tranquillity alike were blasted by the introduction into Congress of the Kansas-Nebraska bill. The Compromise had involved territory whose status had not yet been settled, but now territories that had been reserved for freedom since 1820 were to be fed into the maw of slavery. Promises, agreements and compromises were all to be discarded; there was to be no sanctuary for freedom anywhere; the "ultimate extinction" of slavery was to be made very ultimate indeed. Was it for this that the North had allowed gangsters to roam its streets in search of fugitives and supposed fugitives and suppositious fugitives? Was it for this that the Southwest was being converted into a slave-pen? Was it for this that timid souls "bit their lips and kept silent"?

Many workers reacted vigorously against the Nebraska Act. In New York, an overflow mass meeting of four to five thousand laborers was held to consider this question "of the greatest importance to mechanics," and protested "That the repeal of the Missouri Compromise, in order to introduce Slavery into *our* free territory of Nebraska and Kansas, would be in every point a crime, a breach of plighted faith, a violation not only of our just rights but of the rights of man, in defiance alike of Republican principles and Christian duties."[20] Huge meetings of workers assembled in many other cities in New Hampshire, Pennsylvania, Ohio, Massachusetts, Michigan, Vermont, Connecticut, Indiana, and Wisconsin, passing resolutions similar to that adopted at Newark:

Resolved, That we view with jealousy and suspicion the bold attempts which the Slave Power of the country is now making to degrade the laboring and producing classes of the people by establishing its system of chattel labor in the Free territories of the West; and that . . . we would repel and resent the efforts to introduce the black slaves into our workshops. . . .

Resolved, That the people in this city have abundant reason for sustaining Free and Independent labor . . . and our influence shall never be given to substitute for it slave labor.[21]

The land reformers, meeting at Trenton for the Ninth National Industrial Congress, were careful not to identify themselves with "fanatic abolitionism," but declared that the grasp of slavery was suffocating the spirit of freedom and was inimical to the interests of labor. They demanded the repeal of the Nebraska Act and the Fugitive Slave Law, the protection of "fugitive freemen by the rights of our States, and the strength of our arms," the resignation of the politicians "who sold the priceless principle of freedom to the slave power," and the election of representatives who would resist its aggressions, and invited "workers and foreign immigrants to settle in Nebraska in order to thwart the machinations of the slave power."[22]

The German workers were also roused, and began to modify their policy of indifference to political action. The previous year the Arbeiterbund (Workers' League) had been formed under the leadership of Joseph Weydemeyer, one of the outstanding Marxists in America, and he had persuaded it to abandon the opposition to political struggles that dominated the German-American workers' organizations. At a mass meeting called by the Bund in New York, a resolution introduced by Weydemeyer was adopted, protesting against the Nebraska bill because it favored the capitalists and land speculators at the expense of the people, withdrew vast tracts of territory from the benefits of a future homestead law, and furthered the extension of slavery. Denouncing both black and white slavery, the resolution branded as a traitor to the people every supporter of the bill.[23]

This wave of disaffection in the working class caused consternation in the Democratic party, and the latter assigned to their old wheel-horse, Mike Walsh, the task of putting his finger in the dike. This would-be labor representative spoke most fluently on this occasion when he rose to denounce the workers' demonstrations. He set the halls of Congress rocking with laughter when he reviled the opponents of slavery extension as "a set of peanut agitators and Peter Funk philanthropists" whose object was to revolutionize the country but who "could not revolutionize a barber's shop or an oyster box," and when he made a flippant apology for slavery.[24] Ten years earlier this was the kind of talk to win votes, but now the workers could not see the joke. Walsh had not changed, but the working men had. They were fighting mad over the arrogance and bullying of the slave-power; and the talk was that they would be next to have chains hung about their necks.

The Slave-Power Conspiracy

When the working men insisted on the abolition of *all* forms of slavery rather than exclusive and partial emancipation for the chattel slaves alone, the abolitionists had a stock answer which, in their minds, put an end to the discussion: Why was the Underground Railroad a one-way route? Why, when the slaves were daily risking their lives to follow the North Star, were no working men making the trek in the other direction to accept the wardship of the planters? In asking this question the abolitionists revealed their inability or unwillingness to comprehend the ideology of the labor movement. In comparing the two labor systems, the workers were, of course, speaking of a purely economic relationship and noting the scarcely contestable fact that the workers, like the slaves, were compelled to place their labor at the disposal of the employers, and that in return for this labor, they, like the slaves, often received only a subsistence. But there the analogy ended. The workers, like the slaves, understood clearly enough the difference between John Calhoun's "thirty lashes well laid on" and Francis Lowell's pink slips; between the overseer and the foreman; between "Yes sir" and "Go to hell." They knew that, however limited, they possessed means for improving their conditions that the slaves did not have—trade unions, the right to strike, the ballot, the assembly hall, and the press. They realized that they had the opportunity to rise out of their class and become farmers or employers themselves, and many did. Nor were they unaware of the difference between competing with the low-paid labor of immigrants, Negroes, women and children, and with the labor of slaves.

In fact, so well did the workers understand these things that they were made the basis for the most comprehensive and effective of all anti-slavery propaganda appeals. This campaign was constructed of diverse elements, subtle suggestions and varied formulations, but in its totality it constituted a logical pattern which imputed the existence of a far-reaching, well planned and neatly coordinated slave-power conspiracy whose ultimate object was to destroy the liberty of the American people in general and of the workers in particular.

The plot rested on a foundation of the allegedly intrinsic hostility of slavery and the slaveholders to the working class. This was demonstrated by the conditions of the workers in the Southern states—their low wages, their difficulty in finding employment because of the competition of slave labor, their social and moral degradation, their mass emigration from the slave states, their lack of public education and political rights, and the deprivation of their civil liberties. These conditions, it was asserted, resulted not only from the normal operations of the slave system, but from the aristocratic pretensions of the slaveholders. Their contempt for the working class was emphasized by the endless repetition of a dozen phrases that became household words: "We have got to hating everything with the prefix *free*. . . ."; "Free society! we sicken of the name. . . ."; "the very mudsills of society"; "greasy mechanics"; "filthy operatives"; "the poor and the ignorant"; "sordid, servile, and laborious beings." Extra stress was placed on those expressions which illustrated the slavocracy's opposition to popular government and democratic institutions: "If laborers ever obtain the political power of a country, it is in fact in a state of revolution. . . ."; "The most degraded classes . . . are and must be incapable. . . ."; the capitalists must own the workers, "either collectively through the government, or individually in a state of domestic servitude"; ". . . a dangerous element is introduced into the body politic." In newspapers, pamphlets, lecture halls, and in the Congressional forum, these words were reiterated time without number to prove the actual status of the laborers in the slave states and to suggest the possible status of all workers if they ever fell under the sway of the Southern oligarchy.

The possibility of such an eventuality first became apparent when, during the 1830's, the slaveholders attempted to restrict abolition propaganda by infringing the civil liberties of the people. On the theory that the primary responsibility of the government was the protection of property, they held that it should take every measure necessary to prevent "incendiary" attacks against the institution, and if constitutional rights stood in the way of repression, so much the worse for them. The slaveholders had their own "higher law"—the sanctity of slave property. On the demand of the Dixie dictators, Congress pushed through the gag law prohibiting the reception of abolition petitions, and the postmaster imposed a censorship of the mails to prevent the circulation of abolition literature. Their appetite growing by what it fed on, the slaveholders called upon the Northern legislatures to enact penal laws against the "seditious activities" of the abolitionists, and in several states such bills were introduced.

The defense of the abolitionists became an urgent necessity if the rights of the working people were to be preserved. The Massachusetts Anti-Slavery Society defined the issue with precision in its appeal to the legislature against the proposed subversion of the Constitution. It asserted that the abolitionists were engaged in work that was essential for the preservation of the liberties of mankind in general and of the working class in particular. Abolitionism could not be proscribed without destroying the first principles of republican freedom, for it would require an act of legislative usurpation that would be fatal to the liberties and sovereignty of the people. What encouragement, it asked, would be left for any men to vindicate the rights of any people, when they found themselves under the rod of lawless and unrighteous power? What security would there be for the liberties of mankind when the principle was established that it was "incendiary" and "treasonable" and contrary to law for men to proclaim the precepts of righteousness and to plead the cause of the oppressed? "We ask, especially, what security will remain for the laboring classes of our free Commonwealth, if *legislative censure and proscription* are to be awarded to those who protest against the enforcement of involuntary labor without wages?" The object of the Southern states, concluded the Society, was "nothing more nor less than *the subjugation of the free laboring population of the non-slaveholding states* to a despotism no less appalling than that to which the laboring population of the South are now subjected."[25]

This attempt to suppress abolitionism suffered defeat, but what could not be accomplished legally it was proposed to do with extra-legal vigilante committees. The Northern merchant class organized mobs to put down the abolitionists, and again the democratic rights of the people depended on resisting the assault. A writer in *The Philanthropist* pointed out the menace to labor in a proposed anti-abolition meeting called in Philadelphia:

> *Pay to the laborer!* Never no never!
>   Stoop to persuade whom we love to command;
> Pay to the *laborer* never no never!
>   Till God's vialed vengeance be poured on the land.

Children of Penn! will ye come for the calling
  Of those who will spurn ye like dogs when ye've done?
The pitiful Tyrants whose fortunes are falling,
  McDuffie, and Pickens, and Wise and Calhoun?

They call us "white slaves," aye slaves *shall they* find us
  With shoulders so patient and souls so subdued
As to help forge the fetters with which they will bind us,
  To kiss the same hand our own blood is imbrued?[26]

But the meeting was held; and when, shortly after, the abolitionists erected Pennsylvania Hall as a forum for anti-slavery
meetings, it was burned to the ground by "an orderly, well-
dressed assemblage of men" with the apparent connivance of the
police.[27] The invasion of Constitutional rights became bolder and
more far-reaching as the slave-power strengthened its grip on the
federal government, the most notorious instance being the Fugitive Slave Act of 1850. William Seward warned that this act was
a legislative usurpation which was being boldly enforced by the
courts. Congress had violated the Constitution by compelling non-
slaveholders in the free states to capture and deliver fugitive
slaves. The ancient writ of *habeas corpus* had been made an instrument for the capture of slaves, and the process of punishment
for contempt made sufficient cause to imprison a citizen without
indictment, trial or conviction, without bail and without limit of
sentence. "Are not these invasions of state rights," he asked,
"fearfully premonitory that slavery is to become a universally
ruling power throughout the republic?"[28]

Many believed that slavery had already become the "universally
ruling power," that it was employing its control of the government to pursue a policy which was utterly incompatible with the
interests of the working class, and that if it were not overthrown
it would completely submerge "the principles upon which the
organization of free labor society rests."[29] Others considered the
supremacy of the slave power to be a matter not of controlling the
government but of extending the area of slavery, and it was the

expansionist program which began in 1845 that awakened them to the danger of its universal dominion. The conquest of Mexico had made the free and slave regions approximately equal, but even more direful was the Kansas-Nebraska Act, which repealed the Missouri Compromise and established the possibility that all the territories of the United States could be thrown open to slavery, so that there would be no place where laborers and farmers could go without subjecting themselves to the competition and degradation that was the lot of the Southern working class. These fears were confirmed when, in 1857, the Supreme Court passed down its decision on the *Dred Scott* case. Going beyond its judicial prerogative, the Court laid down the theory so dear to the slaveholders, that Congress could pass no laws which in any way interfered with its most solemn obligation of "guarding and protecting the owner in his rights" of holding property in man. Consequently the Missouri Compromise was invalid and slaveholders could go into any of the territories and be guaranteed the protection of the government.

Many perceived in the Nebraska Act and the *Dred Scott* dictum a logical pattern which led inevitably to the introduction of slavery even into the free states. The Mechanics and Workingmens' Central Union of New York condemned the decision and saw in it evidence that the slaveholders had a "settled determination" to make their institution legal in all the states, thus depriving free labor of the ability to protect itself against the competition of slave labor.[30] The "nationalization of slavery" was seen not only in the logic of events and arguments, but as a conspiracy that was already in the making. Charles Sumner said that slaveholders were now claiming the right to carry slaves into New York and Pennsylvania while in transit to slave territory, and that the courts of the latter state had sustained them.[31] In 1854, Dumas Van Deren, editor of the *Mattoon* (Illinois) *National Gazette,* spoke of free labor as a "novelty" and a "humbug" and proposed the introduction of slavery into Illinois by amending the state constitution. He wrote to Southerners, urging them to emigrate

to Illinois in order to carry the plot and win for the Southern
people possession of "the key to the western world." Several
Southern newspapers endorsed the idea jubilantly, one proclaim-
ing that "The South should not content herself with maintaining
her ground; she should progress. She should expand her institutions wherever soil, climate, and products are adapted to them."[32]
If these schemes were executed, the United States would be converted into a slaveholding empire which would "blast, as with a
sirocco, those influences which make MAN . . . the first great
aim of Society and Government;" and the workers would be
forced "into Canada, Russian America, Australia, and wherever
else, throughout the whole earth, from which industry can find
refuge."[33] It was this thought that inspired Seward's famous reference to the "irrepressible conflict between opposing and endurable
forces." He foresaw that the United States must become, sooner
or later, either entirely a slaveholding nation or entirely a free
labor nation. "Either the cotton and rice-fields of South Carolina
and the sugar plantations of Louisiana will ultimately be tilled by
free labor, and Charleston and New Orleans become marts for
legitimate merchandise alone, or else the rye-fields and wheat-
fields of Massachusetts and New York must again be surrendered
by their farmers to slave culture and to the production of slaves,
and Boston and New York become once more markets for trade
in the bodies and souls of men."[34]

It was this idea also which inspired a correspondent of the
Anti-Slavery Bugle to write "Men of Labor":

> Men of Labor, ho! the battle
>   Calls to action, calls to arms;
> Shall your toil be free or fetter'd
>   In your workshops, on your farms?
> Plough and loom, and ringing anvil,
>   Trowel, hammer, spade and hod—
> Shall they bear the curse of bondage,
>   Or the Freedom born of God?

Lo! 'tis yours to give the answer,
  Yours to say if Slavery's night
Wider o'er this fair Republic
  Shall extend its awful blight—
Blight to speech, and soil, and labor,
  Blight to all that lifts and saves
Freemen—sovereigns in their freedom—
  From the grade and fate of slaves.

Shall the taskman's human chattel
  Here, or over Kansas plains—
Marching, "like dumb driven cattle,"
  To the music of his chains—
Further curse the land your fathers
  Won for Freedom with their blood?
Further, thrice-accursed Slavery!
  Sweep and whelm you with its flood?

Men of labor, shall your labor
  Be degraded everywhere?
Further shall the taskman's chattel
  Three-fifths of your franchise share?
Further shall this cloud of bondage
  Yonder go, or hither come?
On Free Soil, or in Free Senates,
  Further strike your Free Speech dumb![35]

This much of the "slave-power conspiracy" was constructed
from the observed facts of its operation, implemented only by the
imputation of a premeditated design to proceed step by step to a
fixed end. And the end, the capstone of the plot, was furnished
by the slaveholders themselves, namely, the reduction of the free
laboring class to slavery. While they never actually said that the
workers should be literally enslaved, and probably had enough
sense to realize it could not be done, they had predicted that it
would one day be necessary and had clearly expressed their belief
that the world would be a better and safer place to live in if it
were done. From the slaveholders' indictment of the "failure of
free society" it could be inferred that this was in the back of their

minds; from their panegyrics of the slave system, the corollary could logically be deduced that they could not but favor such a policy; and from their contemptuous references to free labor it could be supposed that they would one day attempt it. It could be, and it was.[36] But the pro-slavery propaganda gave grounds for more than inference, deduction and supposition, and this propaganda was captured by anti-slavery men and turned against the enemy.

Calhoun had been one of the first apologists of slavery to define the "positive good" doctrine. In the first generation after the Revolution, the natural rights theory was yet popular even among the Southern aristocracy, and many of them could still utter mild condemnations of slavery. Most of them defended slavery apologetically, as an institution that had been bequeathed to them, or even forced upon them, by the English, and there was nothing they could do about it except treat the slaves humanely and colonize those who were emancipated. They admitted that slavery was an abomination in the sight of man and God, but if it were abolished the South would be ruined, there would be no one to raise the cotton, there would be race war, and besides the Negroes weren't ready for it yet. But Calhoun announced that the "folly and delusion" that slavery was a moral and political evil were gone, and that the South now saw it in its true light, as "the most safe and stable basis for free institutions in the world." It was no longer an evil, or a relative evil, or even a relative good, but a positive good, for slave, for master and for society. It was a natural progression from this position to a defense of slavery as the best condition not only for "inferior races" but for "inferior classes" as well. And the progression was made. The Richmond *Enquirer* put it boldly:

Until recently, the defence of slavery has labored under great difficulties, because its apologists were merely apologists, took half-way ground. They confined the defence to *mere negro slavery,* thereby giving up the slavery principle, admitting other forms of slavery to be wrong, and yielding up the authority of the Bible, and of the history, practices, and experience of mankind.—Human experience, showing the universal success of slave society, and the universal failure of free society, was unavailing to them, because they were precluded from employing it, by admitting slavery in the abstract to be wrong. The defence of mere negro slavery involved them in still greater difficulty. The laws of all the Southern States justified the holding white men in slavery, provided that through the mother they were descended, however remotely, from a negro slave. The bright mulattoes, according to their theory, were wrongfully held in slavery.

The line of defence, however, is changed now, and the North is completely cornered, and dumb as an oyster. The South now maintains that slavery is right, natural, and necessary. It shows that all divine and almost all human authority justifies it. The South further charges, that the little experiment of free society in Western Europe has been, from the beginning, a cruel failure, and that symptoms of failure are abundant in our North. While it is far more obvious that negroes be slaves than whites—for they are only fit to labor, not to direct—yet the principle of slavery is in itself right, and does not depend on difference of complection.[37]

This article was reprinted in other Southern papers, and some of them wrote their own variations on the theme,[38] but it received widest publicity in the North, where it was broadcast with and without comment as the most damning exposure of the true aims of the slave-power conspiracy.[39]

Even in the case of this final stage of the "conspiracy," people found evidence of attempts here and there to begin putting it into execution. For example, numerous instances were reported of slaves, particularly fugitives, who had no "visible admixture of Negro blood," which was cited as proof that the color line was no barrier to enslavement; and it was said that the language of the Fugitive Slave Act made it applicable to white apprentices and all other white men who owed service, and that one such case had actually been enforced in the courts.[40] The enslavement of free Negroes who failed to depart from certain Southern states within a specified time, and of free Negroes in the North who could not definitely prove their right to freedom, showed that a

legal status of freedom could not be an assurance against the
"man-stealers."[41] Some thought that the scheme was to make a
wedge by enslaving immigrants, for it was said that Robert
Wickliffe of Kentucky had suggested, in case of a labor shortage,
that he was "in favor of making slaves of the damned Irish and
Dutch," and that William Gilmore Simms expostulated: "Pity
it is that the lousy and languishing lazzaroni of Italy cannot
be made to labor in the fields under the whip of a severe task-
master!"[42] Others thought the indigent might be the first victims
of the plot, as indicated by the report that New Mexico had
passed a law decreeing corporal punishment for recalcitrant white
apprentices and by the proposal of the *New York Day Book*
that indigent laborers and their children be sold to anyone who
would agree to take care of them "as long as they live." But however it might be perpetrated, it was a common belief that if the
aggressions of the slave power—aggressions against democracy,
against the territories and against "free society"—were not
halted, the end would be the conversion of the United States into
a slave empire. This was the theme of one of the most famous
poems of the day, "A Letter from Mr. Ezekiel Biglow," by
James Russell Lowell:

> Them thet rule us, them slave-traders,
>   Haint they cut a thunderin' swarth,
> (Helped by Yankee renegaders,)
>   Thru the vartu o' the North!
> We beg to think it's nater
>   To take sarse an' not be riled;—
> Who'd expect to see a tater
>   All on eend at bein' biled?
>
>   . . . .
> They may talk o' Freedom's airy
>   Tell they're pupple in the face,—
> It's a grand gret cemetary
>   Fer the barthrights of our race;
> They jest want this Californy
>   So's to lug new slave-states in

To abuse ye, an' to scorn ye,
    An' to plunder ye like sin.

Wy, it's jest ez clear ez figgers,
    Clear ez one an' one make two,
Chaps thet make black slaves o' n——s
    Want to make wite slaves o' you.

Tell ye jest the eend I've come to
    Arter cipherin' plaguy smart,
An' it make a handy sum, tu,
    Any gump could larn by heart;
Laborin' men and laborin' women
    Hev one glory an' one shame,
Ev'y thin' thet's done inhuman
    Injers all on 'em the same.

'Taint by turnin' out to hack folks
    You're agoin' to git your right,
Nor by lookin' down on black folks
    Coz you're put upon by wite;
Slavery aint o' nary color,
    'Taint the hide thet makes it wus,
All it keers fer in a feller
    'S jest to make him fill its pus.
    . . . .
Wal, go 'long to help 'em stealin'
    Bigger pens to cram with slaves,
Help the men that 's ollers dealin'
    Insults on your fathers' graves;
Help the strong to grind the feeble,
    Help the many agin the few,
Help the men thet call your people
    Witewashed slaves an' peddlin' crew![43]

Re-forming the Lines

The aggression of the slave-power, and its impact on American
life and politics, cut the ground from under the position that the

labor movement had maintained until 1845 and created the conditions which made possible the fulfillment of McDuffie's dread prediction that the abolitionists and workers would one day unite. Most working men had been opposed to slavery, but many had refused to join the abolition movement because of their fear that emancipation would produce a mass exodus of freedmen to the North to compete with them in the labor market. A large number of workers never shed this fear, but many more came to feel that the imminent danger of slave competition in the territories and possibly even in the states was of greater concern than the ultimate danger of competition with free Negroes. The threat was both more immediate and, if realized, more momentous. Some of the workers therefore were ready to support abolitionism, while others retained their hostility to it but at the same time were willing to make a stand against the slave power and thus glided cautiously into the anti-slavery camp.

A large section of the labor movement had remained aloof from abolitionism because it believed that the labor issue must be settled first, that it was a problem of greater magnitude, that abolitionism was a diverting influence, and that slavery was on the way out anyhow. But the course of events from Texas in 1845 to *Dred Scott* in 1857 made it increasingly apparent that slavery was so far from curling up and dying that, on the contrary, it emerged as the greatest obstacle to the solution of the labor question, and the plantation masters as the worst enemies of the working class. This was the case with the land reformers also, whose program for the emancipation of labor was blown sky-high by the slaveholders' attempt to engross the territory of the nation. To a great extent the issue of labor's emancipation became merged with the slavery question as the resolution of the latter became a condition for the success of the former.

There were other factors also that had deterred labor from participating more actively in the anti-slavery movement—labor's distrust of the abolitionists and their motives, the abolitionists' hostility to the labor movement, and labor's adherence to the Democratic party. These too were to a large extent eliminated by the events after 1845, and especially by the realignment of political parties and the metamorphosis of the anti-slavery movement.

The abolitionists were one of the most faction-ridden reform movements in the history of the United States. Aside from colonization, which was a bogus anti-slavery scheme, the cause was rent with internecine quarrels which at times became quite nasty. There were advocates of immediate abolition, of gradual emancipation, and of "immediate gradualism," but the brawling of these groups was largely a tempest in a teacup. A more important cause of friction was the extreme egomania of Garrison, born in the self-righteous certainty that he alone knew the will of God, weaned on the adulation of his followers, and matured by criticism which in his eyes could only be the voice of the devil. His pharisaism became insufferable to all but his most loyal adherents. His self-esteem grew to such proportions that he resented the success of Frederick Douglass and opposed any independent efforts of the Negro people to work for their own emancipation, excusing this injury by the insult that "The anti-slavery cause, both religiously and politically, has transcended the ability of the sufferers from American slavery and prejudice, *as a class,* to keep pace with it, or to perceive what are its demands, or to understand the philosophy of its operations."[44] It was apparent that Garrison was beginning to confuse himself with another hallowed name with the same initial.

The first major split in the abolition movement resulted from the controversy between the one-idea men and the universal reformers. Garrison embraced virtually all the social reforms of the day (except labor reform) and insisted on espousing them in the *Liberator,* whereas many abolitionists either could not accept these reforms or felt that they would divert the efforts of the cause and repel potential converts. The most important issue was women's rights: Garrison gladly accepted the support and assistance of women and insisted on their right to hold office in the Anti-Slavery Society and to speak from its platforms. Chiefly as a result of hostility to this policy a large section of the membership seceded and formed the rival American and Foreign Anti-Slavery Society, which eventually overshadowed the parent body. Another source of discord was the insistence of many abolitionists on the exclusive use of passive resistance and moral suasion, thus denying effective means of struggle to both Northern abolitionists and the slaves themselves. Frederick Douglass exposed the hopelessness of such a philosophy, pointing out the futility of using moral considerations or reason with slaveholders. "One might as well hunt bears with ethics and political economy as weapons, as to seek to 'pluck the spoiled out of the hand of the oppressor' by the mere force of moral law." Slavery was a system of brute force, he stated, and must be met with its own weapons.[45]

The philosophy of passive resistance was related to a more deep-rooted disease—an organic disease—that infected a large body of abolitionists, and not only the Garrisonians: namely, purist and puerile sectarianism. With the Garrisonian school abolition was neither a political, a social nor an economic question, but a moral and religious one. The bottom line of their philosophy was, "Slaveholding is a *sin.*" This could have been, and for many was, the beginning of earnest anti-slavery work. But for Garrison and his adherents it was the end. They started by trying to convert the slaveholders, and when that was revealed as a hopeless endeavor, they turned to converting themselves. Every day of their lives was but another opportunity to make public revelation of a religious "experience" and renew their dedication to the faith. They rose up with phylacteries on their arms and lay down thanking God and praising themselves for having lived another day without succumbing to the temptations of the unclean spirits. Their mission was not to destroy evil—"God will vindicate the oppressed"—but to keep themselves from contamination by evil.

Their mission was not to free the slaves but to wash their hands of responsibility for enslaving them.

This peremptory passion for purity was the basis of the Garrisonian political philosophy—or anti-political philosophy—which was summed up in the doctrine "No union with slaveholders." Since the Constitution of the United States recognized and sanctioned and upheld property in man, it was a covenant with death and a compact with hell, and Garrison exorcised the devil every Fourth of July by publicly burning a copy of the Constitution. Since the Union was an instrument of the compact for the preservation of slavery, by armed force if necessary, the Union must be dissolved. Since every office-holder must swear allegiance to the Constitution, no true believer could share in his guilt by electing him to office. Did Garrison think that non-resistance, dissolution of the Union, and non-participation in politics would help the slaves? That was not his concern. If one vote of his would emancipate every slave in the country, he had said, he would not cast that vote. What was his plan for emancipation? He had none, and boasted of it as a mark of his integrity. The best he could offer was, ". . . let no cement of the Union bind the slaves, and he will right himself"—by passive resistance, no doubt.

The American and Foreign Society shared the prophet's bias against political action, but another and growing group came out for political abolitionism. They were able to break the tyranny of Garrison's logic by the simple process of denying that the Constitution was a pro-slavery document. Since the Declaration of Independence, with its proclamation of freedom and equality, formed an integral part of the Constitution, according to their views, the latter could not possibly be interpreted to sustain slavery. Slavery in fact was unconstitutional and illegal, and it was the plain duty of freedom-loving people to elect men to office who would use the powers of the government to destroy the unholy institution. This was a forward step in the abolition movement of inestimable importance, for it finally placed a traditional weapon in the hands of anti-slavery men—political struggle on the basis of the liberating philosophy of the Declaration of Independence. The first result of political abolitionism was the formation in 1840 of the Liberty party, organized mainly by the wealthy Tappan brothers of New York, which entered the election campaign on a straight abolition platform.

The Liberty men quickly learned the first lesson of the political primer, that a party cannot succeed on the basis of one idea, that it must present a program with the widest appeal to the people. Winning voters was different from winning converts. They appealed to the working men of the North and South to cast their votes for the overthrow of the aristocracy that degraded them, exploited them and reviled them, for the emancipation of labor through the emancipation of the slaves;[46] and they broadened their platform to include the special demands of the working men. Gerrit Smith, himself a wealthy landowner, was converted to land reform, mainly by George Evans personally, and at the 1847 convention of the party a program was adopted which included, besides the abolition of slavery, the repeal of all tariffs, the abolition of the military and naval establishments, the ending of the war with Mexico and the restoration of her conquered territory, the abolition of all monopolies, restrictions on land holding, inalienable free homesteads and temperance. The slaveholders and the Northern commercial and industrial aristocracy were allied, declared the convention, against moral law and natural rights, and both must be fought. "Every effective blow struck at either of them, weakens all the rest. . . ." For the first time a serious and practical appeal was made for united political action by the workers and the abolitionists.

In asking you to assist us in vindicating the claims of the oppressed colored man, whose wrongs, being most grievous, demand a commensurate prominence, we do not ask you to stand neutral or non-committal, in your political activity, and in your votes, in respect to the wrongs, greater or smaller, of any other class of men. . . .

As a political party, we will hold no truce with a *Northern* Aristocracy for the purpose of checkmating the *Southern* one. We will take no shelter under the wing of a *Southern* aristocracy, from the spreading branches of a *Northern* one. Whether they choose to measure swords with each other, as rivals, as they sometimes do—or mutually court and strengthen each other, as at present inclining to do,—we will wage an uncompromising and exterminating warfare with each, so long as either of them show their heads in the field, not forgetting to watch after them, if they retire. . . . When all the elements of aristocracy on the one hand, and of true democracy on the other, shall thus find their latent affinities, and marshal their forces, we shall have "an open field and fair play," and we ask nothing more. . . .[47]

The program and the appeal for a common struggle were perfectly symbolized by the party's candidates for president and vice-president: Gerrit Smith, abolitionist and land reformer, and Elihu Burritt, "the learned blacksmith," worker and pacifist. The party was endorsed by the New England Labor Reform League and the National Industrial Congress—McDuffie's fearful forecast was on its way to realization, though not in the manner he had supposed.[48]

There was yet another problem that the anti-slavery men had to solve, namely, the relationship between the ultimate goal and immediate issues. The purists, the "ultra-leftists" in the abolition movement, had no conception of political strategy. They maintained the naive conviction that if they only kept up their agitation for immediate abolition long enough and loud enough, the light would one day break through the minds of the benighted people and slavery would crumble to the ground like the walls of Jericho before the trumpet-blasts of righteousness. They did not understand that most people would arrive at a realization of the need for abolition only as the result of a fight against the slavocracy on issues that touched their immediate interests, and that in the course of this fight they could become organized and united for the eventual overthrow of slavery. Although the working class was opposed to slavery, it was not yet ready to engage in an active fight for its destruction. But it was ready to fight to confine it to the states where it existed and to wrest the government from the hands of the slave-power and the money power. That was not enough for the purists, even among the political abolitionists; in fact it was in their eyes nothing less than "union with slaveholders." They would make no compromises, accept no half measures, never retreat one step in order to advance two. Nor could they countenance cooperation with men who were not animated by the same noble and philanthropic motives that drove them to battle with the legions of darkness. In the 1830's the abolitionists had performed a service that entitles them to a place beside the great heroes of mankind's fight for liberty; they raised the banner of immediate and unconditional freedom for the slaves and kept it flying in the face of a host of enemies, traducers and faint-hearts. In the 1840's and '50's and the war years they made a contribution of no less importance: they kept ever before the people the final goal towards which their efforts must lead. But they could not lead the people to that goal, for they ran too far ahead and lost contact with the people.

The Liberty party could not make the transition, and after garnering a few thousand votes in two Presidential campaigns, sank into oblivion. The new party would have to be one that could absorb the progressive elements in the old parties and among the independent voters as well as abolitionists, and must be based on the issue that could unite them against the slave power. That issue was the exclusion of slavery from the territories, and the party assumed the appropriate name of Free Soil, which suggested not only its major plank but also its endorsement of free homesteads for farmers and workers. Some of the Liberty people came into the new party, forming its abolitionist wing. Like its predecessor, the Free Soil party represented itself as the champion of the slaves as well as the farmers and workers—both those in the South, "more trampled upon, if possible, than the very Africans themselves," and in the North, the "children of toil . . . who would annually seek a new home and a refuge from want and oppression in the vacant territories" and whose protection "in their rights to political and social equality, and in the secure enjoyment of the fruits of their industry" was the true object of government.[49]

The "children of toil" were ready to welcome such an appeal, for they were becoming increasingly aware of the restraint that the slave-power was exercising on all their cherished reforms. "The question of slavery is in truth the question of labor," asserted the *Voice of Industry,* for whenever the rights of labor or any other reform was advanced, the influence of the slaveholders was thrown against it. "Do we ask for a Free Soil, a land limitation law, or any other measure which looks to the protection and elevation of the laboring class, we are told by the McDuffies and the Calhouns that slavery is the natural and necessary condition of the producing classes. . . ."[50] Another labor paper, viewing the influence of slavery in the same light, drew the logical conclusion to which the working men were being propelled. The slavery question could not be downed, it asserted, but was becoming daily more vexing, and was now the only issue before the country. Whether the question was one of free trade, taxation, internal improvements, peace, free soil or anything else, "this enormous dragon" of slavery had something at stake. It was clear to this writer that "Either slavery must have full liberty and sweep to expand itself in influence or else it must meet in fell encounter with death. . . . We go for direct and internecine war with the monster."[51] Throughout the North workers continued to flow into the anti-slavery camp at an accelerating tempo. In Vermont, the advocates of land limitation condemned both land monopoly and slavery and joined the abolitionists to form the state Free Soil organization, and in every other state anti-slavery men and workers joined forces on a program of opposition to slavery, homestead exemption, and the freedom of the public domain; in industrial centers such issues as the ten-hour day were also endorsed by the Free Soilers.[52]

The formation of the Free Soil party was a symptom also of the disintegration and reorganization of the old parties that began in 1845. Both Whigs and Democrats were heterogeneous parties, made up of members of all classes in all sections of the country. Neither could withstand the impact of the slavery and territorial issues when they came to overshadow all others. The Northern wing of both parties had to make a decision sooner or later: either capitulate to the planters and accept their ascendancy in the Union, or resist them and establish its own hegemony. The natural inclination was toward the latter policy, and many made the decision by transferring their support to the Free Soil party in 1848 and the Republican party in 1856. This group represented mainly the farmers, the lower middle class, and the small industrialists on the make.

But others could not make the decision—not yet, at least. Bankers, merchants and cotton manufacturers were bound to the slave system by a network of commercial links, and could not take the risk of antagonizing business associates and possibly disrupting the Union—they believed that the South meant business, in both senses of the term. Besides, many of them were convinced that, as the South had warned them, abolitionism was a species of radicalism that must not be encouraged; men of property must hang together or they would hang separately. The first and greatest concern of conservatives everywhere and at all times is to "maintain the stability of political institutions against the disorganized excitement which [takes] possession of men's minds; the immutability of principles. . . . The stability of the laws, and their uninterrupted action—never their change."[53] How could they go into upstart parties tainted with the dangerous ideas of abolition and agrarianism? These elements, with a few exceptions, stayed in the old parties, possibly hoping to keep control in their hands but willing to temporize, compromise and accommodate themselves to the planters' wishes. The Democrats found this easiest to do, for they had rooted political ties with the South and a traditional policy of state rights, whereas the Northern Whigs had always been a high-tariff, pro-bank and internal improvement, strong government party in the tradition of the Federalists. Furthermore, their opposition to the Mexican War and support of the Wilmot Proviso had been too vociferous, too much tinged with abolitionism. So the Southern planters migrated wholesale into the Democratic party and called it their own. The Whigs floundered in the sea of confusion and indecision, with only one claim on people's loyalty—they had saved the Union by the Compromise of 1850; when that was torpedoed by the Kansas-Nebraska Act, the Whig party was dead.

As the Democratic party made the transition from Jackson to Calhoun, and as the workers became more concerned about the menace of the slave-power, the party found it increasingly difficult to maintain its hold over them, and they began to look for more congenial associates. One symptom of this was the revolt of the Barnburners from the New York organization. This faction of the party was a lineal descendant of the Workingmen's party of 1830 and the Loco-Focos of the Jacksonian days. In 1848 the Barnburners joined the Free Soil movement in protest against the defeat of the Wilmot Proviso, and their leader, former President Martin Van Buren, became its candidate in that year.

Another example of what happened to the Democratic party was revealed in the history of the Fall River *Weekly News,* published by a Mr. Almy and John C. Milne, who was apparently the chief editorial writer. The *News* was a Democratic organ and Milne was decidedly pro-labor. He supported the ten-hour day, wage lien laws and free homesteads, gave full notices of local and New England labor meetings, was sympathetic with Associationism and opposed the anti-union policy of the capitalists—"that miserable race of parvenus, parasites and popinjays"—who "hated everything connected with labor, except its dividends." From the time of the annexation of Texas, the editorial policy of the paper reflected the dilemma of the editor: it tried to maintain "the principles and doctrines of the democracy, as inculcated by Jefferson" and at the same time retain its loyalty to the Democratic party, which was rapidly abandoning those principles as it fell under the domination of the slaveholders. Milne was strongly opposed to slavery and, while he disagreed with Garrison's disunion doctrine, he praised him for his power and ability, and gave lengthy and sympathetic reports of local abolition meetings. However, during the same years he was supporting the annexation of Texas and the Mexican War, as party measures.

Milne was convinced that the workers could achieve their demands only through the Democratic party, and therefore remained loyal to it and supported its national policies, but he did not like the growing symptoms he saw of "fawning sycophancy upon the slaveholders of the South; and this disposition to sacrifice any man at the North who dares to be a thoroughgoing and consistent democrat, in holding the doctrine 'that all men are created equal. . . . ' " In 1847, the *News* unequivocally supported the Wilmot Proviso, stating that the territories should be "speedily purified from the presence of the Slave system, a system so opposed, so antagonistic to every interest and principle upon which our Liberty and happiness are founded." If the slave-power was strengthened by gaining control of the territories, "The North will then be a servant of servants—and democracy may exist here, but only in name—equal rights will die here among the democrats, as it has long ago died at the South among those called by this name." Milne demanded that the Democratic party take a stand against slavery extension, and if it failed he would favor the organization of a new party made up of all friends of freedom.

But the next year he was again supporting the Democratic candidate, Lewis Cass, whose policy called for popular sovereignty in the territories. By 1850 he was willing to give up the fight on the Wilmot Proviso and come to a settlement with the South in the interests of peace and the Union. However, this mood soon passed, and the arrogance of the slaveholders and the complete submission of the Democratic party on the Fugitive Slave Act particularly disgusted him. He was giving up his hopes for saving the party. The North had reluctantly had the slavery question forced upon it, and had determined to decide it in favor of freedom. "Let us do everything in our power," he wrote, "to put an end to a system which permits and enjoins such accursed deeds, and first and immediately to blot and erase forever from the statute books of our own nation, the infernal slave act of 1850."[54]

In 1851 Milne supported the election of Sumner to the Senate: " . . . there are some crises when party considerations should be sunk, or kept out of sight, in view of some commanding and all-worthy object." He gave considerable attention to the proceedings of the Free Soilers and finally, in 1852, broke with the Democratic party and dissolved his connection with the *News*. In a farewell statement to his readers he said that he had supported the party while it was the party of progress and liberty; even when the majority had been derelict to the principles of the democratic faith, he remained with it in hopes that it would return. But he had been disappointed in that hope when the party gave its support to the fugitive slave law. "The respective democratic and whig conventions at Baltimore, seemed to vie with each other in humility to the degrading and unconstitutional measure, both declaring it a finality, and each denouncing its repeal. My judgement abhors the measure, and my feelings revolt at the dereliction evinced by those who bow to it and support its atrocious provisions."[55] Milne was typical of many workers and workers' leaders who were driven out of the Democratic party by its subservience to the slaveholders.

The Free Soil party was composed of farmers, workers and the progressive elements among the middle class and the industrial capitalists who were determined to halt the progress of the slave-power; and by the latter term was meant not only the slaveholders but the Northern business classes that were allied with them. As Sumner said at the Massachusetts Free Soil convention in 1849, the efforts to place the national government on the side of freedom had received little sympathy from the wealthy, but had encountered their opposition. It was easy to explain this, he stated, for the instinct of property was stronger than the instinct of freedom. "The money-power has joined hands with the slave-power. Selfish, grasping, subtle, tyrannical, like its ally, it will not brook opposition. It claims the Commonwealth as its own, and too successfully enlists in its support that needy talent and easy virtue which are required to maintain its sway."[56]

The hostility of the early abolition movement to the workers had made it impossible for the latter to join it without sacrificing their own demands. But now it was clear that the greatest enemies of labor were ranged against them on the side of the slave mas-ters; the exploiters of the chattel slaves and the wage slaves, "the lords of the lash and the lords of the loom," had joined hands, and the workers and the slaves were fighting each other's battles, whether they knew it or not. The fight against the slave-power became "a battle against conservatism, reaction, aristocracy, and the power of capital—in Ohio and Massachusetts as well as in South Carolina."[57] The lines were forming for the Second American Revolution.

Free Soil and Free Labor

With the defeat of the Free Soil party in the election of 1848, many of the Barnburners and Conscience Whigs returned to the haven of party regularity, and the alleged "finality" of the Compromise of 1850 caused others to return. The Free Soil party, with those influences removed, became again mainly a coalition of anti-slavery men, workers and farmers. But the conditions which inspired its organization were recreated in 1854 by the Nebraska Act, this time on a much larger scale. The Nebraska Act not only destroyed the compromises of 1820 and 1850 but, in the eyes of most people, precluded the possibility of future compromises. This time the exodus from the Democratic and Whig parties was of mass proportions and a new party was required to organize the dissidents—not a third party but a party to replace the defunct Whigs and challenge the supremacy of the Democrats. The Free Soil organization could not fill the requirements, because it had suffered the loss of prestige that comes with defeat, and was too "radical" for most of those looking for a new home. Thus the Republican party was born; spontaneously and simultaneously through the North organizations were formed, and then coalesced into a national body.

The Republicans took over their predecessor's slogan: Free soil, free labor, free men, and (for the campaign of 1856) Fremont. But it no longer had precisely the same meaning. The term "free soil" had connoted three different things with the Free Soil party: its dislike of slavery, its determination to keep the territories free, and its support of a free homestead law. With the Republican party, the first and last of these were relegated to a minor position. The party was not, strictly speaking, an anti-slavery party at all in the sense that it avowed opposition to the institution itself; in fact it was specifically pledged not to interfere with slavery in the states where it was recognized.[58] It was anti-slavery only in the sense that it challenged the supremacy of the slaveholders in the territories and in the Union and, if successful, must bring about the downfall of the slave system, willy-nilly; and in its fight against the slaveholders it could not avoid, if it wanted to, a criticism of the institution as such. It was precisely this that dismayed the abolitionists: from Garrison to Smith to Van Buren to Fremont to

Lincoln the anti-slavery creed was steadily diluted and adulterated until it became too distasteful for strong men to swallow. On the other hand, with each dilution the number of men who came to participate was multiplied. From the point of view of some, the process appeared as a steady corruption of the nation's moral character; others could see only the growing strength of the array of hosts come to battle against the slave-power. As for free homesteads, the Republicans scarcely mentioned them in the campaign of 1856. The big issue, almost the only issue, was the exclusion of slavery from the territories, and their preservation for the free laborers of the North and South. As the Cleveland *Leader* stated, the question to be decided at the forthcoming election was whether the unsettled territory would be devoted to the use of free workingmen or whether it would be taken from them and be cursed by the establishment of slavery throughout its entire extent.[59]

The term "free labor" likewise did not have the same significance on the Republicans' banner as it had on the Free Soilers'. The latter party had supported many of the specific demands of the labor movement and was, in truth, a farmer-labor party; the Republicans kept only the homestead plank and consigned it to a dark corner. Farmers and workers made up the bulk of the Republican party, but it was dominated by the middle class leadership and outlook imposed by the Democrats, Whigs and Know-Nothings who swarmed into it. It represented the interests of the working class only in that it was ranged against the money power and the slave-power, the greatest enemies of labor, and in that the slavery question itself was the issue of greatest importance to the labor movement at that time. In fact, the guiding theme of the campaign was the representation of the Republican party as the party of labor. In his letter of acceptance, Fremont wrote that his policy "would leave no aliment to that sectional party which seeks its aggrandizement by appropriating the new Territories to capital in the form of Slavery, but would inevitably result in the triumph of Free Labor—the natural capital which constitutes the real wealth of this great country, and creates the intelligent power in the masses alone to be relied on as the bulwark of free institutions."[60]

From press and platform this idea was harped upon. Seward asserted that the history of the United States was determined by the conflict between slaveholders and nonslaveholders. The slaveholders had sought to fortify themselves with a blind disregard of the rights and interests of non-slaveholders. The latter, increasingly conscious of the danger of slavery, sought to counteract the policy of the slaveholders by diffusing the spirit of freedom. Only the Republican party upheld the cause of the nonslaveholders.[61]

The interests of the Southern workers were also said to be defended by the Republicans. The Cleveland *Leader* congratulated the working men of St. Louis on their turning a Republican victory, and hoped that their example would be emulated in the slave states. Asserting that the interests of labor and Republicanism were identical, the paper declared that the Republican party was the working man's party, its object being to protect free labor from degrading and unfair competition with involuntary labor.[62]

While some of the Republicans expressed the hope that the triumph of free labor would also result in striking the shackles from the slaves, most of them made no pretense of being concerned with the fate of the Negroes, and many went out of their way to insist that theirs was the party of *white* labor. Although the experiences of the Liberty and Free Soil parties had indicated that many workers might be brought to strike at the roots of the slave system in the fight to overthrow the slave-power, the conservative elements in the Republican party introduced the note of white supremacy, and in doing so hoped to win the votes of Negrophobes and anti-abolitionists who were opposed to slavery extension. For example, Senator Trumbull said, at the party's national convention, "It is not so much in reference to the welfare of the negro that we are here, but it is for the protection of the rights of the laboring whites, for the protection of ourselves and our liberties."[63] The Hartford *Courant* expressed the attitude of the more chauvinistic sections of the party. The Republican party was the white man's party, it asserted. It did not oppose the progress of slavery from any feeling of sympathy for the Negroes. On the contrary, it did so because it liked the white men better than the Negroes. "We believe the Caucasian variety of the human species superior to the Negro variety—and we would breed the best stock, and fill this noble land of ours . . . with the noblest race of human beings possible. . . . The Republicans mean to preserve all of this country that they can from *the pestilential presence of the black man*."[64]

While the Republican party presented itself as the champion of free labor, it portrayed the slave power as labor's mortal foe. Its spokesmen carefully spelled out the effect of slavery on the conditions of the Southern workers,[65] and emphasized especially the "northerly direction to the development of the negro race," the threat of slave competition in the territories, and the harmful influence that it already exerted on labor in the free states. A widely circulated pamphlet was devoted to proving that Southern slavery reduced Northern wages by its employment in industries that competed with Northern products. "The system of reducing the laborer to a bare subsistence, is hostile to the individual and personal well-being of the great mass of the fifteen millions of people who wield the political control of the free States; and it will be passing strange if they do not so wield it as to protect themselves and their own."[66]

A great deal was said about the Southern aristocracy's contempt for labor and laborers, and one of the popular campaign songs went:

> The great "F.F.'s" are nobly born,
> A whip each baby waves;
> Our base mechanics they hold in scorn—

They are but *whiter slaves!*
They raise their cash by chain and lash,
And trade and toil ignore.
Why wasn't I born in old Virginia,
On old Virginia's shore?[67]

Much political capital was made when the Democratic congressman Philip Herbert of California shot and killed Thomas Keating, the Irish head-waiter at Willard's Hotel in Washington, allegedly for refusing to serve his breakfast after hours. Herbert was acquitted by Judge Crawford of the Criminal Court of the District of Columbia, and efforts to expel him from the House and to investigate the affair were defeated. This was bad enough, and some of the Southern newspapers added fuel to the flames by defending Herbert, as the *Alabama Mail* did: "It is getting time that waiters at the North were convinced that they are servants, and not 'gentlemen' in disguise. We hope this Herbert affair will teach them prudence."[68] The New York *Tribune* wrote that the doctrine laid down by Crawford was "slaveholder's doctrine and slave driver's law."

It is a customary, natural, and perhaps necessary part of the slavedriving system, that the driver should go armed—should carry a pistol or bowie knife in his pocket, to enforce his command, and to punish all audacious resistance, and especially all insolent demeanor. . . . 'tis a part of the law of slavery that the servant thus chastized for his insolence, has no right to make any reply, retort, or resistance . . . [which] may be forthwith punished by the instant shooting or stabbing of the insolent servant, the killing, so far from being murder, or even manslaughter, will be excusable homicide. . . .
Our laboring people at the North may see in these rulings of Judge Crawford, the natural consequence of the ascendancy which slaveholding and slavedriving have already obtained in our policy, and which the party calling itself Democratic is seeking so eagerly to extend and perpetuate. . . . [69]

Buchanan was portrayed in the 1856 campaign not only as the candidate of the labor-hating oligarchy, but as a man who per-

sonally favored the degradation of labor. He was accused of
having advocated a daily wage of ten cents and thereby won the
sobriquet "Ten-Cent Jimmy." Several campaign songs were composed on this theme, like "Buck Shooting":

> Can poor men forget to remember,
> When old Buck was willing to greet
> The day when mechanics should labor
> For ten cents a day and no meat?
> He may take in his horns and forswear it,
> Can he blot out the record? Not he!
> Our platform is *Freedom for Kansas!*
> Our motto, *"Free Homes for the Free!"*
>
> Oh! the Free Working Men of the Union
> Can think! and will act for themselves!
> They'll slaughter Old Buck for his antlers,
> And let him dry up on the shelves.[70]

A major role in Republican campaign tactics was assigned to
the propagation of the "slave-power conspiracy." McDuffie, Calhoun, Pickens, the Richmond *Enquirer, et al.*, were trotted out
and put through their paces again. One of the most widely circulated and copied broadsides of the campaign was one entitled:
"White Slavery. The New 'Democratic Doctrine.' Slavery not to
be confined to the Negro Race, but to be made the universal
condition of the Laboring classes of society." Most of it consisted
of the choicest quotations from the Southern press about the
mudsills and greasy mechanics. An editorial in the New York
Tribune was typical of what was written in hundreds of Republican and abolition papers. It asserted that the slavery question was
not a Negro question, a question of the abstract rights of man,
or even a question whether slavery should continue to exist; it
was rather a question whether the mass of Americans would
retain their liberty or whether it would be nullified like that of
the poor whites in the South. "It has come at last to this; that the

free millions of the North insist, before everything else, and at all hazards, Slavery shall not extend another step. 'Why?' Because there is but one step more for it to take, and after that there can be no more free labor at the North."[71]

It is very difficult to judge the effect of the 1856 campaign on the workers. It seems certain that the majority of immigrant laborers, and particularly the Irish, did not vote for Fremont, not only because of their traditional Democratic affiliation, but because of the strong nativist strain in the Republican party. After the Southerners captured the Know-Nothing party, most of its Northern members joined the Republicans and furnished them some of their outstanding leaders. In New York and Massachusetts nativist influence in the party was particularly strong, and immigrants could hardly be expected to give their votes to a party which harbored such elements and did not repudiate their hatred of the foreign born. Furthermore, the appeal of free territories could not have much effect on workers who did not have the means to emigrate to the West even if they wanted to.[72] The Germans, however, deserted the Democratic party in large numbers after the Nebraska Act was passed, and most of them went into the Republican fold. The "Forty-eighters" were aggressively anti-slavery, and the Turnvereine, the socialist Turnerbund and the German labor unions, which were all outspoken in their opposition to slavery, gave their support to the Republican party.[73]

Edward H. Rogers, a worker who was active in the abolition movement, stated that the working class played a crucial part in the anti-slavery movement in the 1850's, attributing this largely to the fact that the ten-hour day was won by many workers during that decade, enabling them to participate more actively than before.[74] 25,000 workingmen of Pittsburgh, including German, Irish and native Americans, addressed the workers of Pennsylvania, calling upon them to protect their rights, which were imperiled by the slaveholding aristocracy. If the latter succeeded in extending slavery over all the territories, warned these workers of Pittsburgh, they would establish their supremacy over the government and extend the sway of slavery over the free workingmen. The only hope of the workers was in the Republican party, under whose banner would be fought the battle of the rights of man. The working men were urged to lay aside minor differences in the face of the great danger, and to unite for the preservation of the territories against slavery.[75]

If the Republican party had taken a more positive stand on labor issues other than the territorial question, it would have won more support from the workers. But then it wouldn't have been the Republican party.

In many respects the campaign of 1860 was a carbon copy of 1856; but there were important differences, for while the issues were essentially the same, the developing crisis had reached a new stage. The attempts of the administration to force slavery on Kansas, the attempt of the Supreme Court to force it on all the territories, the demands for reopening the slave trade, the increasing talk of secession, the Ostend Manifesto, the filibustering expeditions—these events convinced the Northerners more than ever that compromise was impossible, that the decision to submit or make a stand could not be avoided much longer. It was becoming clear to those who wanted nothing more than concord and order that the price demanded by the slaveholders was too high. Many businessmen wanted a high tariff, a Pacific railroad, river and harbor improvements, a national banking system, and control of the national resources and the national market; while the Democrats were in power they could not get them, but the Republicans promised them all. The majority of Northern businessmen, and particularly the merchants, bankers, and cotton manufacturers, remained in the Democratic party, and in fact a number of Whigs among them moved into the Democratic camp as their only hope for defeating the Republicans. But a significant section of the capitalist class, especially among the iron masters of Pennsylvania and New Jersey and others who had no business connections with the South, shifted their support to the Republican party, determined to end the domination of the slave power.[76] As the Republicans gained in strength and bade fair to win the next election it became even more important to jump on the bandwagon and convert the party to their own purposes. The depression that set in after the panic of 1857 produced a wave of militant labor struggles; the unions folded up but the unemployed workers demonstrated in the streets for relief and jobs. Their discontent might be siphoned off by directing it against the slave power. Politicians too, sniffing victory in the air, scampered to join the winning side. Lincoln put "the man before the dollar," but by 1860 the idealism of his party was tempered by the realism of businessmen who considered the man a means of making the dollar, and of politicians who saw him only as a means of making votes. The platform of 1860, the Republican legislation of the war years and the subsequent history of the party bear witness to this fact.

The rank and file had their own reasons for supporting the party: they were "the man" in person, the common people to whom the Declaration of Independence was more than "glittering generalities" and "self-evident lies." It was the creed of their life and the foundation of their liberties; it was given life by the revolution against King George, and it would be preserved by a second revolution against King Cotton. They would return America to the path of democratic development. Many workers believed that a democracy instituted and managed by the Republican party would be spurious, and refused to give their support to it: The capitalists have no sympathy for the Negroes or the white workers, wrote one worker; their only purpose in joining the Republican party was "that capital shall obtain political power to direct the legislation of the Federal Government as it does now that of New England, and thus enable the few to govern the many."[77] But this was the issue of the future; the immediate job was to save the country from the slave power. And since the workers were not strong enough in numbers and organization, or mature enough politically to carry on the fight independently, they attached themselves to the party of the middle class and accepted its leadership in the fight against the common enemy.

In the struggle against reaction, waged by a coalition of farmers, workers, middle class and capitalists, inevitably the ideology of the coalition was expressed in a curious amalgam of conservatism and liberalism, property rights and human rights, the dollar and the man. It represented antagonistic forces, yet they were united in a common fight for progress, each attaching its own meaning to the term. A perfect embodiment of this unity of contradictions was found in the standard-bearer of the party, Abraham Lincoln. He was a firm believer in the philosophy of the Declaration of Independence, but maintained that the Negro was inferior to the white man and opposed their right to be citizens, voters, jurors or office-holders or to have social equality. He was opposed to slavery on moral grounds, but when he introduced a bill in Congress proposing gradual emancipation in the District of Columbia, he added a strong fugitive-slave clause for the restoration of slaves escaping into the District; later he said, "I confess I hate to see the poor creatures hunted down . . . but I bite my lips and keep quiet." He had a profound faith in democracy and the common man, but during most of his political career he was a Whig regular. His views and his actions were at all times governed by caution, moderation and expediency, but he always tempered them with Christian morality, justice and humanity.[78]

Lincoln's deep fellow-feeling for the workingmen was merged with the ideology of the middle class. His sympathy for labor and his understanding of the labor movement were greatly exaggerated in his own time and have been ever since. One of Lincoln's widely quoted expressions was that "To secure to each laborer the whole product of his labor, or as nearly as possible, is a worthy object of any good government."[79] This sentiment was written during his Whig days in the course of an argument for a protective tariff, and if it were translated into modern terminology, it would be more accurately rendered as "To secure to each manufacturer the whole profit of his production . . . is a worthy object of any good government." In Lincoln's view, a manufacturer was a laborer, and the product of his employees' labor was the product of his own labor.

The most radical-sounding of all his pronouncements on labor was contained in an address to the Wisconsin State Agricultural Society in 1859, in which he said, " . . . labor is prior to, and independent of, capital; . . . in fact, capital is the fruit of labor, and could never have existed if labor had not first existed; . . . labor can exist without capital, but . . . capital could never have existed without labor. Hence . . . labor is the superior—greatly the superior—of capital."[80] What was the context of this remark? Lincoln was refuting two other labor theories, both of which were based on the assumption that "labor is available only in connection with capital—that nobody labors, unless somebody else owning capital, somehow, by the use of it, induces him to do it." If the single word "else" were deleted from this passage, its assumption would have been more correct, but Lincoln was talking about laborers (not wage-earners) who owned their own "capital," either in the form of tools or, especially, in the form of land—that is, the farmers whom he was addressing, who did not labor for capitalists but did their own work on their own land. Those who held this assumption, Lincoln continued, were divided into two groups: those who thought it best "that capital shall hire laborers, and thus induce them to work by their own consent," and those who preferred to "buy them, and drive them to it, without their consent." The latter system, chattel slavery, of course he disapproved. The wages system he found quite unobjectionable, providing it was not based on the premise that "whoever is once a hired laborer, is fatally fixed in that condition for life."

As long as class stratifications were fluid, a laborer could save his money and become a capitalist himself, thus proving that labor was "independent of capital" and "superior to capital." This was really but another way of saying that there was no contradiction or conflict between capital and labor.

This was the sum of Lincoln's labor philosophy, and he adverted to it many times. The mudsill theory was false, he asserted, because "There is no permanent class of hired laborers among us. Twenty-five years ago I was a hired laborer. The hired laborer of yesterday labors on his own account today, and will hire others to labor for him tomorrow. . . . "[81]

He did not realize that he was admitting one of the basic contentions of the mudsill theory when he went on to say: "The power of hope upon human exertion and happiness is wonderful. . . . The slave whom you cannot drive with the lash to break seventy-five pounds of hemp in a day, if you will task him to break a hundred, and promise him pay for all he does over, he will break you a hundred and fifty." In short, Lincoln wanted workers to become capitalists, and he wanted slaveholders to become capitalists—the world would be a bourgeois heaven for every one except those who were working twice as hard as the slaves under the compulsion of "the power of hope" that they too would one day join the charmed circle.

In 1860 Lincoln made a speaking tour of New England, where he found a shoemakers' strike in progress. In Hartford, he told his audience, "Thank God that we have a system of labor where there can be a strike."[82] This was hardly in the category of bold assertions, particularly for a Presidential aspirant in an election year. The next day he repeated this remark to the New Haven strikers and explained it more fully:

. . . I am glad to see that a system of labor prevails in New England under which laborers can strike when they want to, where they are not obliged to work under all circumstances, and are not tied down and obliged to labor whether you pay them or not! I like the system which lets a man quit when he wants to, and wish it might prevail everywhere. One of the reasons why I am opposed to slavery is just here. . . . I want every man to have the chance—and I believe a black man is entitled to it—in which he can better his condition—when he may look forward and hope to be a hired laborer this year and the next, work for himself afterward, and finally to hire men to work for him. . . . I desire that if you get too thick here, and find it hard to better your condition on this soil, you may have a chance to strike and go somewhere else, where you may not be degraded, nor have your family corrupted by forced rivalry with negro slaves. I want you to have a clean bed and no snakes in it![83]

Thus, Lincoln conceived of labor's advancement in terms of individual betterment rather than through group action. Even his conception of a strike was very narrow: it meant to him merely the right to quit and "go somewhere else," presumably to the territories where one could get a homestead and become "independent of capital." He held to the Calvinist doctrine that prosperity was a sign that one was a chosen vessel of God, and that failure was a mark of disfavor and a result of indolence, prodigality and careless work habits.[84] His outlook was that of the bourgeois who believes that every man holds in his two hands the means of salvation (that is, prosperity) through hard work, thrift and ambition—in short, it was the philosophy of rugged individualism. It was not the men of toil that Lincoln extolled, but "those who toil up from poverty"[85]—a distinction that was full of meaning.

Lincoln's philosophy of labor was not essentially different from that of many abolitionists, but he differed from them in one important respect: whereas they had counterposed the labor question and the slavery issue and made the abandonment of one the condition for accepting the other, Lincoln merged them into a single problem and made the resolution of the latter a condition for the solution of the former. Lincoln's position was much more practical from the viewpoint of both capitalists and Republican politicians, and more realistic from the viewpoint of labor's interests. His ideology was a reflection of the alliance between labor and capital in the fight against the slave power. It is noteworthy that every expression of his labor philosophy was coupled with a refutation of the mudsill theory, and often with the issue of keeping the territories free of slavery.

Lincoln was quite concerned with the Southern attack on "the failure of free society." He clipped the worst anti-labor articles from the Southern press and pasted them in his scrapbook, and when he read Fitzhugh's *Sociology for the South* he "revolted in anger and disgust." This was unquestionably a sincere reaction, but Lincoln also perceived the propaganda value of such arguments, especially if some of the Northern papers would endorse them. In 1856 he arranged, through his partner Herndon, to have the *Conservative* reprint the famous article from the Richmond *Enquirer* which defended the principle of slavery for all laborers, regardless of race. In the same issue of the paper, however, appeared an editorial denouncing the doctrine that slavery was the best condition for all laborers. Lincoln used the article throughout the campaign to show the danger of the slave-power conspiracy, but never mentioned the editorial.[86] He was reported to have drawn the ultimate conclusion from the slave-power conspiracy in his speech to the Illinois state convention of the Republican party in 1856:

. . . if the safeguards to liberty are broken down, as is now attempted, when they have made *things* of all the free negroes, how long, think you, before they will begin to make *things* of poor white men? Be not deceived. Revolutions do not go backward. The founder of the Democratic party declared that *all* men were created equal. His successor in the leadership has written the word "white" before men, making it read "all *white* men are created equal." Pray, will or may not the Know-nothings, if they should get in power, add the word "protestant," making it read *"all protestant white men"*? . . .

But we cannot be free men if this is, by our national choice, to be a land of slavery. Those who deny freedom to others, deserve it not for themselves; and, under the rule of a just God, cannot long retain it.[87]

In the debates with Douglas, however, and in his own campaign of 1860, he only hinted at the possible enslavement of all workers, choosing rather to emphasize the probability of the institution's becoming nationalized. This was most clearly expressed in his famous House-Divided Speech:

We are now far into the first year since a policy was initiated with the avowed object and confident promise of putting an end to slavery agitation [The Nebraska Act]. Under the operation of that policy, that agitation has not only not ceased, but has constantly augmented. In my opinion, it will not cease until a crisis shall have been reached and passed. "A house divided against itself cannot stand." I believe this government cannot endure permanently half slave and half free. I do not expect the Union to be dissolved—I do not expect the house to fall—but I do expect it will cease to be divided. It will become all one thing, or all the other. Either the opponents of slavery will arrest the further spread of it, and place it where the public mind shall rest in the belief that it is in the course of ultimate extinction; or its advocates will push it forward till it shall become alike lawful in all the States, old as well as new, North as well as South. Have we no tendency to the latter condition?[88]

It has been said that Lincoln tried to "forget" this speech as being too radical for a Presidential candidate, but he repeated its essence several times in 1860,[89] and his party rode it hard and fast throughout the campaign.

On the basis of Lincoln's remarks concerning labor, he was built up by the party as a great champion of the working class. But even more, his own origins and his homely demeanor were exploited to picture him, in Ben Wade's words, as "the very incarnation of American labor."[90] He was already known among the Swedes as "the son of a working man," and the campaign managers made a brilliant effort to impress this image on all the workers. The Chicago *Press and Tribune,* for example, proclaimed that Lincoln was a man of the people, that he had been a laborer during all of his early life, and that he consequently had sympathy with the men who toiled. "Himself an outgrowth of free institutions, he would die in the effort to preserve to others, unimpaired, the inestimable blessings by which he has been made a man."[91] The omnipresent symbols of the campaign were the rail and the ax, and every one in the world knew, as little Tad said, that Abe was a rail-splitter. Banners were carried in parades, reading: "SMALL-FISTED FARMERS, MUDSILLS OF SOCIETY, GREASY MECHANICS, FOR A. LINCOLN."[92]

As in 1856, the Republican party was presented as the party of free labor ranged against its only enemy, the slaveholders. "I say to you, men of Massachusetts, slavery is the one enemy of the free laboring men of America, of the North and of the South," declared Henry Wilson; its mouthpiece, the Democratic party, has ceased to talk of the rights of man "and speaks now solely of the rights of property in man." The contest is "between the interests and claims of the few, who eat their bread—not in the sweat of their brow, but by the forced and unrequited toil of bondsmen—and the enduring interests and indefeasible rights of millions of toiling men who eat their bread in the sweat of their faces."[93] Seward was more explicit. He stated that slavery was objectionable not only on account of the slaves; on the contrary, the Negro was only an incident to it, a subject of disputes but not one of the litigants—like a horse in a justice's court when two neighbors were litigating about its ownership. The controversy was not with the Negroes, but with two classes of white men, those who had a monopoly of the slaves, and the others who had none. The pith of the conflict was that the former wanted to extend themselves over the new territories in order to retain their power, while the latter intended to resist that extension. "It is an eternal question between classes—between the few privileged and the many underprivileged—the eternal question between aristocracy and democracy."[94]

The Democrats were assailed as "the same men, who born with a silver spoon in their mouths, and entertaining a supreme contempt for all who are not rich, think to beat the honest masses of the voters by specious appeals to their prejudices;" and Herschel Johnson, Douglas' running mate, was accused of having declared that "capital should own labor."[95] The central issues, of course, were the exclusion of slavery from the territories, the complete incompatibility of the interests of the slaveholders and those of the workers, and the halting of the slave-power conspiracy.[96] In addition, the Republicans made an appeal to the workers on three other issues.

First, a concerted effort was made to prove that the party had been purified of all traces of Know-Nothingism—an effort made especially difficult by the Massachusetts law passed in 1859 by a Republican-Know-Nothing coalition, which required a two-year waiting period before immigrants could vote, and by the circulation as a campaign document of Helper's *The Impending Crisis,* which contained a scurrilous attack on the Irish Catholics. But the damage was counteracted by the repudiation of the Massachusetts law by Republican state conventions, by the assurances of party leaders, including Lincoln, by the numbers of German leaders who held fast to party loyalty, and by the special "Dutch plank" of the party platform, written by Carl Schurz: "The Republican party is opposed to any change by which the rights of citizenship heretofore accorded to immigrants from foreign lands shall be abridged or impaired, and in favor of giving a full and sufficient protection to all classes of citizens, whether native or naturalized, both at home and abroad."[97]

A second important issue was the homestead bill, which the Republicans not only endorsed but actively campaigned for. The South was opposed to such a law, primarily because it would promote the occupation of the territories by native and immigrant workers and farmers; this would assure the freedom of the territories more certainly than any act of Congress, thereby annihilating any hope of new slave states and upsetting the political balance. Twice in the 1850's the homestead bill was defeated, once by Southern votes in Congress, once by the Democratic President

Buchanan. The Republicans interpreted this as a clear demonstration of the slaveholders' hostility to free labor. Representative Windom declared that it was a struggle between the Republican party, as the friend of the toiling millions, and the Democratic party, as the champion of the aristocratic few who regarded the laboring men as slaves. And this was merely a new version of the age-old, irrepressible conflict between the workers, struggling for food, raiment and a humble home for their families, and "grasping, insatiate capital, seeking to erect for itself luxurious palaces upon the bones and muscles and heart's blood of those whom it is pleased to call the 'mud-sills' of society."[98] The Republicans would make the laborers independent freeholders, while the Democrats would enslave them![99]

Finally, the tariff was presented as a labor plank on the grounds that its primary purpose was to protect American workers against the competition of cheap foreign labor, and that it would relieve the distress resulting from the depression. The Hartford *Evening Press* turned this issue, like all others, into a conflict between slavery and free labor. Since the slave states could not engage extensively in manufactures, it asserted, the slave-power had always opposed such tariffs as free labor desired. But since free labor had an immense preponderance of numbers and wealth, why should it not have such legislation as it wanted? This was the position of the Republican party, stated the writer.[100] This type of appeal was so effective that the Democrats in Pennsylvania actually promised a tariff in order to steal the thunder of their opponents.[101]

The Democrats tried to counteract the tremendous appeal that the Republicans made to the laboring men by playing on their prejudices and especially by raising the old bugaboo of emancipated Negroes flooding the North to compete with them. They also emphasized that if Lincoln were elected the South would withdraw its trade, and probably secede from the Union, throwing Northern industry into paralysis and bringing unemployment and ruin to the workers.[102] By the latter threat they attempted also to scare the capitalists into swinging the election for them. An Indiana Douglas journal warned that following a Republican victory, "soon the cry of the strong man for *bread* will be heard in accents of woe and dread, in every part of the land. A people who have never heard *that cry,* have but a poor conception of the gloom and terror it will carry to every heart. And what shall follow it? Can we hope that such a day of tribulation would pass, without bringing with it fire and blood—the torch of the incendiary, the blow of the assassin, the war of the poor for food, the struggle of men for life?"[103]

As the election approached and a Republican victory appeared probable, the New York *Herald* urged manufacturers to use "pressure" to secure the votes of workingmen against Lincoln. The employers who manufactured for the Southern market did not require much coaxing to carry out this assignment. In every Eastern state they poured out lavish expenditures to turn the tide, attempted to bully and intimidate their employees by threatening their dismissal in case of Lincoln's election, told applicants for jobs that no hiring would be done until after the election and then only if the anti-Republican ticket carried. A circular sent to every workman in the clothing houses of New York a few days before the election, printed in German for the numerous German-American employees in the trade, urged the workers to vote the Union ticket in the coming election, and to persuade their friends to do likewise. By doing so, they were assured, they would get plenty of work at good wages. But if the Republican candidate were elected, they were warned, the South would withdraw its patronage and unemployment and low wages would follow. On election day, practically every store and shop in the city was closed, and many had signs posted: "Closed—gone to vote and work for the Union."—that is, against the Republicans.[104]

These efforts unquestionably had their effect, but it seems clear, nevertheless, that the majority of Northern workers, with the exception of the Irish, voted the Republican ticket. Although there were many demonstrations of Irish workers in support of Lincoln, they voted by an overwhelming majority for Douglas; but their vote was not for slavery, but rather against the party which they were convinced was the party of nativism, capitalism, temperance and disunion.[105] The German working men, on the other hand, were a strongly anti-slavery and pro-Republican group, the principal exceptions being the Catholics among them.

During the 1850's the German-American workers were influenced by men of varied and conflicting views, and there was considerable confusion among them on the slavery question. Karl Heinzen, a leader among the Free Germans, was a radical abolitionist and made his paper a crusader for Negro freedom;[106] but Hermann Kriege violently opposed abolition as a measure, supported by "sentimental philistines" and "liberty-intoxicated ladies," which would not improve the lot of the Negroes by converting them into wage slaves but would depress labor "to the last extremity."[107] Wilhelm Weitling, a utopian communist, strongly condemned slavery and the theories of racial supremacy, but always retained the position that was so popular in the 1840's, that abolition agitation could only divert the workers from their struggle against the wage system, and consequently he gave little attention to the issue.[108] This confusion was reflected in the shifting position of the Arbeiterbund. That organization had been led on to the path of political action and opposition to slavery by Weydemeyer, but in 1857 it was reorganized and fell under new leadership which was not interested in the slavery question, believing the institution to be firmly intrenched, and it warned against overlooking "the other burning issues of the day." A splinter group headed by W. Banque became a virtual advocate of slave imperialism. However, after his influence was cast off, the Bund began to take a stronger position, pledging itself to combat slavery "in whatever form it may appear . . . with all the means at our disposal." In the last months before the war it came to be a vigorous champion of abolition.[109]

A more consistent anti-slavery element in the German-American labor movement were the socialists. Most of the German-American unions in the East, as well as the Sociale Turn-Vereine, were under their leadership and they were all uncompromising opponents of slavery and the slave power; and the German Communist Club was active in spreading abolition propaganda.[110] Joseph Weydemeyer, the leading Marxist in America, believed that the free labor movement could not develop as long as slavery existed and hampered the growth of industrial capitalism. He wanted labor to play an active and independent part in the anti-slavery political movement, especially in the Republican party, so that the workers, while hastening the downfall of slavery, would also strengthen their organization for the subsequent fight against capital. Through his positions in the German labor organizations, his articles in the Illinois *Staats-Zeitung,* and his lectures, his arguments gained widespread recognition among the German-American workers.[111]

By 1860 the great majority of the German-American laborers had become committed to a radical anti-slavery position and to support of the Republican party. In fact, they played a crucial role in paving the way for the nomination of Lincoln. There was a strong tendency in the party to nominate a conservative ticket, and German workers feared that in such an event the party's position on slavery extension and a homestead bill would be compromised and that nativist elements would strengthen their influence in the party. Consequently the German-American workers of New York called a special meeting in which they announced that they could support the party only if it nominated candidates on the basis of those principles, and they called for a national conference to prevent the ascendancy of conservatism.[112] Such a conference was held in the Deutsches Haus in Chicago two days before the opening of the Republican convention. It included representatives of the German workers, particularly Weydemeyer, speaking for the Chicago Workers' Society, and Adolph Douai, shortly arrived from Texas with a pro-slavery mob on his heels. The conference insisted on a firm anti-slavery stand, opposition to the Massachusetts amendment, support of a homestead act, the admission of Kansas as a free state, and the nomination of candidates who would defend these planks. The importance of the German-American voters was universally recognized, and their influence was reflected in the party platform and in the defeat of such men as Judge Bates who were being groomed by the conservative forces in the party for the Presidential nomination.[113]

The German workers were not intimidated by the employers' bullying. In October, the manufacturing establishments of New York began to curtail production, fire workers and restrict supplies to the tailors, who were nearly all German-Americans, on the pretext that the South was not placing orders for fear of Lincoln's election. They were told that if he were elected, operations would cease entirely. The employers called a meeting of the tailors for October 30, but several days before, the tailors' union issued a leaflet condemning this "stupid trick" of the "lackeys of the slave power" and called on the workers to "stand by Lincoln and freedom and do not be intimidated into voting for the Fusion ticket." When the employers arrived at the scheduled meeting, they found that it had already been organized by the Turners, and they were unable to make their speeches because the audience interrupted them. Some of the tailors had prepared a circular warning their fellow workingmen of the plot to make them vote against their interests. "Do not let slide the banner of free labor, of free homesteads, and the protective tariff—to go in hand with dealers in human flesh." The tailors' union took over the meeting and turned it into a demonstration for Lincoln, Weydemeyer making the main speech. Many other German-American unions also held Lincoln-for-President meetings.[114]

In all the Northern cities labor leaders organized Republican workingmen's clubs, conducted mass meetings in support of Lincoln, and worked actively to bring out the labor vote. Their efforts were highly successful, for the Republicans carried the day or at least increased their vote in practically every city. The workingmen received praise for their activities from party spokesmen, and one leader declared at a victory celebration that "We owe a debt of gratitude to the laboring class who gave us this victory, not to the mass of the merchants who were frightened by the cry of wolf."[115]

CHAPTER V

"THE UPRISING OF A
GREAT PEOPLE"[1]

───────────

The Secession Crisis

The slaveholders had been preparing a long time for the contingency that faced them at the end of 1860, and now they stepped up their efforts to nullify the will of the people: The Republicans must be forced to submit to their demands or they would destroy the new administration by unleashing civil war. To accomplish the former objective, they hoped to take advantage of the economic distress that was spreading through the Northeast. This was a result partly of the continuing effects of the depression that had been hanging over the country since 1857, and partly of the uncertainty and hesitation that accompanied the political crisis; but the immediate aggravation of the decline was due at least in part to the deliberate policy of the planters and their Northern business associates, first to prevent Lincoln's election and then to undo it.

Again the slaveholders employed the dual tactic of intimidating the workers and frightening the capitalists. At the time of the crisis in 1850, the South had attempted to force the workers to accept slaveholder domination of the territories by threatening secession. The fall of wages would be heavy and instantaneous were the union dissolved, wrote a Southern pamphleteer, for the North would have to assume the $20 million of taxes that the South was paying, and $140 million of Southern capital which was giving employment to Northern laborers would be withdrawn. The workers were warned that they would have to bear the entire burden of this loss of business. For the capitalists would send their capital to the South, where profits were higher, until the wages of Northern workers had been reduced to the point which would again permit the profitable investment of capital. The employers would thus escape the burden of new taxes and throw it upon labor.[2]

In 1860, *Anticipations for the Future and Lessons for the Present* was written by Edmund Ruffin, who fired the first shot on Fort Sumter. In this "prediction" of future events, Ruffin foresaw horrible calamity for Northern workers as a result of the cessation of purchase of Northern goods and the employment of Northern ships, the diminished supply of cotton and the sequestration of debts. In spite of unprecedented relief efforts, he envisioned huge demonstrations, succeeded by plundering mobs and riots in every city, ending in complete anarchy. The troops sent to suppress the revolts would be paralyzed by mutiny and desertion; Boston, New York, Philadelphia and Lowell would be the scenes of hitherto unknown bloodshed and carnage, and at last would lie in ruins, burned to the ground, and every man of property butchered. Finally, after the defeat of the North, on "April 7, 1869," it would be reported that "many politicians, and others, and some newspapers, openly maintain the Southern doctrine of the benefits of the institution of negro slavery, not only for the South, but also for their Northern region, (for domestic and menial services,) and argue in favor of slavery being permitted and protected in their states."[3]

Perhaps this was not in the realm of purely fanciful speculation. In December, 1859, a circular was sent in the mails to many Irish-Americans in New York, presumably by Southerners. It stated:

The South looks to its Irish friends in the large free cities to effect a diversion in its favor; and for this purpose the Union Constitutional Irish Association has been formed, of which some of you are (and doubtless

all will be) members. In the great cities prominent free soilers and abolitionists own large factories, stores and granaries, in which vast sums (made
out of the South) are invested. This fact furnishes a means of checking
their aggressions in the South, and the Irish friends of the South are
relied on to make the check effective.—Property is proverbially timid.
Whenever a hay stack or cotton gin is burned at the South by free soil
emissaries, let a large factory, or a plethoric store, or an immense granary
be given to the flames. . . .

Let us urge you to disseminate among your fellow-laborers the idea that
you have not wages proportionate to the present high scale of prices.
When once the mass of our countrymen are filled with the notion that the
free soil capitalists are withholding the price of Irish labor, while trying
to incite the negro of the South to rebellion, it will be easy enough to
gather large mobs of your brethren, . . . [4]

Was this the beginning of the long-threatened invasion of the
North by agitators to "preach up insurrection to the laborers"?

Many Northern business men shared, or pretended to share,
these apprehensions. The Detroit *Free Press* prophesied that the
approaching conflict "will not be with the South, but with tens of
thousands of people in the North. When Civil War shall come it
will be here in Michigan, and here in Detroit, and in every
northern state."[5] Another Democratic paper thought that, in case
of war, the slaves would be found true to their masters, but not
the laboring classes of the North. With the removal of the restraints of law, which presumably would follow in the wake of
war, mobs of starving and desperate men would strike out to
redress their grievances. "So these Republican agitators who have
been sowing seeds of disunion by appealing to the hearts of the
people instead of their heads; playing upon their passions, arous-
ing their sympathies, all to get their votes for places of pelf and
preferment, had better look to their own homes and hearthstones
when the evil days which they have brought about shall come."[6]

The Democrats accused the Republican party of playing with
the prosperity and the very lives of the working class in order
to enrich the capitalists and of proposing "to overthrow this white

Republic in a vain search after 'negro freedom.' "⁷ They tried to
inflame the workers against their employers and the Republicans,
and the New York *Herald* urged the workingmen to express their
sentiments in mass meetings "in such a way that the South will
see that the rabid republicans, who, with their mad cry of elevation of the negro, would destroy the prosperity of the nation,
cannot rely upon them to back them up in this wild crusade, that
will land us—Heaven only knows where."⁸ The workers did hold
mass meetings, but they did not read the lines that the Democrats had written in the script.

The majority of the workers were intensely loyal to the Union,
and placed its preservation above all other considerations. But
they fervently desired its maintenance by peaceful means if possible, and were willing, in order to avoid war, to make concessions consistent with the sovereignty of the federal government. They knew, of course, that they would have to bear the
brunt of the sacrifices demanded by war, they did not believe that
the conflict could be solved only by a resort to force, and they
were reluctant to take up arms against their fellow workers on
the opposite side of Mason's and Dixon's line. It had been only a
few months since a revival of unionism had begun, and a number
of unions embraced both Northern and Southern mechanics; war
would disrupt the bonds of fraternity and seriously set back the
progress of the labor movement. The resolution of the Painters'
Society of Brooklyn represented the sentiments of the workers:
they saw "with regret the crisis brought on . . . by extremists of the
North and South," but reluctantly declared their willingness "to
fight if need be, for the maintenance of the flag of our country."⁹

The Irish-American, which was not a workingmen's paper but
reflected the attitudes of the Irish working men in a distorted
way, called upon its readers to stand by the Union. It was stead-
fastly opposed to secession and poured its contempt upon

Buchanan for his vacillating and submissive policy toward traitors, demanding that the government take a firm stand against the disunionists.[10] The German-American workers likewise stood firm in their loyalty to the Union and the President-elect. When Lincoln passed throught Cincinnati on his birthday in 1861, he was serenaded by the band of the German Workingmen's Society, whose leader, Frederick Oberkleine, read an address. On behalf of the German free workingmen of Cincinnati, he assured the President-elect of their sincere regard. They had voted for him as the champion of free labor and free homesteads, and firmly adhered to the principles of liberty without compromise. They assured Lincoln that if he needed men to maintain those principles, they and other workers "will rise as one man at your call, ready to risk their lives in the effort to maintain the victory already won by freedom over slavery." Lincoln made a rather noncommittal reply, agreeing that workingmen were the basis of all government, because they were the most numerous class, and giving his assurance that he favored a homestead law, free immigration and "those means which will give the greatest good to the greatest number."[11]

The workingmen in the slave states were among the staunchest opponents of disunion. As early as 1849, when there was talk of secession, a leading Georgia Democrat wrote confidentially: "It is impossible to rally the working people of the country to dissolve the Union for the protection of the slaveholders against a measure which three-fourths of the slaveholders will be sustaining and justifying"; another complained that the non-slaveholders could not be excited about the protection of slavery.[12] When the crisis actually came in 1860-61, Southern politicians were again bemoaning the fact that the workers had no interest in defending the human property of the rich and could not be depended on for supporting the plot to subvert the Union.[13] This helps explain the refusal of the secessionists to submit their actions to popular ratification.

It was in the border slave state of Kentucky that the workers initiated their broadest independent political campaign up to that time. On December 27, 1860, workers in all branches of industry assembled in the largest hall in Louisville, on the initiative of the Iron Molders' Union. The guiding thought of the workers was the preservation of the Union "as it is," for on it depended "our hope of happiness and future security." Disclaiming any interest in the "mere abstract questions which have been used . . . to distract and divide the honest masses," they could recognize no just cause or pretext for questioning the election of Lincoln or for abandoning "the gallant old ship of Union—freighted as she is, with the liberty, happiness and prosperity of more than twenty-five millions of human beings—so long as one timber remains above the surging sea, or one shred of the glorious emblem of our national unity is to be seen at her masthead." The meeting viewed "with scorn and deep indignation the course being pursued by the disorganizing traitors who are now at the Federal Capital plotting treason against the greatest and best government instituted by man," and hoped that the public sentiment of an "outraged and indignant people, may reach and overwhelm them." Since the workers had no hope that the politicians would solve the problem, they called upon their brothers throughout the nation to abandon party affiliations and to take united action to prevent the "ultra or sectional men" who were imperiling the safety of the nation. A committee was appointed to prepare an address to the working men of the United States, to urge the calling of meetings in every congressional district and to hold a national labor convention at Philadelphia in February.[14]

The response to this appeal was immediate and widespread, possibly encouraged by the opinion of the Cincinnati *Commercial* that it was "the heaviest blow which the secessionists of Louisville have received from the workingmen of that city." Meetings were held in many cities in the slave states, such as Kentucky, Tennessee, Virginia and Maryland. They all endorsed the resolutions of the Louisville workers, emphasizing their loyalty to the Constitution and the Union, denouncing secession as treason, which was being engineered "by designing and mad politicians, calculated to deluge the Valley of the Mississippi with the blood of freemen," and warning that the federal government and the working people were strong enough "to punish transgressions of every kind." Most of these meetings elected delegates to the coming national labor convention in Philadelphia, and the workers of Baltimore selected James Touchstone, well known for his strong anti-slavery views.[15]

In many cities throughout the North, the workers held similar meetings during January and February, expressing their confidence that "The remedy of all grievances can be had under the constitution and the only way to safety is by the maintenance of it." In many places, the workers went farther, as at Pittsburgh, where they deplored party spirit and recommended the acceptance of any mutually satisfactory agreement, but resolved that it was the President's duty to take prompt and energetic measures to quell treason and rebellion; in Cincinnati one worker was applauded for saying that every rebel should be hanged and that he was ready to put down rebellion by force of arms.[16] A meeting of working men in New York resolved that "the Union must and shall be preserved," by all lawful and constitutional means, and the government sustained and protected. The resolution favored any conciliatory settlement which would be just to all sections and would secure peace and union, "*after a fair and candid discussion before the people.*" It further proposed that the slavery question be removed from the realm of partisan politics, leaving it to the settlement of each state. The resolution also reiterated the workers' demand for a homestead act.[17]

On the other hand, some of the meetings were dominated by Democrats, and while they too expressed their earnest support of the Union and the Constitution, they often blamed the crisis impartially on the politicians of both parties and sections. Most of them favored concessions to the South, usually by endorsing the Crittenden plan to divide the territories into free and slave areas along the line of 36°30'.[18]

Such was the case in Boston, where a mass meeting was held in Faneuil Hall on February 20. Of the thirty-five sponsors of the meeting, only twenty were laborers, the remainder being lawyers and businessmen; Jonathan Preston, who presided, was the head of an architectural firm. The first and only worker who addressed the meeting was Daniel Kelly, a shipwright, and he was indiscreet enough to deride the Republican leaders because none of them "ever did any work or ever taught any of his sons to labor, or ever allowed his daughter to marry a mechanic or a laborer." He went on to blame the abolitionists for unemployment among the Boston workers, and to praise the living standards of the Southern slaves, who "know nothing of the cares and responsibilities that torment their white brethren, and so live a happy, peaceful life." The main speech furnished the substance of the "Address of the Workingmen of Massachusetts to their brethren throughout the United States." It blamed the threatening disruption of the Union on the politicians who betrayed the people of both North and South by fomenting sectional hatred, and singled out the abolitionists for special vilification. If the Southern states chose to return to the Union, they were assured that the workingmen would give them a hearty welcome and endeavor to protect them in their rights. If they preferred to remain out of the Union, the workers would bid them go in peace. "We wish no Union but a Union of friendship, not of force. . . ." The resolution concluded by endorsing the Crittenden compromise.[19]

In Philadelphia, workers held meetings in their shops and then paraded to Independence Square, carrying banners which read: "The Union is the keystone of the country." "The Union and the Crittenden resolutions." "We want Working Men not talking men in Congress." 5,000 workers stood in the snow for four hours listening to speeches by labor leaders and employers. The meeting was conducted in a very arbitrary manner, and because of this some of the delegates, including Jonathan Fincher, the outstanding leader of the Machinists' and Blacksmiths' Union, disavowed their connections with it. There was considerable disagreement over the endorsement of the Crittenden compromise, but none on that part of the resolution which stated "That, if after all fair and honorable means have been exhausted without effecting the desired object so earnestly cherished by all Union-loving citizens, we as workingmen, will sustain the Federal Government in all just and legal measures to enforce the laws of our land and nation." Machinery was set up to prepare for the national convention to meet there the following month.[20]

William Sylvis, president of the Iron Molders' Union which had initiated the Louisville meeting, wrote about the national convention in the *Mechanics' Own* ten days before its opening: "Under the leadership of political demagogues and traitors scattered all over the land, North and South, East and West, the country is going to the devil as fast as it can. And unless the masses rise up in their might, and teach their representatives what to do, the good old ship will go to pieces." He urged workers in every state to send delegates to Philadelphia, where they would "make one more strong pull for the Union."[21] Workers from a large number of cities in eight states—four free and four border slave states—responded, and on the morning of Washington's birthday a huge parade marched to the old State House. Ten divisions were formed by mechanics representing some two score of trades; floats symbolizing the Union were carried, and banners reading "Concessions not secession." At Independence Square a mass meeting was held, in which pleas were made to sacrifice political partisanship for the sake of the Union, and the Crittenden compromise was approved.[22]

The convention sessions were held the following day, when James B. Nicholson welcomed the delegates in behalf of the Philadelphia workingmen. He urged the setting aside of partisanship in favor of a conciliatory attitude in order to preserve the Union and "transmit to our children the inheritance bequeathed to us by our patriotic sires." He believed the Crittenden plan could be honorably accepted as a basis of settlement. One of the Virginia delegates, who had voted for Douglas in 1860, said he would support any party capable of saving the Union; he opposed secession and proudly labeled himself a "submissionist." Several speakers urged the immediate organization of a farmer-labor party and the election of workers to office as the only way to save the Union, but this question was not permitted to come to a vote. Finally, an eight-point resolution was presented and adopted: (1) the Crittenden compromise was endorsed as a Constitutional settlement of the territorial issue; (2) devotion to the Union and defiance to traitors were reaffirmed; (3) disunion was denounced as repugnant to the people; (4) the politicians of both North and South were anathematized and it was determined to replace them with men who would truly represent the people; (5) the right of secession was denied, but the preservation of the Union by coercion was deprecated; (6) the workers pledged to vote against any candidate who opposed compromise; (7) the repeal of personal liberty laws was urged as a conciliatory measure; (8) a committee was chosen to organize the nation's workers for political action.[23]

As the convention prepared to adjourn, James Touchstone of Maryland rose and delivered a stinging broadside against the Southern aristocracy who were organizing treason for the purpose of "placing their feet on the necks of the mechanics," overturning Constitutional liberty and rearing a despotism on its ruins. He thought the workers' convention should say so, instead of deceiving the people by "a contemptible subterfuge." He therefore submitted resolutions for upholding the Constitution and the laws by all measures, and expressing the sympathy of the convention "with their brother workingmen of the seceded states and . . . pledge to them their effort to regain their constitutional rights, which have been wrested from them by violence." These resolutions were greeted by loud applause, but when it was pointed out that their passage would wreck the compromise platform already adopted, Touchstone withdrew them. It is evident that political forces on the resolutions committee had distorted the real feelings of the workers by softening the opposition to the slave-power and the determination to defend the Union and over-emphasizing the desire for conciliation.[24] Considering all the manifestations of labor's attitude from the election to the inauguration of Lincoln, the conclusion is inescapable that, while the depression, the desire to prevent war and the activities of the Democratic party had resulted in some defection from the Republican ranks, the new administration could take a firm stand against the slave-power with the assurance that the working class in the North would rally to the support and defense of the Union, and that the Southern workers, particularly in the border states, would constitute a potent deterrent to the schemes of the disunionists. The workingmen were not committed to any political party, but they were committed to the defense of their country and their liberties.

Labor, Emancipation and the Civil War

When the war began with the attack on Fort Sumter, the workers rose to the defense of their country. Many military units of native-, German- and Irish-American workers had already offered themselves to the President and they now rushed to the colors, as did a Polish-American and an Italian-American workingmen's guard. Trade unions organized fighting companies and enlisted as a body, posting notices on their union halls: "Closed for the duration." Behind the lines the workers labored long hours under difficult conditions to turn out the materials of war for their brothers at the front. As William Sylvis said at the close of the war, "I presume it is hardly necessary for me to enter into any arguments to prove that the workingmen, the great body of the people, the bone and muscle of the nation, the very pillars of our temple of liberty are loyal; that, I take it, would be sheer mockery, would be adding insult to injury; for the evidence of our loyalty one need only point to the history of the war; to the fact that while armed treason and rebellion threatened our institutions with destruction, while the proud and opulent of the land were plotting the downfall of our government, the toiling millions stood like a wall of adamant between the country and all its foes."[26]

The Negro workers also made an outstanding contribution to the victory of the Union. From the very beginning of the war they offered their services to the government, and as soon as they were allowed, joined the army, recruiting their own men, and sometimes refusing pay, as did the 54th Massachusetts regiment which served for an entire year. In spite of their receiving half the regular pay, in spite of being consigned frequently to menial services in the army camps, and in spite of unfriendly commanders in many cases, they did whatever they could—and in a manner which evoked the highest praise. General Rufus Saxton, for example, reported: "It is admitted upon all hands that the Negroes fight with a coolness and bravery that would have done credit to veteran soldiers. There was no excitement, no flinching, no attempt at cruelty when successful. They seemed like men who were fighting to vindicate their manhood and they did it well."[27]

Some 80,000 Northern Negroes served in the Union armies, and they were joined by 125,000 slaves who escaped to the Union lines and joined the army as soldiers, workers, and scouts. In the latter capacity they performed an indispensable job that could have been done by no one else. That the Negro people played a decisive role in the struggle for their emancipation was attested to by many authorities, and by none less than President Lincoln, who said in 1864: ". . . the experience of the present war proves their [the South's] success is inevitable if you fling the compulsory

labor of millions of black men into their side of the scale. . . .
Abandon all the posts now garrisoned by black men, take 150,000
men from our side and put them in the battle-field or corn-field
against us, and we would be compelled to abandon the war in
three weeks."[28]

The workers, of course, were fighting for the purpose, as the
Troy Iron Molders put it, of "maintaining the supremacy of Law
and Order and defending the Constitution so wisely drafted by
the Sons of '76 and also the Federal Capital and last but not least
to protect that good old flag, the Stars and Stripes. . . ."[29] But
they were motivated by more than patriotism alone. By their
political struggles for over a decade they had shown that they
understood the character of their enemy and the fact that they
were defending the democratic tradition of their country, although
some of them did not yet realize that the fulfillment of that
tradition was dependent on the overthrow of chattel slavery.
They identified the fight against the slave-power with the defense
of the labor movement—the word "Union" had a double meaning for them. When the delegates to the National Typographical
Union convention held their annual dinner in Cleveland in 1863
they drank a toast to "Our brethren in the field—True to their
love of 'Union,' they fearlessly stand face to face with its
enemies."[30] The New York local of the same union defined
the issue similarly if not so concisely: if the workingman would
be free "and enjoy the blessings of liberty for himself and his
children—if he would be true to himself and the workingmen
of the South—if he would be true to the interests of labor
throughout the world he must work and vote to overthrow
rebellion and treason and maintain the government at every
cost."[31]

It was only their patriotism and understanding of the issues
of the war that enabled the workers to make the contributions
they did in the face of provocations and injustices from their
employers and from the government. During the elections the

Republicans had worked hard to convince the workers that labor had only *one* enemy, the slave-power; but by their conduct during the war they seemed to be trying to reverse this attitude—everything they did lent credence to the opinion that it was "a rich man's war and a poor man's fight." While working class families were suffering from the absence and death of their breadwinners, the masters of industry were making fortunes from war contracts and increasing their profits by the manufacture of shoddy uniforms and shoes that disintegrated in the rain and rifles that blew off the hands of the soldiers. While living standards deteriorated under the impact of runaway inflation, the rich were getting richer by profiteering and speculation. While workers were promised the benefits of the Homestead Act, the railroad manipulators and stock-jobbers were grabbing millions of acres of the best land and being paid to build the roads. While soldiers and workers received depreciated greenbacks for pay, government bondholders were guaranteed payment in hundred-cent dollars. When workers were forced to strike for a living wage, their strikes were broken, sometimes by foreign laborers imported under the terms of the new Contract Labor Law, sometimes by hastily enacted state legislation which virtually outlawed the right to strike, as in Minnesota and Illinois, sometimes by Federal troops, as in the strike at the Parrott Gun Works in Cold Springs, New York, the walk-outs of machinists and tailors in St. Louis, the engineers on the Reading Railroad, the miners of Tioga County, Pennsylvania, and two hundred mechanics in Tennessee.[32] And while the workingmen were fighting their country's battles, the government and the army brass were honeycombed with Copperheads and pussy-footers who vacillated, temporized, hampered the prosecution of the war and sowed confusion and defeatism.

This state of affairs provided grist for the mill of the Copperheads, who sought to turn labor's discontent with the manner in which the war was conducted into opposition to the war itself.

For example, when two hundred workers in Louisville refused to work at the wages which were offered to them, the New York *Daily News* reported that General Thomas, commanding the region, had arrested them. He is "employed in freeing the Negro," said this Democratic organ, "even at the expense of transferring the chains to the limbs of free laboring men," and the punishment of the workers would last "as long as the Abolitionists can keep up the war spirit, and run riot on the money they fleece from the government." During the election campaign of 1864, when the Copperheads were attempting to save the slaveholders by a negotiated peace, they directed their propaganda to the workers who were suffering as a result of the "aimless strife." They pointed out that while the war was enriching the "shoddy contractors, shoulder-strap politicians and bounty jumpers," it was starving the workingmen and tearing them from their families to bleed and die in an unnatural and patricidal strife. Only peace would put an end to the slaughter, the demoralization of industry, and the starvation wages of labor.[33]

This quisling campaign had little effect on the organized workers of the country, who understood that, even though the rich were using the war to get richer, it was still a war for the liberties of America and the working people. But the propaganda of the Copperheads undoubtedly did influence many of the unskilled and unorganized workers, whose economic conditions were the worst, who did not have the guidance of the most advanced working class leaders and the labor press, and who were still attached in large numbers to the Democratic party. It was to this group especially that the Copperheads, Peace Democrats and Negrophobes directed their propaganda, and they used with greatest force the old tactic of frightening the workers with exaggerated predictions of the free Negroes flooding the Northern labor market. An editorial in the Columbus (Ohio) *Crisis* in 1861 was typical. It reported that a large-scale immigration of free Negroes had already begun and claimed that the Republicans desired to emancipate all the slaves. This would send an influx of a million Negroes into Ohio, predicted the writer, "to mix with the white population, and compete with the white laborers for a living, or steal from those who have got property. . . ." He protested against such an interference with the prosperity and manhood of the farmers and laborers and expressed the desire that the Negroes be kept in slavery.[34]

During the election of 1862 this was a major theme in the Democratic campaign. The state organizations of the party adopted resolutions which designated the Republican party as "the party of fanaticism or crime, whichever it may be called, that seeks to turn the slaves of the Southern States loose to overrun the North and enter into competition with the white laboring masses, thus degrading and insulting their manhood by placing them on an equality with negroes in their occupations. . . ."[35] The Democratic press reported instances, often false, to show that this was already happening. It was alleged that some hotel keepers had discharged white employees to make jobs for Negroes who had escaped into the Northern lines, and that the abolitionists were working to secure positions for all of them, each of whom would replace a white worker. The Philadelphia *Public Ledger* warned laborers to "beware of the contractors, robbers and jobbers who were fattening upon the spoils of their hard earned labor" and who wanted the war continued in order to introduce cheap labor into the North. Another Pennsylvania paper reported that the Cambria Iron Works in Johnston had employed several "contrabands" at twenty-five cents a day, thus provoking a strike by the white employees. "The Government was made for the benefit of white men," decreed the editor, "and the white men will not submit to be crowded out by the worthless runaway negroes of the South. Our friends can see in this the beautiful workings of the Emancipation policy of President Lincoln." This story was refuted by the employees of the company themselves, but it was nevertheless reprinted in almost every Democratic paper in the state.[36] The Democrats in many Northern states conducted a campaign to prohibit the immigration of free Negroes or to retain such exclusions where they already existed, as in Illinois, Indiana and Ohio.[37]

The Republicans and abolitionists denied that free Negroes would come North once slavery was abolished, and asserted that those who came during the war were needed to fill the labor shortage, and that they were being employed at standard wages. General D. H. Hunter, who as commander of the Department of the South declared all the slaves in South Carolina, Georgia and Florida free,[38] issued a specific denial of the Democrats' charges, stating that he had given passes north to all Negroes asking for them, but not more than a dozen had applied for them. "My experience leads me to believe that the exact reverse of the received opinion on this subject would form the rule, and that nearly if not quite all the negroes of the North would migrate South whenever they shall be at liberty to do so without fear of the auction block."[39] Lincoln made a special point of this in his annual message to Congress in 1862, pointing out that whether free or slave, there would still be the same number of Negroes doing the same amount of work. Besides, he asked, why should emancipation send the free people North? "People of any color seldom run unless there be something to run from. . . ." As evidence of the truth of this statement, he pointed to the abolition of slavery in the District of Columbia, which had not produced any influx of Negroes to the North.[40] The Republicans would perhaps not have been in such an embarrassing position if they had not, for eight years past, made their contribution to anti-Negro prejudice by insisting that theirs was a white man's party, that their object was to preserve the territories for white men, and that the Negroes were "no party" to the controversy at all.

Although the Democrats magnified and embroidered the problem, a problem did exist—not in emancipation, but in the anti-labor and anti-Negro policies of employers who could be counted on to create divisions and to employ Negroes in order to depress the wage standards of both white and Negro workers, as they had done in the past both North and South, and as they were doing with immigrant contract labor, with women and children, and with convict labor.

Fincher's Trades' Review, the outstanding labor paper edited by Jonathan Fincher, placed the blame for the problem on "the cupidity of the more avaricious" who would seek to employ the Negroes to "gratify their notions of economy." Fincher did not allow his apprehensions to blind him to the fact that the rebellion was an "attempt . . . to establish a government on the destruction of the rights of labor," and that the workers had to make every necessary sacrifice to win the war, and he did not question the propriety of emancipating the slaves. But, he said, "we will not conceal our fears of the injury likely to be visited upon the innocent, in the attempt to punish the guilty. It will be but a poor return, indeed, to the mechanics and workingmen of the North, who are now fighting the battles of the Union, to find on their return, every source of employment choked up by the freed negroes of the South." He proposed that the government "repay the patriotic thousands who have responded to their country's call by placing proper restrictions upon the ingress of emancipated slaves into the Northern states. . . . We demand that protection from the Government, which we have won by our sacrifice of life, blood and treasure, and which we will continue to give in her defense."[41]

Misgivings were naturally strongest among the unskilled and unorganized workers who would feel any competition the worst, who had the least means of protection, and many of whom were already experiencing such competition. Having learned from hard experience that they could rely on no one to defend them, having no trade unions to help preserve their wage standards, and being subjected to the anti-Negro propaganda of the Democratic press, they sometimes turned their resentment against their rivals, using whatever weapons came to hand. Thus in Cincinnati, in the summer of 1862, Negroes were hired on the river boats for $30 a month when the current rate was $40 to $75. The Cincinnati *Enquirer* reprinted an article from a Philadelphia paper which reported that Negro labor there was causing a decline in wages and alleged that Negro workers pouring in from the South were willing to work for ten cents a day. "Like causes will produce like results here," wrote the *Enquirer*. "How do our white laborers relish the prospect that the emancipation of the blacks spreads before them?" A few days later, the white boatmen, mostly Irish, attacked the Negroes and rioting raged over the waterfront for five days. The Cincinnati *Gazette* denounced both the assaults and the agitation that incited them, saying that "the very men who today are endeavoring to incense the honest white laboring men in Cincinnati against black competition, are the supporters of Slavery, and would tomorrow initiate slave labor into every workshop in your city, if it were possible." Such agitators who "wilfully excite the worst passions of the white workers," recommended the Cleveland *Leader*, "deserve a halter."[42]

Similar occurrences took place in many Northern cities, often as a result of the introduction of Negroes as strike-breakers. In Chicago the workers in the slaughtering and packing industry met to protest "the intention of one or more of the leading packers of this town to bring negro labor into competition with that of the white men for the purpose of reducing the wages of the latter to the lowest possible standard." They pledged not to work for any employers who hired Negroes and voted to expel from the union any members who violated the pledge.[43] When the commanding general in Illinois tried to find employment for "confiscated" Negroes sent north by the Union armies, there was considerable protest. Workers in Quincy held a mass meeting and announced that "we hereby give notice to those engaged in this business of attempting to ride down and crush out the free white workingmen of Illinois, by thus seeking to bring free negro labor into competition with white labor, that we cannot and will not tolerate it; that we will seek our remedy, first, under the law; second, at the polls; and third, if both these fail, we will redress our wrongs in such a manner as shall seem to us most expedient and most practicable."[44] Many other instances of this kind could be cited.[45] In the spring and early summer of 1863 there was a wave of riots between Negro and Irish longshoremen in Chicago, Detroit, Cleveland, Buffalo, Albany, New York, Boston and other places, almost invariably produced by the employment of Negroes to break strikes. In June 3,000 dock workers in New York struck for higher wages to meet the increased cost of living, and their jobs were filled by Negroes brought in under police protection.[46]

These conditions were aggravated to the bursting point by the passage of the first conscription act in March 1863, for it virtually established by law that this was to be a "poor man's fight." In providing that any person subject to the draft might be exempted by furnishing a substitute or paying a $300 commutation fee, it permitted men of means to avoid service and saddle their share on the backs of those who could not pay. The labor movement was not opposed to conscription, but it was vehemently opposed to this discriminatory feature of the act; and while demanding the democratization of the law, it urged complete obedience to its provisions. William Sylvis thought Congress had a perfect right to compel the workers to serve in the army if necessary.[47] Jonathan Fincher agreed that the government had a right to appropriate the lives of its citizens and that the people owed it to their government to give their lives in its defense and "to yield obedience to ALL laws enacted by the proper powers, even if the most objectionable. . . ." But in this case, he pointed out, the government has committed the unpardonable crime of dividing the people into classes of the worst distinction—rich and poor . . . We cannot silently see the poor conscript torn from family and friends, and forced to the ranks, while the worthless drone upon society, a rich man's son, can, by paying the cost of a week's debauchery, be relieved from the hardships and dangers of a soldier's life. . . . For the sake of the country let the conscription come. But let it come alike upon the rich as well as the poor. No exemptions! No, not one—either for worth or worthlessness, distinction or obscurity, wealth or poverty.[48]

Again the Copperheads swung into action, striving to turn dissatisfaction with the draft law into opposition to the war and the government. The most unconcealed incitement to riot was preached, as in an article in the New York *Daily News* on July 13:

Only a few among the workingmen of this city who may be conscripted into the ranks of the abolition army, will march to the field with the proud conscience that they are the soldiers of a Republic about to do battle for Republican institutions. The very fact that a power exists that can *drive them from their homes to the slaughter pen will teach them that they are no longer free agents.* . . .

If the workingmen of this city are disinclined to be forced into a fight for emancipation, let them clamor so loud for peace that their voices shall be potential with our rulers. It is a strange perversion of the laws of self-preservation which would compel the white laborer to leave his family destitute and unprotected, while he goes forth to free the negro, who, being free, will compete with him in labor. Let the laboring population assemble peaceably in mass meeting, and express their views upon the subject. Let it be no political gathering . . . but a spontaneous congregation of the working class to give vent, within legal bounds, but firmly, to the sentiments of their fraternity with regard to this odious war. . . .[49]

On the same day that this article appeared, a mob gathered at the main recruiting office, disrupted the proceedings and wrecked the building. The mob quickly gained momentum and soon had the upper hand throughout the city. The rioters attacked the *Tribune* offices; assaulted factories and foundries where Negroes were employed and tried to close them down or drive out the Negroes; overran the docks and piers, where their strike had recently been broken by the employment of Negro longshoremen, and attacked every Negro in sight. Blind fury took possession of the mob, which was joined by the riff-raff of the city and pro-slavery sympathizers; they roamed the streets looking for victims, attacked Negroes and Republican leaders, destroyed property, and climaxed their frenzy by burning down a Negro orphan asylum. It was not until three days had passed that the rioting was brought under control by Federal troops rushed into the city. Similar occurrences took place in several other cities, but on a much smaller scale.[50]

It is not difficult to fix the responsibility for this eruption in view of all that had gone before. Opposition to the discriminatory features of the draft was only one element in the "draft riots." The outbreaks were a blind revolt against class legislation, against strike-breaking, against intolerable economic conditions, against the orgy of profiteering and speculation at the expense of the workers and soldiers; they were nourished on the white supremacy propaganda of politicians, both Republican and Democratic, and the divisive policies of employers, both Republican and Democratic; and they were stimulated by treasonous agents of the slave-power. Fincher observed that the working men were loyal and patriotic, and their opposition to the draft was not the result of their being puppets of the Democratic party. The mobs in New York, he said, were composed of men who had families to look after and lacked the $300 to purchase their exemption. "This is the whole matter in a nutshell. It is an outbreak of the poor against the rich. It is the poor conscript against the rich exempt." The rioting was wrong, he concluded, but the wrong did not begin with the mob. It began with the law, which was "so glaring an outrage" as to invite what happened. If men with families were exempted and the $300 clause repealed, the laborers would give a "hearty acquiescence" to their duty.[51]

These provocations could only have inflamed many people beyond the limits of human endurance. The remarkable fact is that such a small number succumbed to them. Before, during and after these outbreaks, the overwhelming majority of the workers demonstrated their loyalty to the government and their determination to carry the war to a successful conclusion. That the majority of workers was not responsible for the riots was proved, Fincher pointed out, by the fact that thousands of workingmen were driven from their shops by the rioters, and many others continued at their work at the risk of their lives. Hundreds of others cooperated with the authorities to restore order. And the riots were suppressed by the army and militia, 90 per cent of whom were workingmen, who were always to be found on the side of law and order. "They suppressed the riots, as they are suppressing the rebellion—perhaps to be rewarded in the one case, as they have been in the other, with the ingratitude of political demagogues."[52]

Working men printed and distributed posters admonishing their fellow laborers not to fall into the trap of Southern traitors:

Workingmen! when any man asks you to break the law, and tries to stir up your passions, while he skulks out of sight, you may set him down as your worst enemy. Spurn him as you would a viper. The patriotic workingmen of the North can not afford to spend time in killing each other.[53]

Another leaflet said, in part:

Do not listen to bad men who are only leading you to your ruin. . . . Stand up as Democratic Workingmen should stand up before the world, and show the traitors of the South, and the friends of tyranny all over the world, that *the Workingmen of New York are able to govern themselves!* Stand by the Union, the Constitution, and the Laws! Then peace, freedom and prosperity will be secured to you and to your children after you. KEEP HONESTLY AT YOUR WORK! GIVE NO HEED TO BAD ADVICE![54]

After the riots, there were numerous mass meetings of workers in New York which protested against the demonstrations and strongly condemned and disclaimed the disloyal sentiments which were uttered during their progress.[55] Subsequent calls for volunteers were responded to enthusiastically by the workers, and later drafts were welcomed by the labor press and carried out without incident.[56]

While the Northern workers remained loyal throughout the war, the laborers in the South were permeated by a profound and widespread resentment against the slaveholders who had forced them into a conflict in which they had no interest. The Confederacy was also racked by profiteering, speculation and inflation, and had its own brand of discriminatory conscription which exempted overseers and owners of twenty or more slaves. But these conditions produced much more opposition than in the North, because the workers did not have the motivation to fight that inspired the Northern laborers; they had nothing to gain and everything to lose by a strengthening of the slave-power. Senator James Phelan told Jefferson Davis that no law had ever met "with more universal odium than the exemption of slave-owners. . . . Its influence upon the poor is most calamitous, and has awakened a spirit and elicited a discussion of which we may safely predict the most unfortunate results."[57] The workers employed every possible means of evading service: they entered into the exempted jobs and professions in large numbers, managed to get affidavits of physical incapacity, went into hiding in caves and swamps, organized shotgun squads to receive conscription officers, and deserted from the army in fantastic numbers. In many cases resistance to the draft was so widespread that the officials were openly defied, and in some places anti-conscription and pro-Union organizations were formed. The unwillingness of the Southern workingmen to fight the battles of the slaveholders was a significant factor in the defeat of the South.[58] To the activities of the free workers must be added the struggles of the bondsmen against their enslavers. By strikes, sabotage and insurrection, by guerilla warfare conducted by outlaw communities of runaways, by supplying Union armies with important military information, by serving as scouts for the Union forces, and by escaping to the Union lines where about one third of them enlisted in the armies of liberation, the slaves immeasurably hastened the downfall of their oppressors and thus earned their emancipation by their own efforts.[59]

The events of the war helped to clarify labor's understanding of the need to destroy the chattel system. Many workingmen earlier had feared that abolition agitation would divert them from their struggles for the emancipation of labor, but now it was obvious that the aggression of the slave-power and not the struggle against it was what stood in the way of the labor movement. Many had believed that the emancipation of labor must precede the abolition of slavery, and now it was equally plain that the workers would not be able to advance their cause until the great issue of the day was settled by the complete uprooting of the system that had produced it. William Sylvis had voted for Stephen Douglas in 1860 and strove to prevent war, but once it came he knew that it must terminate in emancipation. "Whatever our opinions may have been as to the cause of the war," he said in 1868, "we can all agree that human slavery (property in man) was the first great cause; and from the day the first gun was fired, it was my earnest hope that the war might not end until slavery ended with it."[60]

As the war progressed it became clear that it not only should but must end in freedom for the slaves, and in fact that it could not end in victory *unless* the slaves were liberated. Any other conclusion to hostilities would have been, by its very nature, a negotiated peace, for the economic basis of the slave-power would be left unimpaired (unless the Southern whites and the slaves themselves put an end to it). The North was fighting with one arm tied behind its back as long as it did not enlist the slaves in the struggle by emancipating them and welcoming their support. The logic of war was forcing the adoption of emancipation, if not as a policy of principle, then as a military necessity. Many people who had taken a very conservative position on the slavery question before the war underwent a complete change within a short time. For example, the attitude of John B. Purcell, archbishop of Cincinnati, was typical of the pre-war Catholic view, but he became a staunch Unionist and supported emancipation. His brother, Father Edward Purcell, editor of the *Catholic Telegraph*, shared his views, and added that it was in the interest of the white laboring men of both the North and South to save the Negro workers from slavery. Many Catholics agreed with his stand.[61] The personal experience of the workers was also an important part of their political education. Greeley stated that "The soldiers who, though generally enlisted with strong anti-Negro prejudices, quite commonly experienced a gradual change under the discipline of service at the front, where they found every Black their ready, active, zealous friend, and nearly every slaveholder or overseer their quiet but deadly, implacable foe."[62]

Of considerable importance in helping the workers to understand the issues of the war was the action of the European working class. The common people of Europe were lukewarm towards the American conflict as long as the North was professedly fighting only for "the Union as it was and the Constitution as it is." Carl Schurz, from his ambassadorial post in Europe, warned Lincoln that the aristocracy of Europe contemplated intervention in behalf of the slavocracy, and that it would be prevented by the people if they knew that the war was being conducted for the emancipation of the slaves.[63] In no place was this more true than in England, for that country could determine the role of the Continent in the war. The aristocracy and the cotton manufacturers were solidly on the side of the Confederacy and were more than once on the verge of throwing their weight into the scale. That they did not do so was due to a large extent to the unmistakable warnings of the workers that they would not tolerate a crusade for the perpetuation of slavery and against their fellow workingmen on the other side of the ocean. The workers took this stand in spite of the fact that they were suffering the most cruel privation as a result of the Confederacy's inability to ship cotton to the industrial centers, a situation which could have been relieved by the British navy.

At the end of 1861 English reaction seized upon the Mason and Slidell affair as a pretext for war against the United States, but mass meetings in the working class districts of London warned that "no intervention on the part of the English government will be permitted," and that they would "raise their voices and, in case of need, their hands for the prevention of so great a crime." Mason and Slidell were denounced as "slaveholders as well as confessed agents of the tyrannical faction that is at once in rebellion against the American republic and the sworn enemy of the social and political rights of the working class in all countries."[64] When the Emancipation Proclamation was announced in September 1862, it was greeted with enthusiasm by the English workers. On December 31 a mass meeting of London workers adopted an address to President Lincoln, in which they expressed their admiration for the strugggle to deliver the country from the curse and shame of slavery.

We regarded with abhorrence the conspiracy and rebellion by which it was sought at once to overthrow the supremacy of a government based upon the most popular suffrage in the world, and to perpetuate the hateful inequalities of race. . . . We have watched with the warmest interest the steady advance of your policy along the path of emancipation; and on this eve of the day on which your proclamation of freedom takes effect, we pray God to strengthen your hands, to confirm your noble purpose, and to hasten the restoration of that lawful authority which engages . . . to realize the glorious principle on which your Constitution is founded— the brotherhood, freedom and equality of all men.[65]

On the same day the workmen of Manchester congratulated Lincoln on his action:

Since we have discerned that the victory of the free North, in the war which has so sorely distressed us as well as afflicted you, will strike off the fetters of the slave, you have attracted our warm and earnest sympathy. We joyfully honor you as the President, and the Congress with you, for many decisive steps toward practically exemplifying your belief in the words of your great founders, "All men are created free and equal." . . . Heartily do we congratulate you and your country on this humane and righteous course. We assume that you cannot now stop short of a complete uprooting of slavery. . . . While your enthusiasm is aflame, and the tide of events runs high, let the work be finished effectively. . . .[66]

In a long editorial, the London *Daily News* applauded the working class for "maintaining the honor and character of the British nation in the eyes of the world" when others had defaulted.[67] Both the address and the editorial were widely reprinted in the American press, and as broadsides they were distributed among the workers. So was Lincoln's reply, in which he told the workers that their "decisive utterances" in the face of the severe trials to which they were subjected was "an instance of sublime Christian heroism which has not been surpassed in any age or in any country. It is indeed an energetic and reinspiring assurance of the inherent power of truth, and of the ultimate and universal triumph of justice, humanity, and freedom."[68]

Also widely publicized in American newspapers and pamphlets were the speech of John Bright at a Trades Union meeting in London on March 26 in which he characterized the slaveholders as the foes of labor and democracy throughout the world,[69] and the remarks of a Trade Union deputation to the American ambassador, Charles Francis Adams. They expressed their "abhorrence of the American institution of slavery, their disapprobation of the rebellion of the Southern States of that country, their sympathy with the North in its efforts to put down that rebellion, and their admiration of the general policy—more particularly that relating to slavery—pursued by President Lincoln." Adams tendered his thanks to the workers and observed that it was natural for a body of workingmen to look with disfavor upon any party which infringed on the rights of labor. "You perceive that in the struggle now going on in America an attempt is being made to establish a government on the destruction of the rights of labor—a government of physical power to take away the rights of labor. . . ."[70]

In January 1865, the International Workingmen's Association congratulated Lincoln on his re-election in a letter written by Karl Marx:

If resistance to the Slave Power was the reserved watchword of your first election, the triumphant war cry of your re-election is Death to Slavery.

From the commencement of the titanic American strife the workingmen of Europe felt instinctively that the Star-spangled banner carried the destiny of their class. The contest of the territories which opened the dire epopee, was it not to decide whether the virgin soil of immense tracts should be wedded to the labor of the emigrant or prostituted by the tramp of the slave driver?

When an oligarchy of 300,000 slaveholders dared to inscribe for the first time in the annals of the world "slavery" on the banner of armed revolt . . . then the working classes of Europe understood at once . . . they were unable to attain the true freedom of labor, or to support their European brethren in their struggle for emancipation; but this barrier to progress has been swept off by the red sea of civil war.

The workingmen of Europe feel sure that, as the American War of Independence initiated a new era of ascendancy for the middle class, so the American anti-slavery war will do for the working classes. They consider it an earnest of the epoch to come that it fell to the lot of Abraham Lincoln, the singleminded son of the working class, to lead the country through the matchless struggle for the rescue of an enchained race and the reconstruction of a social order.[71]

Adams replied in behalf of Lincoln that the American people "derive new encouragement to persevere from the testimony of the workingmen of Europe that the national attitude is favored with their enlightened approval and earnest sympathies."

Labor's support of emancipation was greatly stimulated also by a thorough and well organized publishing program. The

Republicans and abolitionists made a systematic effort to discuss slavery in terms of its effect on the working class, both in their regular press and by the publication of numerous pamphlets and leaflets written especially for workers.[72] Prominent in the coordination and distribution of such literature were the New England Loyal Publication Society, organized in Boston in 1862, and the Loyal Publication Society of New York. These societies gathered anti-slavery material from a wide variety of sources and sent it to newspapers throughout the North for reprinting. By the end of 1863 nearly a thousand papers were using the services fully and gratefully, expressing praise for the merit and value of the material they received. Many of the clippings and other documents were printed as broadsides and sent to some five hundred individuals and organizations for mass distribution, particularly among the workers.[73] A large number of these leaflets were devoted to exposing the conditions of workers in the slave states, the anti-labor policy of the slavocracy and its intention of establishing a universal slave empire. Many of them gave special attention to the nativist policy of the Confederate leaders, their contempt for the foreign born, and their aim of disfranchising immigrant workers and restricting their rights of citizenship as a prelude to enslaving them.[74]

The pre-war depression and the war dealt a crippling blow to the labor movement and its press, but at least one important labor paper managed to survive and in the last two years of the war there was a revival. These journals, many of them of a very high standard, were able to play an important part in clarifying the issues of the rebellion to the workers. *The Iron Platform*, published by the New York Typographical Union, constantly explained to its readers the necessity of overthrowing treason in order to insure the protection of labor's rights in America and throughout the world, and that this could be achieved only by freeing the slaves. "There is one truth," it said, "which should be clearly understood by every workingman in the

Union. *The slavery of the black man leads to the slavery of the white man.* . . . If the doctrine of treason is true, that Capital should own labor, then their logical conclusion is correct, and all laborers, white or black, are and ought to be slaves."[75] *Fincher's Trades' Review,* published in Philadelphia from the middle of 1863, took a similar position on the issues of the war, calling on the workers to make every sacrifice necessary to crush the rebellion which was attempting "to establish a government on the destruction of the rights of labor."

In addition to the labor newspapers, workingmen published many leaflets and pamphlets to mobilize support for the war and emancipation. These were particularly important in 1863 and 1864 when the Copperheads were agitating for a negotiated peace which would save the slaveowners and their property. One series of broadsides published by "A Democratic Workingman" in New York brought to the workers' attention the ambition of the Confederate leaders "to destroy their republican institutions, and build up an aristocracy or a monarchy upon the ruins," to disfranchise foreign born workers, to "check the spread over our territory of that spawn of ignorance and crime, which flows in endless issue from the prisons and dens of corruption in the marts of Europe," and to "reduce free white workingmen to the same political, social, and moral condition as their slaves." It admonished the workingmen not to interfere with the vigorous prosecution of the war and thus help the sworn enemies of labor. It urged them to stand by their government until the enemies of the Union and of democracy were overthrown, and peace and prosperity were restored by the victory of the Union.[76] Another leaflet, addressed to the Irish laborers, quoted Daniel O'Connell's remark that "The spirit of democratic liberty is defiled by the continuation of Negro slavery in the United States." It explained the Southern doctrine that "Capital shall own Labor," and asserted that slavery was anti-democratic because it was a war on the interests and rights of workingmen.

"We call upon you, in the sacred name of humanity, never again to volunteer on behalf of the oppressor, nor even for any self-interest to vindicate the hideous crime of slavery. . . . Give your votes in behalf of Freedom and not in behalf of slavery!"[77] The last broadside in the series printed the Southern peace terms —complete submission, recognition of the Confederacy, giving up all the territories west of the Confederate states, and reimbursement of the slave states for the costs and losses of the war— and added: "Comrades! Vote for the party that stands by the government, and vote for the man who stands by us, and by your brave brothers in the field, and let the ballot box tell the story of your patriotism and your resolve not to be the 'white slaves' of traitors or their friends."[78]

One other pamphlet may be cited as representing a somewhat different approach to the workers. In a series of questions and answers it explained the means by which the slaveholders controlled and oppressed the white workingmen as well as the slaves, and concluded with this exchange:

Q. 9. Shall we suffer these 350,000 men, who have committed all these enormities, and who are now drenching this nation with blood, to continue to hold their unjust, ruinous power?

A. No! never! They have forfeited their lives and property. Let us free their slaves. . . . Nothing short of this can ever make this nation a Union. Let this be done, and the down-trodden white people of the South will soon feel deliverance and shout for joy. The welfare of the whole nation demands the entire abolition of the slaveholding power. . . . I call upon my fellow working men, and all who desire the welfare of this nation, and entreat them . . . to unite in demanding of the Government the abolition of the slaveholding power.[79]

The publications of the workingmen helped considerably to defeat the plans of the defeatists and Copperheads, to maintain the fighting spirit of the people, to insure the election of the Union ticket in 1864, to bring the war to a successful conclusion and to secure the complete abolition of slavery.

CHAPTER VI

FRATERNITY IN FREEDOM

The United States, and the working class with it, was transformed by the events of the Second American Revolution, by the overthrow of the slave power and by the struggle for freedom by the workers themselves. To spell out the details of this transformation would require another study as long as the present one, but some of the more immediate effects may be traced. The organized labor movement disintegrated under the blows of economic depression and war, as union members lost their jobs or joined the army, labor newspapers were unable to keep their heads above water, and the few national organizations were split by the impossibility of maintaining connections between Northern and Southern locals. But a revival of the labor movement began with the recovery of business produced by the war economy. The real wages of the laboring men and women deteriorated disastrously as prices soared, and they were compelled to organize to protect their living standards. From 1862 to 1865 most of the old unions were reconstituted or reinvigorated and many new ones were established, and steps were taken to restore the Southern unions and secure their renewed affiliation with the national bodies.

But the post-war labor movement did not merely take up where it had left off before the war. It operated under different conditions and was strongly influenced by the experiences gained in economic and political struggle during the conflict. The process of industrialization and consolidation that had been going on for two generations received a tremendous stimulus from the war, and the capitalist class was in firm control of the national economy by 1865. A "shoddy aristocracy," rich and blustering, had grown up from war contracts, fraudulent dealings with the Union and the rebels, sharp speculation in government bonds, cheap labor and industrial expansion. Iron manufacturing, the production of sewing machines, lumbering, textiles and other industries received a momentous fillip from army contracts and vast new capital resources, and other fortunes were made by railroad construction. Tendencies toward consolidation and monopoly were accelerated, and employers in many industries organized associations for lobbying, price agreements and union-smashing. The rapid growth of population in the Middle West increased the home market, and the sale of farm machinery tripled. Furthermore, the new "captains of industry" had also become, through their influence in the dominant Republican party, the captains of the state as well.

The post-war labor movement, developing under these conditions, was pervaded by a higher degree of militancy and class-consciousness than it had previously known. This may be seen, for example, in the case of two of the largest national unions. Both the Iron Molders' Union and the Machinists' and Black-smiths' Union, and their leaders, Sylvis and Fincher, held to the doctrine of harmony of interests between employers and employees before the war. But in 1865 Sylvis said that society was divided into two great classes, separated by an impassable gulf—"the rich and the poor, the producers and the non-producers; the busy bees in the industrial hive, and the idle drones who fatten upon what they steal."[1] Fincher opposed political activity by labor on the ground that it would blur the antagonism between the two classes and restrain the workers from asserting and maintaining their rights.[2]

For a decade the Republicans had been telling the "hard-handed sons of toil" that their only enemy was the slavocracy, while the Democrats said that it was the capitalists. The workers themselves for the most part agreed that both classes were hostile to their interests. But during the war their primary aim was to defeat the slave-power, and while they did not forget their own immediate economic problems, they subordinated them for the sake of victory. When strikes were broken by the army during the war, Sylvis declared, only labor's loyalty to the Union had prevented "scenes that would appall the stoutest heart." These outrages on the rights of the workers created a profound sensation, he stated, and although "the muttering thunders of the confined volcano were scarcely audible above the surface . . . they were none the less deep because in secret." He warned that the point might be reached where forbearance would cease to be a virtue.[3]

With the defeat of the slave-power, the emancipation of the slaves and the unbridled reign of capital, this question which had agitated the labor movement for a generation was settled once and for all: the field was clear, and capital and labor stood face to face. The continuity of the struggle for the emancipation of the slaves and that for the advancement of labor was symbolized by Wendell Phillips, who devoted his genius and energies to the cause of the slaves and, when that was won, took up the cause of the working class. In 1865 he addressed a mass meeting of workers in Faneuil Hall and recalled the first time he had stood on that platform twenty-nine years earlier at an abolition meeting. He had felt then that he was speaking in the cause of the laboring men, for he was contending not only in behalf of a race that was bought and sold, but against the contention of Harper, Calhoun and Pickens that the laborer must necessarily be owned by capitalists. "That struggle for the ownership of labor is now somewhat near its end; and we fitly commence a struggle to define and to arrange the true relations of capital and labor."[4] When Phillips had concluded his speech, Ira Steward of the Machinists' Union, and leader of the eight-hour movement, proposed the following resolution, which was adopted by the acclamation of the assembled workers:

. . . we rejoice that the rebel aristocracy of the South has been crushed, that . . . beneath the glorious shadow of our victorious flag men of every clime, lineage and color are recognized as free. But while we will bear with patient endurance the burden of the public debt, we yet want it to be known that the workingmen of America will demand in future a more equal share in the wealth their industry creates . . . and a more equal participation in the privileges and blessings of those free institutions, defended by their manhood on many a bloody field of battle.[5]

The *Daily Evening Voice,* published by the Workingmen's Assembly of Boston and vicinity, also recognized that the struggle to place labor "beyond the reach of misused power" was but a new phase of the contest between liberty and aristocracy. While the capitalists "whine at the degradation of labor at the South," it declared, they are "at this very time forging a golden chain . . . to bind the Free Laborer of the North."

An oligarchy at the South, holding in its grasp the destinies of millions of the human race, and made mad by their lust for additional power, and, from the very nature of things, antagonistic to free labor, has struck a blow at the National life, and men stand appalled at the magnitude of the struggle. And here at the North, where every village, town and hamlet gives evidence of the industry of the people; where we have, through our institutions, instilled into our minds and fixed in our hearts a sacred love of liberty, an oligarchy, comparatively small, strikes a blow at the independence, nay, the very manhood of the industrial classes, when it denies their right to combine for mutual protection and advancement.[6]

William Sylvis forcefully expressed the new tasks of labor in a circular issued by the National Labor Union:

The working-people of our nation, white and black, male and female, are sinking to a condition of serfdom. Even now a slavery exists in our land worse than ever existed under the old slave system. The centre of the slave-power no longer exists south of Mason's and Dixon's line. It has been transferred to Wall Street; its vitality is to be found in our huge national bank swindle, and a false monetary system. The war abolished the right of property in man, but it did not abolish slavery. This movement we are now engaged in is the great anti-slavery movement, and we must push on the work of emancipation until slavery is abolished in every corner of our country. . . . Then will come such a social revolution as the world has never witnessed; honest industry in every department will receive its just reward, and public thieves will be compelled to make an honest living or starve. LET US ALL GO TO WORK.[7]

Even more for the Negro workers, in the North and the South, emancipation inaugurated a new stage in their fight for freedom. They were the most exploited of laborers, and in the South their oppression was trebled by cheating them of their earnings and by the desire of employers to "keep them in their place." Pressed by unbearable economic conditions, and stimulated by the resurgent labor movement and the electrifying effects of the anti-slavery struggle, Negro workers began to organize trade unions and to strike for higher wages. In 1867 a wave of strikes, particularly among Negro longshoremen, swept over the South. Most of these were for higher wages, and one in Savannah, Georgia, succeeded in securing the repeal of a ten dollar poll tax on all dock workers.[8]

By 1869 the growth of Negro labor organizations had been so rapid that they began to consolidate into state-wide bodies which would coordinate the work of the locals, further the organization of the laborers and press for protective legislation. In the four years after the War, conventions of Negro workers were held in Indiana, Pennsylvania, New York, Kentucky, Maryland, and the District of Columbia, and the roster of delegates represented virtually every trade in which Negroes were employed in those places. In December 1869, two hundred and three delegates from every section of the country met at Washington to "consolidate the colored workingmen of the several states to act in cooperation with our fellow workingmen in every state and territory in the union, who are opposed to distinctions in the apprenticeship laws on account of color, and to so act cooperatively until the necessity for separate organization shall be deemed unnecessary." The convention organized the National Colored Labor Union, whose principal activities for the next three years centered around the demands for higher wages, equal employment opportunities, educational facilities, cooperatives, homesteads and equality before the law.[9]

The agrarian laborers of the South, the bulk of the freedmen, also began to organize to achieve those measures which would secure the fruits of emancipation. Realizing that the formal proclamation of freedom would be hollow without the means of acquiring economic independence and securing their political rights, the Negroes demanded that the land of the traitorous slaveholders be confiscated and divided among the landless farmers, and that they be granted the civil and political rights which alone would guarantee the maintenance of their newly won status: the protection of life and property by law, freedom to sell their labor without intimidation, public education, freedom of speech, press and religion, equal suffrage and equality before the law. In order to secure these essential requirements of free people, the Negroes, with many white people as well, organized Union Leagues and militia units, joined the Republican party and assisted in the writing of democratic constitutions and in organizing state governments. These reconstruction governments have been contemptuously designated as "carpet-bag" governments and "Black Parliaments," but never before or since did the South know such a period of progress and democratic attainment: the civil rights of the Negroes were secured, public school systems established, state and county governments were reorganized on a more democratic basis, the tax systems were revised on a uniform basis applied to all property at its full value, fair labor relations were assured, the landless were given assistance in purchasing homesteads, and aid was granted for the building of railroads and much-needed public improvements. The Negro people and their white allies had placed the South on the high road to democratic progress—until they were betrayed by the Republican party.

Another marked result of labor's struggles in the Civil War era was the revival of independent political activity. This was an inevitable result of the exodus from the Democratic party which began in the early 1850's, for many workingmen, while supporting the Republican party as the party of resistance to the slave-power, could not identify themselves with it as the party of capital. This was evident in the anti-war and pro-Union campaign during the secession crisis. The workers who participated in that movement had little confidence in either party to solve the problems of the country in the interest of labor and viewed independent political organization as the only solution. The campaign itself was an example of such action, and from it emerged a definite movement towards a labor party. Within a few weeks after the mass meeting in Cincinnati in January 1861, there was a local labor party ready to participate in the city elections. After the national convention in Philadelphia, the delegates from Kentucky and Ohio returned home with definite political aspirations in mind, and the only others from whom anything further was heard—the Philadelphia workers—held meetings which demanded the establishment of a political body in opposition to both the Republican and Democratic parties.[10] Sylvis was the corresponding secretary of the committee chosen to implement the decisions of the convention and to arrange its next meeting, and on March 23 he wrote: "The business of this committee is to perfect and perpetuate an organization among the industrial classes of the city and State, for the purpose of placing in positions of public trust men of known honesty and ability; men who know the real wants of the people, and who will represent us according to our wishes; men who have not made politics a trade; men who, for a consideration, will not become the mere tools of rotten corporations and aristocratic monopolies; men who will devote their time and energies to the making of good laws, and direct their administration in such a way as will best subserve the interests of the whole people."[11]

Plans for the formation of a separate party were disrupted by the outbreak of the war, but the idea was kept alive. Most laborers wanted to support the war and the government without committing themselves to any party, and as early as 1862 the *Iron Platform* urged the formation of a Democratic-Republican party in New York to unite the Union supporters of both parties, but the Democrats refused to cooperate. In 1864 groups of trade unionists in several cities formed Workingmen's Democratic-Republican Associations with the aim of uniting the workers in support of Union candidates, educating them on the issues involved in the war, and mobilizing support for the administration.[12] The New York Association addressed a letter to both candidates, expressing its belief that the war was a defense not only of the Union but of the principles of democracy and the rights of labor and that it should be fought to a victorious conclusion without compromise.[13] When it became clear that the Democratic party would not prosecute such a war, the Association threw its support to Lincoln and worked energetically to secure labor's vote for Lincoln on the Union ticket.[14] At the same time it attempted to secure support for an eight-hour law, but was ignored by the Democratic party and brushed off by the Republicans with polite phrases about the antagonism between the slave-power and labor and the "hope that the great struggle . . . shall end in the interest of justice and free labor."[15] The campaigns in New York and Massachusetts against the proposed anti-strike bills gave a strong impetus to independent political activity by labor.

As the belief grew that the Republican party was not "the

party of free labor" but the party of big business, demands for a genuine labor party were heard more insistently. Through 1864 Fincher repeated time and again that the old parties could not be trusted to meet the new issues that would arise after the war, and asserted that the workers must form their own organizations and become a power that could command recognition.[16] Andrew C. Cameron of the Chicago *Workingman's Advocate* stated that labor could not win its struggle against capital except by taking the law-making power out of the hands of the latter and shaping the law in the interests of labor. "The relation that labor bears to the state . . . is the great issue. . . . The eight hours movement is the indispensable inaugural of the new era. But it cannot be carried, unless the thorough political organization of workmen and laborers all over the country is perfected."[17]

Many state and municipal trade union bodies organized independent political parties to campaign for the legal recognition of unions, eight-hour laws, the discontinuation of the importation of foreign contract labor, and equal pay for women employed at public expense. In 1866 the National Labor Union was formed, with Sylvis as its president, and the first convention adopted a resolution asserting that history had proved that the working class could not place its confidence in the existing political parties, and that they must cut themselves loose from party ties and predilections and organize themselves into a labor party for the purpose of securing eight-hour legislation. This eventually led to the organization of the National Labor Party, though not until 1872, and then it was dominated by currency reformers who made the greenback program the major demand of the party. The party also called for the eight-hour day, the granting of public lands to settlers only, an end to the emigration of forced Chinese labor, and tariff reduction.[18]

The ties of friendship between American labor and the European working class that had been established during the war were greatly strengthened in the post-bellum years. Several labor papers fully reported the decisions of the International Workingmen's Association (First International) and the activities of its American section, and many leaders of the trade unions and the National Labor Union understood the value of international labor unity, particularly for the purpose of preventing the importation of strike-breakers and checking the immigration of workers when there was no demand for their labor, but also because it was recognized that "the interests of labor are identical throughout the world . . . a victory to them will be a victory to us."[19] Several unions took independent action leading toward cooperation and possible affiliation with the workers in the corresponding British trades, and from its inception the National Labor Union showed interest in furthering international labor solidarity. Its first convention failed to send a delegate to the International only because there was not sufficient time left, but wished them "Godspeed in their glorious work." In 1867 a delegate was chosen to attend the congress of the International, and the National Labor Union promised cooperation to the workingmen of Europe. This delegate did not attend because he could not collect the necessary funds, but in 1869 Andrew C. Cameron was sent to the Basle conference of the International. Proposals for cooperation between the two bodies were accepted, and a resolution was adopted asserting that the National Labor Union adhered to the principles of the International and expected to join it in a short time. But because of Sylvis' death and Cameron's belief that the methods of struggle advocated by the International were not applicable to American conditions, this expectation was never realized.[20]

A month before Sylvis' death in 1869, he received a letter from the General Council of the International, written by Marx, which appealed for labor unity to prevent war between England and the United States over the *Alabama* claims arising from the Civil War. "Another war which did not have for its objective the cause of the working people would prevent the development of an independent labor movement," Marx observed, and he concluded:

"Yours then is the glorious task of seeing to it that at last the working class shall enter upon the scene of history, no longer as a servile following but as an independent power . . . capable of commanding peace where their would-be masters cry war." Sylvis responded promptly in the spirit of international friendship, asserting that the cause of workingmen on both sides of the ocean was a common one: "It is war between poverty and wealth; labor occupies the same low condition and capital is the same tyrant in all parts of the world." On behalf of the American workers, he extended the right hand of fellowship to "all down-trodden and oppressed sons and daughters of toiling Europe" and wished them success in the good work they had undertaken.[21]

The course of events leading to the Civil War had taught labor that its own strivings could not advance materially until the slaves were emancipated, that "The slavery of the black man leads to the slavery of the white man," as the *Iron Platform* said. Would the workers learn now that their interests and those of the Negro laborers were still bound inexorably together? The competition of Negro and white working men before and during the war had wrought serious injury to both, and as Negroes began to enter into industry in larger numbers and to form their own labor organizations, it became urgent that the labor movement give careful consideration to this question. Already in 1864 the Boston *Daily Evening Voice* had declared that it would advocate and sustain "the rights of Labor—without distinction of sex, complection or birthplace. . . ."[22] Sylvis also was aware of the common interests of Negro and white workers; in a speech in 1868 he declared that he had rejoiced at the downfall of Negro slavery. "But when the shackles fell from the limbs of those four millions of blacks," he stated, "it did not make them *free* men; it simply transferred them from one condition of slavery to another; it placed them upon the platform of the white workingmen, and made all slaves together. . . . We are now all one family of slaves together, and the labor reform movement is a second emancipation proclamation."[23]

In its first address to the workers of the United States, written by Cameron, the National Labor Union dealt with this matter forthrightly. The address stated that the Negro people, almost entirely workingmen and women, must become an element of strength or of weakness in the labor movement, depending on the decision of the white workingmen. Would the whites reject the Negroes' offer of cooperation?

By committing such an act of folly we would inflict greater injury upon the cause of labor reform than the combined efforts of capital could accomplish. . . . So capitalists North and South would foment discord between the whites and blacks and hurl one against the other . . . to maintain their ascendancy and continue the reign of oppression . . . What is wanted is for every union to help inculcate the grand ennobling idea that the interests of labor are one; that there should be no distinction of race or nationality; no classification of Jew or Gentile, Christian or infidel; that there is one dividing line, that which separates mankind into two great classes, the class that labors and the class that lives by others' labor.[24]

This resolution, however, represented the views only of some of the more farsighted men of the labor movement, and even they for the most part looked upon the Negroes not as brothers in a common struggle but as competitors who must be organized if only for the protection of white labor. The majority of the workers, on the other hand, still believed that the menace of competition could be met only by the exclusion of Negroes from the labor unions. At the second annual convention of the National Labor Union in 1867, President J. C. Whaley recommended that, in order to deal with the competition of Negro laborers, they should be organized into unions and brought into harmony with the interests of the labor movement. A committee appointed to prepare a resolution on the subject brought in a report stating that there was such divergence of opinion and the matter was so full of complexity and "mystery" that it was inexpedient to take action. The debate revealed that there was truly a wide variety of opinion on the subject, including advocates of unity between Negro and white labor, of exclusion of the Negroes, and of co-operation between separately organized labor movements. Action was avoided, however, by the assertion that the constitution of the National Labor Union invited all laborers to join and therefore there was no necessity for any special notice of a particular class. At the session of the following year, no mention of Negro labor seems to have been made other than a statement in the platform: "Resolved, That inasmuch as both the present political parties are dominated by the non-producing classes, who . . . have no sympathy with the working millions beyond the use they can make of them for their own political and pecuniary aggrandizement; therefore, the highest interests of our colored fellow-citizens is with the workingmen, who, like themselves, are slaves of capital and politicians, and strike for liberty."[25]

One of the obstacles to unity centered around differences of opinion concerning political action. While the labor movement as a whole was moving in the direction of independent organization and concentrating on issues like the eight-hour day and monetary reform, the Negro workers were firmly attached to the Republican party as the bulwark of their hopes for political and civil equality, and they were more concerned with the problems of reconstruction. The failure of the National Labor Union to consider the special political demands of the Negroes created serious difficulties.

But the principal issue was the admission of Negro workers into the existing trade unions, and at the 1869 convention of the National Labor Union a more positive stand was taken. This was partly because of the constant insistence of such leaders as Sylvis, Richard Trevellick of the Ship Carpenters' Union and successor to Sylvis as President of the National Labor Union, and most of the labor press, and partly because of the widespread organization and successful struggles of the Negro unions—the presence of nine delegates from the Negro labor movement demonstrated the impossibility of further ignoring Negro labor. This convention was the first national labor assembly in the United States in which Negro delegates participated. The resolution adopted by this congress declared that "The National Labor Union knows no North, no South, no East, no West, neither color nor sex on the question of the rights of labor, and urges our colored fellow members to form organizations in all legitimate ways, and send their delegates from every state in the Union to the next congress." A special committee was appointed to organize the Negro workers into unions to be affiliated with the National Labor Union.[26]

This action was greeted by the Negro delegates at the convention. Isaac Myers, of the Colored Caulkers Trade Union Society of Baltimore, congratulated the delegates on this important step in advancing the unity of Negro and white workers. "Silent, but powerful and farreaching is the revolution inaugurated by your action in taking the colored laborer by the hand and telling him that his interest is common with yours." The Negro workers, he said, desired the opportunity to labor at wages which would secure a comfortable living and security. They were eager for cooperation, although it had not always been possible because the workshops and the unions had been closed to them, and they had to sell their labor for whatever it could bring. "We mean in all sincerity a hearty cooperation. . . . Where we have had the chance, we have always demonstrated it. We carry no prejudice. We are willing to let the dead past bury its dead. . . . Mr. President, American citizenship for the black man is a complete failure if he is proscribed from the workshops of the country."[27]

In many respects the action of the National Labor Union represented a forward step, for it recognized the importance of the Negro workers and the community of interests between Negro and white labor and envisioned their cooperation in the future.

But it also reflected the persistence of prejudice against the Negroes, the desire to protect white labor against their competition, and the refusal to accept them as equals in the labor movement. As the *Workingman's Advocate* said on December 12, 1869, "It will take time to eradicate the prejudices of the past; to overcome the feelings which, it may be, the teachings of a lifetime have inculcated." The Negro workers were forced to organize their own unions, while at the same time they strove for acceptance by white labor. The *American Workingman* of Boston expressed its sorrow at the necessity for the organization of the National Colored Labor Union, and added: "But we are convinced that for the present at least, they could not do better. It is useless to attempt to cover up the fact that there is still a wide gulf between the races in this country, and for a time at least they must each in their own way work out a solution of this labor problem. At no very distant day they will become united, and work in harmony together. . . ."[28]

REFERENCES

Chapter I: THE LABOR AND ABOLITION MOVEMENTS

1. Of 5,500,000 immigrants from 1820 to 1860, 1,100,000 (20%) were mechanics and artisans and 2,000,000 (37%) were unskilled laborers. If all were still living and still in the same occupations in 1860 (neither of which was true), they would account for two-thirds of the mechanics and all the laborers in the country, or all of both categories in the free states, where practically all of them settled.

2. The ensuing data are derived from: *Sixth Census of the United States* (U.S. State Dept., 1841), *Compendium of the Sixth Census* (U.S. State Dept., 1841), *Statistical View of the United States . . . Seventh Census* (U.S. Census Office, 1854), *Population of the United States in 1860* (U.S. Census Office, 1864), *Statistics of the United States in 1860* (U.S. Census Office, 1866), *Manufactures of the United States in 1860* (U.S. Census Office, 1865), *The Statistics of the Population . . . 1870* (U.S. Census Office, 1872), *and The Statistics of Wealth and Industry . . . 1870* (U.S. Census Office, 1872). See also Victor S. Clark, *History of Manufactures in the United States* (New York, 1929; 2 vols.).

3. This number seems excessively small when compared with the number of persons employed in various industries and with such facts as that there were an estimated 100,000 cotton-mill operatives as early as 1815. See John R. Commons, *History of Labour in the United States* (New York, 1918), I, 105. The discrepancy is undoubtedly due to the fact that there was no definition of a "factory" or clear distinction between factories, mills, and workshops by which census enumerators could follow a common or consistent practice. The manufacturing statistics given below probably give a better picture of the character of the industrial population.

4. Counting half of the mechanics, artisans, and skilled laborers as wage earners.

5. The extent to which manufacturing had passed out of the home, even in the South, is indicated by the fact that in 1850, less than 10% of all manufactures were produced in families, all others being produced in manufacturing establishments of some sort. In North Carolina the figure was 10%; in Ohio 3%; in New York and Massachusetts 1%.

6. See Clark, *op. cit.*, I, 441-445.

7. Edward C. Kirkland, *A History of American Economic Life* (New York, 1951; 3rd ed.), 326-327.

8. Commons, *op. cit.*, I, 104-105.
9. Seth Luther, "An Address to the Working Men of New England . . ." (Philadelphia, 1836; 3rd ed.).
10. The following breakdown was given: New York and Brooklyn, 11,500 members; Philadelphia, 6,000; Boston, 4,000; Baltimore, 3,500; Washington, 500; Newark, 750. Commons, *op. cit.*, I, 424; Frank Tracy Carlton, *Organized Labor in American History* (New York, 1920), 21.
11. Commons, *op. cit.*, I, 424.
12. Philip S. Foner, *History of the Labor Movement in the United States* (New York, 1947), 222.
13. The following is based on John Hope Franklin, *From Slavery to Freedom* (New York, 1947), 204 ff., and J. Saunders Redding, *They Came in Chains* (Philadelphia, 1950), 85 ff.
14. *De Bow's Review*, January, 1850, 25-26.
15. *The Voice of Industry*, February 19, 1847, in John R. Commons' Labor Collection of Newspaper Extracts in the Wisconsin Historical Society Library.

Chapter II: In the Lion's Den

1. Daniel Raymond, *Thoughts on Political Economy* (Baltimore, 1820), 440-441.
2. Cassius Marcellus Clay, *Writings* (New York, 1848), 346-347 and 227; see also Henry Ruffner, *Address to the People of West Virginia* (Louisville, 1847), 19-20.
3. M. Tarver, "Domestic Manufacturers in the South and West," *DeBow's Review*, March, 1847, 188.
4. Chauncey S. Boucher, *The Ante-Bellum Attitude of South Carolina towards Manufacturing and Agriculture*, Vol. III of *Washington University Studies* (St. Louis, n.d.), 249, 260-261; *DeBow's Review*, Jan., 1850, 12.
5. Thomas Marshall, *Speech in the House of Delegates of Virginia on the Abolition of Slavery* (Richmond, 1832), 6.
6. Frederick Law Olmsted, *A Journey in the Back Country* (London, 1860), 17.
7. *The Injurious Effects of Slave Labour* (Philadelphia, 1824), 17.
8. *Niles' Register*, June 15, 1833; Asa Earl Martin, "The Anti-Slavery Movement in Kentucky Prior to 1850" (unpublished dissertation,

Cornell University, 1918), 66-67; Judge Harper's "Memoir on Slavery," cited in *The Philanthropist,* December 11, 1838.

9. *Niles' Register,* December 31, 1831; *Congressional Globe,* 24C. 1S., 1835, Appendix, 86.

10. Cited in Russel B. Nye, *Fettered Freedom* (East Lansing, 1949), 30.

11. Rosser Howard Taylor, *Slaveholding in North Carolina,* Vol. XVIII, *The James Sprunt Historical Publications* (Chapel Hill, 1926), 80; Frederick Law Olmsted, *A Journey in the Seaboard Slave States* (New York, 1856), 564; according to Hinton Rowan Helper, *The Impending Crisis of the South* (New York, 1857), 380-381, and *The Free South* (Newport, Ky.), Sept. 3, 1858, slave labor was paid better than free labor, but this was probably exceptional.

12. Clay, *op. cit.,* 234-235.

13. "Address to the Non-Slaveholders of Kentucky," in the Louisville *Examiner,* cited in the *Anti-Slavery Bugle* (Salem, Ohio), May 4, 1849.

14. Cited by Charles Nordhoff, *America for Free Working Men* (New York, 1865), 10.

15. E. S. Abdy, *Journal of a Residence and Tour in the United States . . .* (London, 1835), II, 219.

16. Nordhoff, *op. cit.,* 6-7.

17. Roger W. Shugg, *Origins of Class Struggle in Louisiana* (Baton Rouge, 1939), 88-89.

18. Cited in Charles H. Wesley, *Negro Labor in the United States* (New York, 1927), 19.

19. Ernest M. Lander, Jr., "Manufacturing in South Carolina, 1815-60," *The Business History Review,* XXVIII (Mar., 1954), 62.

20. Nordhoff, *op. cit.,* 10-11.

21. N. A. Ware, *Notes on Political Economy . . .* (New York, 1844), 201-202; also, see Edward Ingle, *Southern Sidelights* (New York, 1896), 77-78.

22. Shugg, *op. cit.,* 91.

23. *Seaboard Slave States, op. cit.,* 84, 349-350, 373; see also Olmsted, *The Cotton Kingdom* (New York, 1861), 113.

24. *Ibid.,* 112; *The Free South,* Sept. 3, 1858.

25. Charles Lyell, *A Second Visit to the United States . . .* (New York, 1849), II, 36; Nordhoff, *op. cit.,* 13; Camden (South Carolina) *Journal,* cited in French Ensor Chadwick, *Causes of the Civil War* (New York, 1906), 34.

26. Olmsted, *The Cotton Kingdom, op. cit.,* 89, 276. The contraction in

220 REFERENCES

the spelling of the epithet is mine, as it is whenever quoted in this study.

27. *The National Era,* Jan. 11, 1849; New York *Evening Post,* cited in *Publications of the New England Loyal Publication Society* (Boston, 1862-68), III, 278.

28. Cited in the *Anti-Slavery Bugle,* Dec. 15, 1855.

29. John Hope Franklin, "James Boon, Free Negro Artisan," *The Journal of Negro History,* April, 1945, 160-161.

30. Wesley, *op. cit.,* 71; Shugg, *op. cit.,* 117-119.

31. Wesley, *op. cit.,* 32-33, 80-81; Guion Griffis Johnson, *Ante-Bellum North Carolina* (Chapel Hill, 1937), 71-72; John R. Commons, ed., *A Documentary History of American Industrial Society* (Cleveland, 1910), II, 108.

32. Anonymous, *A Summary View of America* (London, 1824), 252-253; see also excerpt from John Finch, *Notes of Travel in the United States,* in Commons, *Documentary History, op. cit.,* VII, 63.

33. Quoted in Lorenzo Dow Turner, "Anti-Slavery Sentiment in American Literature," *The Journal of Negro History,* October, 1929, 386.

34. See "Letter from a Kentuckyan," in *The True American,* Feb. 11, 1846.

35. *The Impending Crisis, op. cit.,* 40-41.

36. Olmsted, *Seaboard Slave States, op. cit.,* 543.

37. Shugg, *op. cit.,* 116-117.

38. The Muscogee (Ga.) *Herald,* quoted in the *Anti-Slavery Bugle,* October 18, 1856.

39. The Richmond *Examiner,* Dec. 28, 1855, quoted in *The Republican Scrap Book* (Boston, 1856), 54.

40. The Charleston *Standard,* quoted in *ibid.,* 53.

41. *DeBow's Review,* XXX, 306.

42. *Republican Scrap Book,* 51.

43. *Congressional Globe,* 24C. 1S., 1836, App., 289-290. See also George McDuffie, "Message to the Legislature of South Carolina," (1835); J. H. Hammond, "Slavery in the Light of Political Science," in E. N. Elliott, ed., *Cotton is King* (Augusta, 1860), 638-639; *DeBow's Review,* Oct. 1849, 295-296; *Anti-Slavery Bugle,* Sept. 20, 1856.

44. *Correspondence of Calhoun,* in Fourth *Annual Report* of the American Historical Association (1899), II, 399-400.

45. Edmund Ruffin, *Anticipations of the Future* . . . (Richmond, 1860), 306-307; my emphasis—B.M.

46. See especially Fletcher M. Green, *Constitutional Development in the South Atlantic States* (Chapel Hill, 1930); Clement Eaton, *Freedom*

of Thought in the Old South (Durham, 1940); Henrietta Buckmaster, *Let My People Go* (New York, 1941).

47. Quoted in Shugg, *op. cit.,* 127.
48. Harper, "Memoir on Slavery," *DeBow's Review,* December, 1850, 614-616.
49. December 28, 1855, cited in *Republican Scrap Book,* 52.
50. See the Address of Robert Wickliffe, in the *Philanthropist* (Cincinnati), October 6, 1837.
51. Quoted in Clarence C. Norton, *The Democratic Party in Ante-Bellum North Carolina* (Chapel Hill, 1930), 200 ff.
52. Quoted in *ibid.,* 200 ff. See also William K. Boyd, "North Carolina on the Eve of Secession," *Annual Report* of the American Historical Association for 1910 (Washington, 1912); Henry M. Wystaff, *State Rights and Political Parties in North Carolina*—1776-1861, Ser. XXIV, nos. 7-8, *Johns Hopkins University Studies in History and Political Science* (Baltimore, 1906), 109-111.
53. The *Philanthropist,* May 31, 1843; see also Abdy, *op. cit.,* II, 227; *Niles' Register,* XLI (1831), 130-131; Wesley, *op. cit.,* 70-71; Nordhoff, *op. cit.,* 19-21; *Anti-Slavery Bugle, A*ugust 19, 1854.
54. Reprinted in the *Anti-Slavery Bugle,* May 10, 1856.
55. See "The Report of a Meeting of Workingmen in the City of Wheeling, Virginia" in John R. Common's *Labor Collection,* Wisconsin Historical Society Library.
56. Kathleen Bruce, *Virginia Iron Manufacture in the Slave Era* (New York, 1930), 224 ff.
57. Quoted in Richard B. Morris, "Labor Militancy in the Old South," *Labor and Nation,* May, 1948, 35.
58. July 1, 1847.
59. Rosser H. Taylor, *Ante-Bellum South Carolina,* XXV, No. 2, *James Sprunt Studies in History and Political Science* (Chapel Hill, 1942), 81; see also Ulrich B. Phillips, "The Central Theme of Southern History," *The American Historical Review,* October 1928, 32; F. L. Olmsted, *A Journey in the Back Country* (London, 1860), 180-181.
60. Guion Griffis Johnson, *Ante-Bellum North Carolina* (Chapel Hill, 1937), 174.
61. Olmsted, *Back Country, op. cit.,* 180n.
62. *Anti-Slavery Bugle,* Sept. 5, 1857; Arthur Raymond Pearce, *The Rise and Decline of Labor in New Orleans* (unpublished Thesis, Tulane Univ., 1938), 13.

63. The *Eagle of the South,* cited in the *Anti-Slavery Bugle,* August 21, 1858.
64. Commons, *Documentary History, op. cit.,* II, 108, 367-368; Julia A. Flisch, "The Common People of the Old South," in *Annual Report of the American Historical Association for 1908* (Washington, 1909), 139-140; "Slaves on a Federal Project," *Bulletin of Business History,* January, 1934, 32-33; Robert R. Russel, *Economic Aspects of Southern Sectionalism* (Urbana, 1923), 219-220; Theodore M. Whitfield, *Slavery Agitation in Virginia, 1829-1832* (Baltimore, 1930), 119 ff; Johnson, *op. cit.,* 71-72.
65. Commons, *Documentary History, op. cit.,* II, 176-177.
66. Nordhoff, *op. cit.,* 6.
67. Arthur Charles Cole, *The Irrepressible Conflict,* Vol. VII, *A History of American Life,* ed. by A. M. Schlesinger and D. R. Fox (New York, 1934), 36-37.
68. Sterling D. Spero and Abram L. Harris, *The Black Worker* (New York, 1931), 10.
69. Wesley, *op. cit.,* 80-81; Whitfield, *op. cit.,* 127 ff.; Green, *op. cit.,* 160-161; U. B. Phillips, in *The South in the Building of the Nation* (Richmond, 1909), X, 477-478; Russell, *op. cit.,* 54.
70. John G. Palfrey, *Papers on the Slave Power* (Boston, 1846), 59.
71. *Republican Scrap Book, op. cit.,* 27.
72. *The Free South,* September 3, 1858.
73. July 15, 1845; in Clay, *Writings, op. cit.,* 268-269.
74. New York *Evening Post,* quoted in *Publications* of the New England Loyal Publication Society (Boston, 1862-1868), III, 278; Olmsted, *Seaboard Slave States, op. cit.,* 308, 357; Ingle, *op. cit.,* 326; *The National Era,* Nov. 18, 1858; Cleveland *Leader,* Sept. 24. 1858; Chauncey S. Boucher, *South Carolina and the South on the Eve of Secession,* Vol. VI, *Washington Univ. Studies* (St. Louis, 1919), 100; Henry Bibb, *Narrative of the Life and Adventures of Henry Bibb* (New York, 1849), 24-25; Frederick Douglass, *My Bondage and My Freedom* (New York, 1855), 169-170; Helper, *op. cit.,* 375-376; Abdy, *op. cit.,* II, 218 ff.
75. *The North Star,* May 25, 1849, quoted in Philip S. Foner, *History of the Labor Movement in the United States.* (New York, 1947), 263-264.
76. Foner, *Labor Movement,* 264; for the participation of white workers in previous slave revolts, see James Hugo Johnston, "The Participation of White Men in Virginia Negro Insurrections," *The Journal of Negro History,* April, 1931, 158 ff.

77. pp. 120-121.
78. *E.g.,* see Gilbert J. Beebe, *A Review and Refutation of Helper's "Impending Crisis"* (Middletown, 1860) and Samuel M. Wolfe, *Helper's Impending Crisis Dissected* (Philadelphia, 1860).
79. See Herbert Aptheker, *To Be Free* (New York, 1948), and Wesley, *op. cit.,* 21-22.
80. Cited in Olmsted, *Seaboard Slave States, op. cit.,* 589-590.
81. *Anti-Slavery Bugle,* December 8, 1855.
82. M. W. Cluskey, *The Political Text-Book* (Philadelphia, 1860, 14th ed.), 220-222.
83. Foner, *Labor Movement,* 264.
84. "Extract from an Address Delivered by Thomas R. Whitney, December 23, 1851," in Commons, *Labor Collection, op. cit.*
85. See Chapter V.
86. "Establishment of Manufactures at New Orleans," *DeBow's Review,* January, 1850, 25-26; see also Governor Hammond's Address before the South Carolina Institute in *ibid.,* June, 1850, 518-520.
87. Cited in Boucher, *op. cit.,* 255-256.
88. Quoted in the *Anti-Slavery Bugle,* Oct. 18, 1856; see also Kenneth M. Stampp, "The Fate of the Southern Anti-Slavery Movement," *The Journal of Negro History,* January, 1943, 18.
89. Charleston *Standard,* cited in Nordhoff, *op. cit.,* 12; Greeley said: "Every free laborer taken to the South is a fresh nail in the coffin of slavery." (New York *Tribune,* June 4, 1853.)
90. Ingle, *op. cit.,* 242; Olmsted, *The Cotton Kingdom, op. cit.,* 229-301; Lander, *op. cit.,* 64-66.
91. James S. Green in the House, Jan. 4, 1850, in *Congressional Globe,* 31C. 1S., App., 426; The Pendleton (S.C.) *Messenger,* quoted in the *Liberator,* Aug. 10, 1849; Martinsburg *Republic,* cited in Howard C. Perkins, ed., *Northern Editorials on Secession* (New York, 1942), 872; Bruce, *op. cit.,* 235.
92. J. D. B. DeBow, *The Interest in Slavery of the Southern Non-Slaveholder* (Charleston, 1860), 5-8; D. R. Hundley, *Social Relations in our Southern States* (New York, 1860), 125.
93. Ingle, *op. cit.,* 240-241, 246; Joseph Dorfman, *The Economic Mind in American Civilization, 1606-1865* (New York, 1946), II, 951.
94. Alexandria *Constitutional,* Jan. 5, 1861, quoted in Shugg, *op. cit.,* 29; "Abolition of Negro Slavery," *American Quarterly Review,* Sept. 1832, 253; Nye, *op. cit.,* 187; T. H. Bayly in the House, in the *Congressional*

Globe, 30C. 1S., App., 579; DeBow, *op. cit.,* 8-9; Henry C. Carey, *The North and the South* (New York, 1854), 7.
95. Olmsted, *The Cotton Kingdom, op. cit.,* 54-55.
96. *A Chapter of American History* (Boston, 1852), 62; Eaton, *op. cit.,* 228.
97. Quoted in George M. Weston, *The Poor Whites of the South* (Washington, 1856); see also Lewis Tappan, *Address to the Non-Slaveholders of the South* (New York, 1843), 8-9; Morris, *op. cit.,* 34.
98. Douglass, *My Freedom and My Bondage, op. cit.,* 309.
99. Quoted in Edward McPherson, *The Political History of the United States of America During the Period of Reconstruction.* (3rd. ed; Washington, 1880), 55-56.
100. See Eaton, *op. cit.,* and instances of repression cited above.
101. *Douglass' Monthly,* February, 1859.

Chapter III: NORTHERN LABOR CONSIDERS SLAVERY

1. James Birney to Charles Hammond, November 14, 1835, in Dwight L. Dumond, ed., *Letters of James Gillespie Birney* (New York, 1938), I, 270-271.
2. Thomas Wentworth Higginson, *Cheerful Yesterdays* (Boston, 1898), 115-117; see also Martin, *op. cit.,* 74; the *Liberator,* May 12, 1837; Samuel J. May, *Some Recollections of our Antislavery Conflict* (Boston, 1869), 141; Henry Middleton, *Economical Causes of Slavery in the United States* (London, 1857), 51-53; The Haverhill *Gazette,* cited in *The Philanthropist,* August 3, 1836.
3. Richard R. Wright, *The Negro in Pennsylvania* (Philadelphia, n.d.), 19-20; see also Dorfman, *op. cit.,* I, 119.
4. In *Collections* of the Massachusetts Historical Society (Boston: The Society, 1877), 5th ser., III, 402.
5. The *Liberator,* Dec. 20, 1834; see also "Proceedings of the Pennsylvania Convention of the State Anti-Slavery Society," 1837, in Williston H. Lofton, "Abolition and Labor," *The Journal of Negro History,* July, 1948, 253-254.
6. Calvin Colton, *The Rights of Labor* (New York, 1847), 6-7.
7. Article in a St. Louis Democratic paper, cited in the *Anti-Slavery Bugle,* February 27, 1858.
8. *Anti-Slavery Bugle,* March 26, 1847, August 7, 1846, Sept. 18, 1846, July 16, 1853; Philadelphia *Daily Record,* cited in *Anti-Slavery Bugle,* Dec. 15, 1848; *Phil. Daily Republic,* cited in Foner, *op. cit.,* 281; Robert

Dale Owen, *Labor: Its History and Its Prospects* (Cincinnati, 1848), 37-38; *Liberator*, Nov. 10, 1848; *The True American*, Dec. 2, 1845.
9. April 27, 1844 and May 11, 1844.
10. Proceedings of the Rhode Island Anti-Slavery Convention, 1836, cited in Lofton, *op. cit.*, 253; see also The *Philanthropist*, May 19, 1841; The *Herald of Freedom*, cited in the *Liberator*, June 9, 1843; The *American Jubilee*, March 1855.
11. *Congressional Globe*, 25C. 3S., 1839, Appendix, 174.
12. Theodore Sedgwick, *Public and Private Economy* (New York, 1836), 254-255, 263; see also Stephen Simpson, *The Working Man's Manual* (Philadelphia, 1831), 15 ff.
13. July 26, 1836.
14. The *Weekly Reformer* (Boston), March 31, 1837.
15. *Frederick Douglass' Paper*, March 4, 1853, in Philip Foner, *The Life and Writings of Frederick Douglass* (New York, 1950), II, 223-225.
16. Spero and Harris, *op. cit.*, 12; Wesley, *op. cit.*, 32, 75-78; *The Philanthropist*, May 26, 1841; Leo H. Hirsch, Jr., "New York and the Negro, from 1783 to 1865," *The Journal of Negro History*, October, 1931, 436; Abdy, *op. cit.*, I, 358-359; The *Liberator*, April 4, 1851; Frederick Douglass, *Life and Times of Frederick Douglass* (Hartford, 1881), 293-294.
17. Buckmaster, *op. cit.*, 80; Douglass, *My Bondage, op. cit.*, 454-455; Carter G. Woodson, "The Negroes of Cincinnati Prior to the Civil War," *The Journal of Negro History*, January, 1916, 5 ff.
18. See Lyell, *op. cit.*, II, 82; Edward Raymond Turner, *The Negro in Pennsylvania* (Washington, 1911), 158-159; Foner, *Labor Movement*, 269.
19. Wesley, *op. cit.*, 79-80; Nehemiah Adams, *A South-Side View of Slavery* (Boston, 1860), 4th ed., 120-121; Cole, *op. cit.*, 266.
20. Abdy, *op. cit.*, I, 181; Cole, *op. cit.*, 339; Turner, *op. cit.*, 150-151.
21. August 27, 1847; see also Theodore Sedgwick, ed., *A Collection of the Political Writings of William Leggett* (New York, 1840), I, 207-209; New York *Evening Post*, July 25, 1835, in Commons, *Labor Collection, op. cit.*
22. June 7, 1845, July 24, 1844, July 27, 1844, and April 26, 1845; see also the *Liberator*, February 15, 1834; Herman Schluter, *Lincoln, Labor and Slavery* (New York, 1913), 72-73.
23. Cited in Ralph Korngold, *Two Friends of Man* (Boston, 1950), 64; see also the *Congressional Globe*, 25C. 3S., App., 358; 29C. 2S., App.,

94; 30C. 1S., App., 45; *DeBow's Review*, XVII, 182; N. Y. *Globe*, cited in Lofton, *op. cit.*, 275; Leander Ker, *Slavery Consistent with Christianity*, cited in *ib.*, 274.

24. *The Philanthropist*, Jan. 15, 1836, Nov. 4, 1840; Foner, *Writings of Frederick Douglass, op. cit.*, I, 339; Charles C. Burleigh, *Slavery and the North* (New York, n.d.), 8-10; *National Enquirer*, April 29, 1837.

25. See Florence E. Gibson, *The Attitudes of the New York Irish Toward State and National Affairs*, 1848-1892 (New York, 1951), 110; Commons, *Documentary History, op. cit.*, VII, 60-61; *The Journal of Negro History*, April, 1927, 157; Carl Wittke, *We Who Built America* (New York, 1939), 158-159.

26. Rice, *op. cit.*, 152 ff.

27. See especially the New York *Irish-American*.

28. Wendell Phillips, *Speeches, Lectures, and Letters*. (Boston, 1892), II, 19 ff.; see also the *National Anti-Slavery Standard*, January 4, 1844; "Daniel O'Connell upon American Slavery: With Other Irish Testimonies," *Anti-Slavery Tracts*, New Ser. No. 5 (New York, 1860).

29. Several less prominent economic arguments were also used in the effort to win the support of labor for abolition, such as that the existence of slavery in the South restricted the market for the sale of Northern-manufactured goods; that workers were excluded from profitable employment in the favorable climate of the South; that the slaveholders prevented the passage of tariff and homestead laws for the benefit of labor; that taxes were high because the government was controlled by the slaveholders; and even that hard times were a result of slavery. See the *National Enquirer*, April 18, 1839 and May 27, 1837; *The Philanthropist*, June 9, 1841; Alvan Steward, "The Cause of the Hard Times," (Boston, 1843), Tract No. 4; The *Friend of Man*, September 2 to September 30, 1840: New York *Tribune*, October 9, 1858; Lofton, *op. cit.*, 256-257; *Liberator*, January 19, 1833; *Niles' Register*, XLI, December 31, 1831 and January 14, 1832.

30. In Commons, *Labor Collection, op. cit.*

31. *The Pennsylvania Freeman*, February 7, 1839.

32. *National Laborer*, September 13, 1836, cited in Foner, *Labor Movement*, 268.

33. T. V. Powderly, *Thirty Years of Labor* (Columbus, 1890), 48-49.

34. *Working Man's Advocate*, October 1, 1831.

35. Joseph Sturge, *A Visit to the United States in 1841* (London, 1842), 143; Lucy Larcom, *A New England Girlhood* (Boston, 1889), 255; Foner, *Labor Movement*, 267, 274.

36. *National Enquirer,* May 7, 1837.
37. E.g., see the issues of June 11, 1840, April 27, 1843, and July 3, 1845; see also *The Philanthropist,* September 18, 1838; the *National Enquirer,* January 3, 1838; the *Liberator,* May 8, 1846; *The Plaindealer,* in Sedgwick, *Writings of William Leggett, op. cit.,* II, 216; *The National Era,* December 23, 1847.
38. *New York State Mechanic,* April 9, 1842.
39. The *Liberator,* February 20, 1846.
40. *Ibid.,* May 26, 1848.
41. Trenton *Daily State Gazette,* Dec. 6, 1851, cited in Foner, *Labor Movement, op. cit.,* 279.
42. *Niles' Register,* October 3, 1835.
43. March 26, 1836, cited in Foner, *Labor Movement,* 267.
44. *The Man,* July 10 to July 14, 1834.
45. Fall River *Weekly News,* August 28, 1845; see also the Boston *Weekly Reformer,* December 15, 1837, and the *Working Man's Advocate,* October 31, 1835.
46. "Address to the Free Laborers of the United States," in the *Emancipator,* cited in *The Philanthropist,* January 15, 1836; see also the issues of January 1, 1836, March 4, 1836, June 16, 1837, December 11, 1838, August 6, 1839, and November 4, 1840; S. B. Treadwell, *American Liberties and American Slavery* (New York, 1838), 162-163; the *National Anti-Slavery Standard,* April 27, 1843; The *Anti-Slavery Record,* September, 1836; The Boston *Weekly Reformer,* March 17, 1837; The *Liberator,* September 28, 1838; Russel B. Nye, "The Slave Power Conspiracy," *Science and Society,* Summer, 1946, 262 ff.
47. *The Voice of Industry,* February 13, 1846.
48. Lofton, *op. cit.,* 262-263.
49. Issue of September 11, 1830, in Commons, *Labor Collection, op. cit.*
50. July 17, 1845, cited in Norman Ware, *The Industrial Worker, 1840-1860* (Boston, 1924), 214.
51. Fall River *Mechanic,* November 2, 1844; *Working Man's Advocate,* March 16, 1844.
52. Vera Shlakman, *Economic History of a Factory Town* (Northampton, 1935), 133-134.
53. *Northampton Democrat,* cited in the *National Anti-Slavery Standard,* August 5, 1847.
54. The Lynn *Awl,* October 9, 1844.
55. *New England Artisan and Laboring Man's Repository,* October 4, 1832.

56. Issue of September 11, 1830, in Commons, *Labor Collection, op. cit.*
57. *Congressional Globe*, 33C. 1S., 1854, App., 1224. The labor press of the period is filled with discussions of this subject. In addition to the above, see especially *America's Own and Fireman's Journal*, April 26, 1851, May 10, 1851, June 21, 1851, and February 12, 1853; the *Voice of Industry*, October 9, 1846; *Working Man's Advocate*, June 22, 1844; *The Harbinger*, June 21, 1845 and July 5, 1845; *The Slavery of Poverty* (New York: Society for the Abolition of ALL Slavery, 1842), 1; The Boston *Laborer*, October 26, 1844; *New England Artisan*, October 3, 1833; The Lynn *True Workingman*, October 22, 1845; and the *Monthly Jubilee* (Philadelphia), May, 1854.

Some labor spokesmen denied that the wages system was comparable to slavery, but this was almost invariably in rebuttal of attacks on them by pro-slavery apologists—a case of "I can say it about myself, but you can't say it." See, e.g., The *Weekly Tribune*, November 29, 1845, in Commons, *Labor Collection, op. cit.;* The New York *Tribune*, November 21, 1845; The *National Enquirer*, January 10, 1830; The Fall River *Weekly News*, September 25, 1845.

As for the Negro workers, there was little question in their minds or any one else's that there was little to choose between their conditions and those of the slaves. See *The Colored American*, November 25, 1837.
58. This contradiction was noted by the Northampton *Democrat*, cited in the *National Anti-Slavery Standard*, August 5, 1847, and by *The Slavery of Poverty, op. cit.*, 4.
59. Dorfman, *op. cit.*, II, 687.
60. Simpson, *op. cit.*, 85-86.
61. Published in Cincinnati, 1847, by Thomas Varney.
62. See pp. 3-4.
63. *Ibid.*, 33-34.
64. *Ibid.*, 43-44.
65. Issue of February 12, 1853.
66. Foner, *Writings of Frederick Douglass, op. cit.*, I, 249. Walsh had published a paper entitled *The Subterranean*.
67. Lofton, *op. cit.*, 263.
68. Those historians who state that labor was against emancipation (and this is common among those who mention the role of labor at all) have been misled by several errors: first, they have identified the anti-slavery movement with the abolitionist organizations, although the latter were at all times a minor element among the forces that

brought about the overthrow of slavery; second, they have confused the policy of the workers, which was in favor of emancipation, with their tactics, which required the subordination of the slavery question to the labor question; third, they have failed to take into account the change in labor's position during the 1850's; and finally, they have too often based their judgment on a few spectacular events, like the draft riots in New York, rather than on a careful study of all the evidence.

69. Issue of August 15, 1833.
70. *Ibid,* Nov. 1, 1832. See also the Lynn *Awl,* September 4, 1844; Boston *Weekly Reformer,* January 20, 1837 and May 5, 1837.
71. *The Workingman's Advocate,* January 25, 1845.
72. Andreas Dorpalen, "The German Element and the Issues of the Civil War," *The Mississippi Valley Historical Review,* XXIX, 55 ff.
73. There is no adequate biography of Evans, nor of any of the important ante-bellum labor leaders.
74. *Working Man's Advocate,* July 6, 1844.
75. *Ibid,* June 1, 1844.
76. *Young America,* January 23, 1848.
77. William West to the editor of the *Liberator,* August 28, 1846.
78. Pickering, *op. cit.,* 68-69. For other material on the land reformers and slavery, see the *Monthly Jubilee,* August, 1854; The *Voice of Industry,* Jan. 22, 1847 and Aug. 13, 1847; The *Liberator,* July 4, 1845; *The Slavery of Poverty, op. cit.,* 4, 15.
79. Albert Brisbane, *Social Destiny of Man* (Philadelphia, 1840).
80. See pp. 97-112.
81. *The Phalanx,* November 4, 1843, cited in Commons, *Documentary History, op. cit.,* VII, 207-210.
82. Cited in *ibid.,* VII, 211-213. See also his explanation of this letter in the *Tribune,* June 20, 1845, and his second letter, printed in the *Voice of Industry,* August 21, 1845; *The Phalanx,* Dec. 5, 1843; *The Harbinger,* June 21, 1845 and July 5, 1845; Robert Owen's address in The *Liberator,* June 6, 1845.
83. *The New Harmony Gazette,* October 1, 1825; A. J. G. Perkins and Theresa Wolfson, *Frances Wright, Free Enquirer* (New York, 1939), 123 ff., 255, 329.
84. *New Harmony Gazette,* October 1, 1825 and succeeding numbers.
85. Elinor Pancoast and Anne E. Lincoln, *The Incorrigible Idealist* (Bloomington, 1940), 47-49, 57-58.

86. *Boston Quarterly Review*, October, 1838, 499-500, and July, 1840, 368 ff.; Boston *Weekly Reformer*, July 21, 1837, April 4, 1838.
87. The *Liberator*, December 24, 1841; see also the issue of November 19, 1836; the *Anti-Slavery Bugle*, Nov. 6, 1846, and Jan. 6, 1855; *The Philanthropist*, February 26, 1836; *The National Era*, March 16, 1848, April 20, 1848, April 27, 1848; *The National Enquirer*, March 17, 1839; *America's Misfortune* (Buffalo, 1856), 38; *Third Annual Report*, American Anti-Slavery Society (New York, 1836), 28; Olmsted, *Seaboard Slave States, op. cit.*, 700 ff.
88. Korngold, *op. cit.*, 155-157.
89. The *Liberator*, January 1, 1831.
90. *Ibid.*, January 29, 1831.
91. *Ibid.*, January 1, 1841.
92. *Ibid.*, July 9, 1847; *The Harbinger*, July 17, 1847; George E. McNeill, ed., *The Labor Movement* (Boston, 1887), 113.
93. Clay, *Writings, op. cit.*, 348-352.
94. *The Voice of Industry*, November 6, 1846.
95. *Voice of Industry*, February 19, 1847, in Commons, *Labor Collection, op. cit.*; Ware, *op. cit.*, 221; Shlakman, *op. cit.*, 111-112. See also the *Liberator*, March 19, 1847, February 4, 1837, and April 22, 1853; and the *Anti-Slavery Standard*, October 14, 1847.
96. *Liberator*, January 7, 1837; The *Emancipator*, October 28, 1840; Foner, *Writings of Frederick Douglass, op. cit.*, II, 168-169; *National Anti-Slavery Standard*, August 5, 1847.
97. Issue of May 8, 1846.
98. Cited in Madeleine Hooke Rice, *American Catholic Opinion in the Slavery Controversy* (New York, 1944), 103.
99. *Workingmen's National Advocate* (Washington), April 30, 1853; The *Working Man's Advocate*, October 5, 1833; The *Irish-American*, May 17, 1851, and June 28, 1851; Fall River *Weekly News*, August 21, 1845 and September 4, 1845; Shlakman, *op. cit.*, 134; Foner, *Labor Movement*, 271.
100. May 14, 1846.
101. *The Radical*, March, 1841.
102. Quoted in Shlakman, *op. cit.*, 61; also see *The Harbinger*, September 6, 1845; Fall River *Mechanic*, May 18, 1844; John Campbell, *Negro-Mania* (Philadelphia, 1851), 469-470; *New Era*, August 3, 1839; *The People's Paper*, September 9, 1843, in Commons, *Labor Collection, op. cit.*
103. Wesley, *op. cit.*, 78-79.

104. Cited in Lofton, *op. cit.*, 276.

105. *The Slavery of Poverty*, *op. cit.*, 8.

106. The *Voice of Industry*, August 21, 1845, in Commons, *Labor Collection*, *op. cit.*; Boston *Protective Union*, March 30, 1850; *Liberator*, September 5, 1845.

107. *Liberator*, March 20, 1846.

108. *National Anti-Slavery Standard*, June 20, 1850; *National Enquirer*, May 13, 1837; *Liberator*, January 9, 1836.

109. *National Anti-Slavery Standard*, December 28, 1848, June 20, 1850, October 25, 1856.

110. *Congressional Globe*, 24C. 1S., 1837, App., 288.

111. "Letter on Slavery," in *DeBow's Review*, March, 1850, 257-258.

112. E.g., see Harper's "Memoir on Slavery" in *DeBow's Review*, April, 1850; *The Southern Quarterly Review*, July, 1851, 118 ff.; Solon Robinson, "Negro Slavery at the South," *DeBow's Review*, Sept., 1849, 222 ff.; Lucien B. Chase, *English Serfdom and American Slavery* (New York, 1854), vii.

113. Elwood Fisher, "The North and the South," *DeBow's Review*, October, 1849, 308-309.

114. *Congressional Globe*, 31C. 1S., 1851, 500; *ibid.*, Appendix, 175; Columbia (South Carolina) *Times*, cited in the *Anti-Slavery Bugle*, Jan. 20, 1855; Washington *Cotton Plant*, cited in *ibid.*, October 8, 1853; Fisher, *op. cit.*; *The Church Review and Ecclesiastical Register*, VII, 431 ff.; Olmsted, *Seaboard Slave States*, *op. cit.*, 701-702.

115. Cleveland *Leader*, January 22, 1855.

116. Harper's "Memoir on Slavery," *DeBow's Review*, November, 1850, 503-504; see also J. K. Paulding, *Slavery in the United States* (New York, 1836), 266 ff.; George Fitzhugh, *Sociology for the South* (Richmond, 1854), 27-28; Fitzhugh, *Cannibals All!* (Richmond, 1857), 25-26.

117. Charleston, 1856.

118. See pp. 21-22.

119. See pp. 43-44.

120. See pp. 49 ff.

121. *Congressional Globe*, 35C. 1S., 1858, 962; my emphasis—B.M.

122. Calhoun, "Report on the Circulation of Abolition Petitions," in *The Works of John C. Calhoun* (New York, 1855), 207-208; Harper, "Slavery in the Light of Social Ethics," in E. N. Elliott, ed., *Cotton is King* (Augusta, 1860), 590-592; Edmund Ruffin, *Slavery and Free Labor Described and Compared* (n.p., n.d.), 1-2.

123. Fitzhugh, *Cannibals All!*, *op. cit.*, 27 ff.; see also *The Southern Quarterly Review*, 1856, 62 ff., and January, 1851, 221 ff.

124. Fitzhugh, *Cannibals All!*, *op. cit.*, 46; *The Southern Quarterly Review*, January, 1851, 223; *DeBow's Review*, October, 1849, 295-296; McDuffie, *op. cit.*

125. J. H. Hammond, in Elliott, *op. cit.*, 638-639; Hammond to Clarkson, in *DeBow's Review*, October, 1849, 295-296; McDuffie, *op. cit.*; Pickens, in the *Congressional Globe*, 24C. 1S., 1836, Appendix, 290.

126. Matthew Estes, *A Defense of Negro Slavery* (Montgomery, 1846).

127. *The Southern Quarterly Review*, January, 1851, 220-221; *Southern Literary Messenger*, 1851, 260; Henry Hughes, *Treatise on Sociology* (Philadelphia, 1854), 187 ff.; Estes, *op. cit.*, 168-172; Thomas R. R. Cobb, *An Inquiry into the Laws of Negro Slavery* (Philadelphia, 1858), ccxiv.

128. Grayson, *op. cit.*, 45.

129. See Thomas D. Jarrett, "Ideas in William J. Grayson's *The Hireling and the Slave . . .*" (Unpublished Thesis, Univ. of Chicago, 1947).

130. See Chauncey S. Boucher, ed., *Correspondence Addressed to John C. Calhoun, 1837-1849*, in *Annual Report* of the American Historical Association for the Year 1929, 328-329; *Congressional Globe*, 31C. 1S., 1850, Appendix, 394; The *Political Reformer* (Richmond), quoted in *The Philanthropist*, July 7, 1840; *The Washington Globe*, Sept. 7 to Sept. 9, 1838; The New Orleans *Delta*, quoted in The *National Anti-Slavery Standard*, November 8, 1856.

131. Arthur M. Schlesinger, Jr., *The Age of Jackson* (Boston, 1947), 410; Richard Hofstadter, *The American Political Tradition* (New York, 1948), 88.

132. *The Harbinger*, October 25, 1845.

133. *The Boston Quarterly Review*, January, 1841, 86 ff.

134. *Congressional Globe*, 24C. 2S., 1837, 82, 106; 25C. 3S., 1839, 21-23, Appendix, 237-241.

135. *Ibid.*, 33C. 1S., 1854, Appendix, 1220; see also *The Slavery of Poverty, op. cit.*, 16.

136. Quoted in Charles A. and Mary R. Beard, *The Rise of American Civilization* (New York, 1930), I, 693.

137. *Congressional Globe*, 30C. 1S., 1848, App. 579.

138. *Register of Debates in Congress*, 25C. 1S., 1837, 1393-1395.

139. *Congressional Globe*, 25C. 2S., 1838, App., 62.

140. Cited in *National Anti-Slavery Standard*, April 27, 1843.

141. Quoted in The *Liberator*, April 30, 1841.

142. Quoted in Schlesinger, *op. cit.*, 246.

143. *Cannibals All!*, *op. cit.*, 127 ff., 368; see also Fitzhugh, *Sociology for the South*, *op. cit.*, 71; Calhoun, *Works*, *op. cit.*, 207-208; *Congressional Globe*, 31C. 1S., 1850, Appendix, 381; New York *Herald*, February 28, 1860, cited in Philip S. Foner, *Business and Slavery* (Chapel Hill: Univ. of North Carolina, 1941), 193; Wilfred Carsel, "The Slaveholders' Indictment of Northern Wage Slavery," *The Journal of Southern History*, 1940, 518-519.

144. Washington *Globe*, December 25, 1834.

145. *The Southern Review*, August, 1830, 1 ff.; Fitzhugh, *Cannibals All!*, *op. cit.*, 127 ff.

146. *Congressional Globe*, 31C. 1S., 1850, Appendix, 242.

147. E.g., see *The Union, Past and Future* . . . (Washington: The Southern Rights Association, 1850), 30 ff.

148. *Register of Debates in Congress*, 25 C. 1S., 1837, 1393-1395; *Congressional Globe*, 35 C. 1S., 1858, 962; see also *ibid.*, Appendix, 394.

149. See Foner, *Business and Slavery*, *op. cit.*, and *A Chapter of American History*, *op. cit.*

150. *The Plaindealer* (New York), May 13, 1837. See also the *Congressional Globe*, 25C. 1S., 1837, Appendix, 255.

151. *Reminiscences of Levi Coffin* (Cincinnati, 1880), 525; *The Philanthropist*, Sept. 23, 1836, Dec. 5, 1837; Boston *Weekly Reformer*, Dec. 9, 1836; The *Liberator*, Nov. 7, 1835; Boston *Times*, cited in *ibid.*, Aug. 20, 1841; May, *op. cit.*, 153 ff.; *Letters of Lydia Maria Child* (Boston: Houghton, Mifflin and Co., 1883), 17-18; William Birney, *James G. Birney and His Times* (New York: D. Appleton and Co., 1890), 240 ff.; Nye, *op. cit.*, 156-157; Foner, *Business and Slavery*, *op. cit.*, 28-29; *The National Era*, Dec. 23, 1847; *Working Man's Advocate* (Phil.), Oct. 3, 1835.

152. *Congressional Globe*, 25C. 3S., 1839, App., 168; see also *The Philanthropist*, March 17, 1837.

Chapter IV: The Slave-Power and the Mudsills

1. Powderly, *op. cit.*, 44.

2. September 1, 1837.

3. The *Liberator*, November 8, 1844.

4. Cited in Foner, *Labor Movement*, 277.
5. Issue of October 25, 1845.
6. *Congressional Globe*, 28C. 2S., 1845, 111.
7. *Working Man's Advocate*, April 20, 1844; New York *Tribune*, August 15, 1850; *America's Own and Firemen's Journal*, December 15, 1849.
8. Foner, *Labor Movement*, 277-278.
9. *Ibid.;* Lofton, *op. cit.*, 281.
10. Quoted in *The Harbinger*, June 20, 1846.
11. *Congressional Globe*, 29C. 2S., 1847, 114.
12. *Ibid.*, especially 29C. 2S., 1847, Appendix, 202-203, 357, 442; 30C. 1S., 1848, Appendix, 1200; 30 C. 2S., 1849, Appendix, 100-101; 34C. 1S., 1856, Appendix, 949 ff.; 35C. 1S., 1858, 220.
13. David Wilmot, *ibid.*, 30C. 1S., 1848, Appendix, 1079-1080.
14. David Wilmot, *ibid.*, 34C. 1S., 1856, Appendix, 1218.
15. T. H. Averett, Va., *ibid.*, 29C. 2S., 1847, App., 87, and 31C. 1S., 1850, App., 394; H. Bedinger, Va., 30C. 2S., 1849, App., 112.
16. New York *Tribune*, June 13, 1850.
17. *Monthly Jubilee*, September, 1852 and October, 1853.
18. New York *Weekly Tribune*, October 26, 1850, in Commons, *Documentary History, op. cit.*, VIII, 329.
19. Issue of September, 1852.
20. New York *Tribune*, February 20, 1854.
21. *Ibid.*, February 4, 14 and 15, March 15 and 23, 1854, and July 3, 1856.
22. *Monthly Jubilee*, August, 1854; this action produced a split in the Congress, the minority withdrawing in protest against the departure from the policy of confining their efforts to labor and land reform.
23. Schluter, *op. cit.*, 75-77.
24. *Congressional Globe*, 33C. 1S., 1854, 1230-1232.
25. William Goodell, *A Full Statement of the Reasons . . .* (Boston, 1836), 27-30. See also *Proceedings* of the Rhode Island Anti-Slavery Convention (Providence, 1836), 37.
26. Issue of March 31, 1837.
27. Russel B. Nye, *Fettered Freedom* (E. Lansing, 1949), 166-167.
28. William H. Seward, *Works* (George E. Baker, ed.; Boston, 1884), IV, 250.
29. Carl Schurz, "Speech at St. Louis, August 1, 1860," in Emerson D. Fite, *The Presidential Campaign of 1860* (New York, 1911), 253-254.
30. New York *Tribune*, April 1, 1857; see also *The Free South*, October 29, 1858 and November 12, 1858; James Harlan, "Shall the Territories

be Africanized?" (New York, 1860; pamphlet reprint of speech in the Senate, January 4, 1860).

31. Charles Sumner, "The Slave Oligarchy and Its Ursurpations" (Boston, 1855), 9.

32. Arthur C. Cole, Lincoln's "House Divided" Speech (Chicago, 1923), 32-33.

33. Cleveland Morning Leader, April 6, 1855; William H. Seward, "Immigrant White Free Labor . . ." (Speech at Oswego, November 3, 1856).

34. Seward, speech at Rochester, October 25, 1858, in Works, op. cit., 292.

35. Anti-Slavery Bugle, August 30, 1856.

36. For example, see the Cleveland Leader, June 15, 1854 and August 13, 1855; Congressional Globe, 35C. 1S., 1858, 1002 ff., 1025; Charles Mackay, Life and Liberty in America (New York, 1859), 248 ff.; Seward, Works, op. cit., 289; Anti-Slavery Bugle, November 21, 1857; Henry L. Dawes, "The New Dogma of the South," pamphlet reprint of speech in Congress, April 12, 1860.

37. Quoted by F. P. Blair in the Anti-Slavery Bugle, October 11, 1856; by Representative Tappan, in the Congressional Globe, 34C. 1S., 1856, Appendix, 949 ff.; and throughout the anti-slavery press.

38. When the editor of the Charleston Mercury held up slavery as the natural and best condition of labor, he was burned in effigy by the mechanics of the city. See Cole, Lincoln's "House Divided" Speech, op. cit., 31.

39. E.g., see George M. Weston, Who Are and Who May Be Slaves (n.p., n.d.); American Jubilee, March, 1854 and April, 1855; Anti-Slavery Bugle, October 18, 1856.

40. William Goodell, The American Slave Code . . . (2nd ed.; New York, 1853), 282 ff.; Anti-Slavery Bugle, August 30, 1856; Frederick Douglass' Paper, September 21, 1855; Cleveland Daily True Democrat, October 16, 1850 and August 3, 1853.

41. The Free South, January 7, 1859.

42. Cincinnati Commercial, cited in the Anti-Slavery Bugle, September 20, 1856; Buckmaster, op. cit., 251.

43. James Russell Lowell, The Biglow Papers (Boston, 1891), 65-68.

44. Frederick Douglass' Paper, Dec. 9, 1853 and April 13, 1855, cited in Foner, Writings of Frederick Douglass, op. cit., II, 58-59, 360-361.

45. Ibid., 460.

46. "The Address of the Southern and Western Liberty Convention, to the People of the United States" (Cincinnati, 1845).

47. William Goodell, "Address of the Macedon Convention" (Albany, 1847).

48. The *Voice of Industry,* July 9, 1847; Ware, *op. cit.,* 224-225. The Liberty party was split into three factions after 1848, but all three groups maintained the principle of unity between labor reform and abolition, and one group advocated, in addition to abolition, free public land for actual settlers, women's political rights, the ten-hour day, and the right of workers to organize. See *Frederick Douglass' Paper,* September 25, 1851; *Anti-Slavery Bugle,* February 11, 1854.

49. Boston *Semi-Weekly Reporter,* September 9, 1848, quoted in Schlesinger, *op. cit.,* 468n.; "Address by the Barnburners of the New York Legislature," cited in *ibid.,* 462-463; Cleveland *Daily True Democrat,* quoted in *The Annals of Cleveland,* XXXII, 135.

50. Cited in Ware, *op. cit.,* 225.

51. *The New Era,* July 27, 1848, cited in *ibid.,* 225.

52. David M. Ludlum, *Social Ferment in Vermont, 1791-1850* (New York, 1939), 269; Helene Sara Zahler, *Eastern Workingmen and National Land Policy* (New York, 1941), 98-99; W. G. Bean, "Party Transformations in Massachusetts" (Thesis, Harvard University).

53. *Memoirs of Prince Metternich,* ed. by Prince Richard Metternich and translated by Mrs. Alexander Napier (New York, 1880-1882), III, 473-474.

54. Issue of April 17, 1851.

55. October 7, 1852.

56. Edward L. Pierce, *Memoir and Letters of Charles Sumner* (Boston, 1894), III, 187; see also *Congressional Globe* 31C. 1S., 1850, Appendix, 268; *The Anti-Slavery Papers of James Russell Lowell* (Boston, 1902), I, 9-10.

57. Russel B. Nye, "The Slave Power Conspiracy: 1830-1860," *Science and Society,* Summer, 1946, 264.

58. The Free Soil party did not advocate abolition either, but its spokesmen did not attempt to conceal their hostility to slavery.

59. Cleveland *Leader,* October 28, 1856, cited in *The Annals of Cleveland,* XXXIX, 324.

60. Cited in *Republican Scrap Book, op. cit.,* 19.

61. Seward, *Works, op. cit.,* IV, 245-246; see also The Cleveland *Leader,* June 28, 1856; *Republican Scrap Book, op. cit.,* 34-36.

62. April 16, 1856; see also the New York *Tribune,* March 10, 1856.

63. The *Radical Abolitionist,* August, 1856.

64. *Ibid.,* June, 1856; see also the Cleveland *Leader,* April 16, 1856; *Anti-Slavery Bugle,* May 16, 1857.

65. For example, see Weston, *The Poor Whites of the South, op. cit.*

66. George M. Weston, *Southern Slavery Reduces Northern Wages* (Washington, 1856).

67. *The Republican Campaign Songster* (New York, 1856), 49-50; see p. 7 also.

68. *Anti-Slavery Bugle,* October 18, 1856.

69. May 14, 1856; see also *Republican Scrap Book, op. cit.,* 9.

70. *The Republican Campaign Songster, op. cit.,* 67-68; also pp. 53-54, 81-82.

71. January 18, 1856; see also The Cleveland *Leader,* July 3, 1856, October 1, 1856, October 14, 1856; The *National Anti-Slavery Standard,* October 11, 1856; *Anti-Slavery Bugle,* October 18, 1856; *Republican Scrap Book, op. cit.*

72. See *The Irish-American,* July 12, 1856, July 19, 1856; Birnbaum, *op. cit.,* 22; *The Tribune Almanac,* 1857; The Cleveland *Leader,* October 15, 1856.

73. Richard T. Ely, *The Labor Movement in America* (New York, 1905), 221-222; F. I. Herriott, "The Conference in the Deutsches Haus . . ." in *Transactions* of the Illinois State Historical Society (Springfield, 1928), 108.

74. *Autobiography,* cited in Foner, *Labor Movement,* 279n.

75. New York *Tribune,* October 31, 1856.

76. Even among the businessmen who remained in the Democratic ranks, there was a split, the Douglas wing representing those who desired to challenge the domination of the slaveholders in the party and the Union, while at the same time they were willing to conciliate them in order to preserve the Union, their political ascendancy, and their business ties.

77. Philadelphia *Public Ledger,* March 13, 1860, cited in Foner, *Labor Movement,* 285.

78. See Hofstadter, *op. cit.,* 106 ff.

79. Abraham Lincoln, *Complete Works* (John G. Nicolay and John Hay, eds.; New York, 1894), I, 307.

80. *Ibid.,* 580-582.

81. *Ibid.,* 179.

82. *Ibid.,* 615-616.
83. *Ibid.,* 625.
84. See his interesting letter to his stepbrother, cited in Hofstadter, *op. cit.,* 103-104.
85. Lincoln, *op. cit.,* II, 104-106.
86. Albert J. Beveridge, *Abraham Lincoln* (Boston, 1928), II, 31, 437-440.
87. "Lincoln's Lost Speech" (Bloomington, May 29, 1856), as reported by H. C. Whitney (n.p., 1896).
88. Lincoln, *op. cit.,* I, 240 ff.
89. *Ibid.,* 614, 629.
90. New York *Tribune,* October 30, 1860.
91. Cited in Osborn H. Oldroyd, *Lincoln's Campaign* (Chicago, 1896), 6; see also p. 87, and New York *Tribune,* September 30, 1860.
92. Beveridge, *op. cit.,* II, 678.
93. Quoted in Birnbaum, *op. cit.,* 27.
94. Seward, *Works, op. cit.,* 372.
95. Boston *Daily Bee,* cited in Birnbaum, *op. cit.,* 28, 31.
96. See Dawes, *op. cit.,* Harlan, *op. cit.,* John Hickman, "Democracy— The Old and the New" (Washington, 1860), Schurz, *op. cit.*
97. Wittke, *We Who Built America, op. cit.,* 246-247.
98. William Windom, "The Homestead Bill—Its Friends and Its Foes," (Washington, 1860), 2.
99. *The Free South,* February 11 and 18, 1859; *The National Era,* September 30, 1852; *Lands for the Landless* (Washington, 1859), also published in German; Seward, *Works, op. cit.,* 426-427; New York *Tribune,* October 12, 1860.
100. In Perkins, *op. cit.,* I, 62-63.
101. Birnbaum, *op. cit.,* 24, 37.
102. Perkins, *op. cit.,* 66-68.
103. *Ibid.,* 71-72; see also the New York *Herald,* October 10 and 26, 1860, cited in Birnbaum, *op. cit.,* 30.
104. New York *Tribune,* October 29 to November 7, 1860.
105. *The Irish-American,* 1860, *passim; The Tribune Almanac,* 1861; Gibson, *op. cit.,* 89 ff.; *Douglass' Monthly,* August, 1859.
106. Carl Wittke, *Against the Current: The Life of Karl Heinzen* (Chicago, 1945), 171 ff.
107. Schluter, *op. cit.,* 72-73.
108. Carl Wittke, *The Utopian Communist* (Baton Rouge, 1950), 159-161.
109. Schluter, *op. cit.,* 77 ff.
110. *Ibid.,* 77; Herriott, *op. cit.,* 133-134.

111. Karl Obermann, *Joseph Weydemeyer* (New York, 1947), 85 ff., 103-104.
112. Foner, *Labor Movement, op. cit.,* 289.
113. Herriott, *op. cit., passim.*
114. New York *Herald,* October 31 and November 1, 1860; Obermann, *op. cit.,* 109 ff.
115. Birnbaum, *op. cit.,* 32 ff.

Chapter V: "The Uprising of a Great People"

1. Title of a book by Count Agenor de Gasparin (tr. by Mary L. Booth; New York, 1861).
2. Carey, *op. cit.*
3. Ruffin, *op. cit.,* 126-127, 141-145, 285 ff., 327. When Lee surrendered, Ruffin wrapped himself in a Confederate flag and committed suicide.
4. Gibson, *op. cit.,* 104-105.
5. Birnbaum, *op. cit.,* 49 ff.
6. Cleveland *Daily Plain Dealer,* January 12, 1861.
7. Birnbaum, *op. cit.,* 89; Gibson, *op. cit.,* 116-117.
8. November 14, 1860.
9. Powderly, *op. cit.,* 44-45; Saul Schindler, *Northern Labor and the American Civil War* (Thesis, Brooklyn College, 1941), 35.
10. *The Irish-American,* November, 1860 to March, 1861.
11. Carl Sandburg, *Abraham Lincoln: The War Years* (New York, 1939), I, 42-43.
12. Arthur C. Cole, *The Whig Party in the South* (Washington, 1913), 148n.
13. See *The Kentucky Statesman,* October 5, 1860, in Dwight L. Dumond, *Southern Editorials on Secession* (New York, 1931), 175.
14. Cincinnati *Commercial,* cited in Birnbaum, *op. cit.,* 101-103.
15. *Ibid.,* 62-67.
16. But another speaker at the same meeting was cheered when he suggested that the politicians should fight their own battles and leave the laboring men in peace. See *ibid.,* 63-65; Schindler, *op. cit.,* 27 ff.
17. "New-York Workingmen's Executive Committee. Report of Committee on Resolutions, adopted February 4, 1861," broadside in the Library of Congress.
18. Frank T. Carlton, *Organized Labor in American History* (New York,

1920), 150-152; Kenneth M. Stampp, *And the War Came* (Baton Rougue, 1950), 126; Birnbaum, *op. cit.*, 67-68.

19. "Mass Meeting of the Workingmen of Massachusetts," February 20, 1861, broadside in the Library of Congress; "Working Men's Mass Meeting in Faneuil Hall," broadside in the Bostonian Society Library; Boston *Daily Evening Transcript*, February 21, 1861; Boston *City Directory*, 1861.

20. Edgar Barclay Cale, *The Organization of Labor in Philadelphia, 1850-1870* (Thesis, University of Pennsylvania, 1940), 42 ff.; Birnbaum, *op. cit.*, 71-73; Foner, *Labor Movement*, 300.

21. James C. Sylvis, *The Life, Speeches, Labors and Essays of William H. Sylvis* (Philadelphia, 1872), 44-45.

22. The Philadelphia *Press*, February 22, 1861; Jonathan Grossman, *William Sylvis* (New York, 1945), 47; Cale, *op. cit.*, 42 ff.

23. The Philadelphia *Press*, February 23, 1861.

24. *Ibid.*, February 25, 1861; Birnbaum, *op. cit.*, 78 ff.

25. McNeill, *op. cit.*, 124; Schindler, *op. cit.*, 3-4; Benjamin A. Gould, *Investigations in the . . . Statistics of American Soldiers* (New York: U.S. Sanitary Commission, 1869), 210 ff.

26. *Fincher's Trades' Review*, January 14, 1865.

27. Cited in Herbert Aptheker, *The Negro in the Civil War* (New York, 1938), 37.

28. Lincoln, *Complete Works, op. cit.*, II, 562, 564, 576; see Aptheker, *The Negro in the Civil War, op. cit.*, 8-10, 34-40.

29. Cited in Foner, *Labor Movement*, 310.

30. Cleveland *Leader*, May 6, 1863.

31. Cited in Foner, *Labor Movement*, 334.

32. See Foner, *Labor Movement*, 325 ff., 352-355.

33. Cited in Leonard Newman, "Opposition to Lincoln in the Elections of 1864," *Science and Society*, Fall, 1944, 317-318.

34. In Perkins, *op. cit.*, I, 444-445; see also examples from the Irish press cited in Gibson, *op. cit.*, 125-126.

35. *The Liberator*, August 8, 1862; see also *ibid.*, August 5, 1862; *New York Copperhead*, May 30, 1863; Williston H. Lofton, "Northern Labor and the Negro during the Civil War," *The Journal of Negro History*, July, 1949, 253-255; *The Irish-American*, November 8, 1862; Senator Cox, in the *Congressional Globe*, 37C. 2S., 1862, Appendix, 248.

36. Stanton Ling Davis, *Pennsylvania Politics, 1860-1863* (Thesis, Western Reserve University, 1935), 246-247.

37. Cleveland *Plain Dealer,* September 18, 1865; Lofton, "Northern Labor and the Negro," *op. cit.,* 255-256; Wood Gray, *The Hidden Civil War* (New York, 1942), 90.
38. This order was countermanded by Lincoln.
39. *Publications* of the New England Loyal Publication Society, *op. cit.,* I, d.
40. Lincoln, *Complete Works, op. cit.,* II, 274-275; Lincoln repeated his advocacy of colonization in this address, stating that this would still further protect white labor against competition from free Negroes. See also The New York *Tribune,* July 11, 1862 and August 8, 1863; "Catechism for Free Working Men," (Cincinnati, n.d.; No. 3), 4; Cleveland *Leader,* August 6, 1862; *Harper's Weekly,* August 23, 1862; Charles C. Burleigh, "Slavery and the North," *Anti-Slavery Tract* No. 10 (New York, n. d.), 9-10.
41. Issue of June 13, 1863.
42. Lofton, "Northern Labor and the Negro," *op. cit.,* 257 ff.; Cleveland *Leader,* July 17 and 19, August 8, 1862.
43. The *Liberator,* December 5, 1862.
44. Gray, *op. cit.,* 99-100.
45. See the New York *Tribune,* August 5, 1862; Frederick Merk, "The Labor Movement in Wisconsin During the Civil War," *Proceedings* of the State Historical Society (Madison, 1915), 168 ff.; *The Liberator,* October 24, 1862; *Three Years among the Working-Classes in the United States during the War* (London, 1865), xiv.
46. Emerson D. Fite, *Social and Industrial Conditions in the North During the Civil War* (New York, 1910), 189-190.
47. Sylvis, *op. cit.,* 229.
48. *Fincher's Trades' Review,* June 6 and 18, 1863; see also "A Workingman's Idea of Conscription," reprinted from *ibid.* in *The Magazine of History* (1918), 103-107.
49. Quoted in the *National Anti-Slavery Standard,* July 25, 1863.
50. See the New York *Herald* and the New York *Tribune,* July 14 to July 19, 1863.
51. *Fincher's Trades' Review,* July 18, 1863.
52. *Ibid.,* July 25, 1863.
53. "Don't Unchain the Tiger." By a Democratic Workingman. New York, July 24, 1863. (Library of Congress.) Also printed in German: "Entfesselt den Tiger nicht!" (Boston Public Library).
54. "To the Laboring Men of New York." By a Democratic Workingman.

New York, July 18, 1863. (Library of Congress.) See also *The Iron Platform,* June, 1864.

55. McNeill, *op. cit.,* 126.

56. *Fincher's Trades' Review,* October 24, 1863, February 1, 1864.

57. Cited in Albert B. Moore, *Conscription and Conflict in the Confederacy* (New York, 1924), 71-72.

58. *Ibid.,* 129-131, 151-152, 221, 240.

59. Aptheker, *The Negro in the Civil War, op. cit.,* 10 ff., 41-43.

60. Sylvis, *op. cit.,* 232-233; Sylvis had a brief term of service in the army.

61. Gibson, *op. cit.,* 127-130.

62. Horace Greeley, *The American Conflict* (Hartford, 1864-1866), II, 244-245.

63. *Speeches, Correspondence and Public Papers of Carl Schurz,* ed. by Frederic Bancroft (New York, 1913), 185 ff.

64. *Die Presse* (Vienna), January 5, 1862 and February 2, 1862, cited in Karl Marx and Frederick Engels, *The Civil War in the United States,* ed. by Richard Enmale (New York, 1937), 131-133, 141-142.

65. Schluter, *op. cit.,* 158-159.

66. "The Working Men of Manchester and President Lincoln," *Union and Emancipation Tracts,* No. 2 (Manchester, 1863), 1.

67. "The Manchester Workmen and Emancipation" (Broadside, Library of Congress).

68. Lincoln, *Complete Works, op. cit.,* II, 301-302, 308-309.

69. *Publications* of the New England Loyal Publication Society, I, 60, no. 53.

70. *National Anti-Slavery Standard,* May 30, 1863.

71. London *Bee-Hive,* January 7, 1865, quoted in Marx and Engels, *op. cit.,* 279-283.

72. See, for example, Charles Nordhoff, *America for Free Working Men* (New York, 1865); *Southern Hatred of the American Government* . . . (Boston, 1862); *The Spirit of the South Towards Northern Freemen and Soldiers* (Boston, 1861).

73. *Publications* of the New England L. P. S., I, 88, II, 143, 169.

74. See Loyal Publication Society, *Pamphlets* (New York, 1864); *Publications* of the New England L. P. S., *op. cit.,* I-III, *passim.*

75. Foner, *Labor Movement,* 312.

76. "A Challenge!" (August 25, 1863); "White Slaves" (September 28, 1863); "An Abolition Traitor" (August 29, 1863), all in the Library of Congress.

77. "Daniel O'Connell on Democracy" (New York, October 13, 1863), in the Library of Congress.
78. "A Traitor's Peace" (New York, October 30, 1863), in the Library of Congress; see also "What Traitors say of Northern Democrats," in the Massachusetts Historical Society Library.
79. *Catechism for Free Working Men, op. cit.*, 1-4.

Chapter VI: FRATERNITY IN FREEDOM

1. Sylvis, *op. cit.*, 31, 82.
2. *Fincher's Trades' Review*, October 10, 1863.
3. Sylvis, *op. cit.*, 140-141.
4. Wendell Phillips, *Speeches, Lectures, and Letters* (Boston, 1892), II, 139.
5. Boston *Daily Evening Voice*, November 3, 1865.
6. *Ibid.*, December 5, 10, 12, 13 and 20, 1864.
7. Sylvis, *op. cit.*, 82; also see page 129.
8. Foner, *Labor Movement*, 397 ff.
9. Spero and Harris, *op. cit.*, 27 ff; Commons, *History of Labour, op. cit.*, 136-137; Wesley, *op. cit.*, 168 ff.; W. E. B. DuBois, *Black Reconstruction* (New York, 1935), 361 ff.
10. Birnbaum, *op. cit.*, 63-64, 78 ff.
11. Sylvis, *op. cit.*, 45-46.
12. Foner, *Labor Movement*, 335.
13. *Publications* of the New England L. P. S., II, 250.
14. Lincoln, *Complete Works, op. cit.*, II, 501-503; "A Workingman's Reasons for the Re-election of Abraham Lincoln," (Broadside in the Library of Congress); "The Workingman," (New York, 1864), 1; Obermann, *op. cit.*, 125-126.
15. "The Workingman," *op. cit.*, 3.
16. *Fincher's Trades' Review*, 1864, *passim*.
17. *The Workingman's Advocate* (Chicago), March 25, 1865.
18. Sylvis, *op. cit.*, 67; Commons, *Documentary History, op. cit.*, IX, 134-136; Foner, *Labor Movement, op. cit.*, 423 ff.
19. Sylvis, *op. cit.*, 186-187.
20. Foner, *Labor Movement*, 409 ff.
21. Commons, *Documentary History, op. cit.*, IX, 338-340.
22. Issue of December 2, 1864.
23. Sylvis, *op. cit.*, 232 ff.

24. Commons, *Documentary History, op. cit.,* IX, 157 ff.
25. Sylvis, *op. cit.,* 295.
26. Commons, *History of Labour, op. cit.,* II, 134-136; Wesley, *op. cit.,* 156 ff.; Sylvis, *op. cit.,* 295, 337.
27. *The Workingman's Advocate* (Chicago), September 4 and 11, 1869, cited in Foner, *Labor Movement,* 399.
28. Quoted in DuBois, *Black Reconstruction, op. cit.,* 364.

Acknowledgments

This book could obviously not have been written without reliance on the many scholars whose work is cited in the footnotes. Its accomplishment was likewise dependent on the innumerable persons who have contributed to the collection of source materials in libraries, universities, and historical societies, and on the never-failing cooperation and skill of the staffs of those institutions. In particular I wish to record the assistance which was given by the libraries of Western Reserve University, Columbia University, and the University of Wisconsin; the public libraries of Cleveland, New York, Boston, and Lynn; the Library of Congress; The Western Reserve, Massachusetts, New York, and Wisconsin Historical Societies; the American Antiquarian Society in Worcester; the Oberlin College Library; the Bostonian Society and the New York Society; and the numerous libraries which furnished material through interlibrary loans. Finally, I am indebted to Dean Carl Wittke and Professors Harvey Wish and C. H. Cramer of Western Reserve University, who read the manuscript with great care and called my attention to many errors of fact and method. Of course, I am solely responsible for all deficiencies and interpretations in the final product.

Acknowledgment is gratefully given to the editors of Smith College Studies in History for permission to quote from Vera Shlakman's *Economic History of a Factory Town* (1935); to Harcourt, Brace and Company for W. E. B. DuBois' *Black Reconstruction* (1935); to Richard B. Morris for his article, "Labor Militancy in the Old South," in *Labor and Nation* (May-June, 1948); to Appleton-Century-Crofts, Inc., for Howard C. Perkins' *Northern Editorials on Secession* (1942); to the Board of Publication of Washington University for Chauncey S. Boucher's *South Carolina and the South on the Eve of Secession* (1919); to International Publishers for Philip S. Foner's *History of the Labor Movement in the United States* (1947); to *The Negro History Bulletin* for permission to reprint the substance of two articles by me in the issues of December, 1953, and February, 1954; and to *Science and Society* for permission to reprint the substance of an article by me in the issue of Summer, 1954.

Bernard Mandel

Cleveland, Ohio
November, 1954

Index

Abolitionists, 25-26, 61-62, 147-148, 186; Southern, 50-55; say free Negroes will not go North, 68; appeal to Irish laborers, 68-70; attacks on their rights, 74-76, 109, 124-126; inconsistency, 79-80; attitude toward labor movement, 89-93; attitude of labor toward, 93-95; division, 135-138; *National Anti-Slavery Standard,* 47, 73, ci., 95; *Anti-Slavery Bugle,* 128, ci., 32, 36, 39, 40, 43, 47-48, 63, 64, 128; *National Enquirer,* 72. See Anti-slavery movement, Bailey, Clay, C.M., Douglass, Free Soil party, Garrison, Greeley, Helper, Higginson, Hunt, Lowell, Loyal Publication Society, Phillips, Rogers, Smith, Whittier.

Adams, Charles Francis, and English labor, 197-198.

Adams, John, on abolition in Massachusetts, 63; on slavery of working class, 77.

Agrarians. See Land Reformers.

American and Foreign Anti-Slavery Society, 136, 137.

American Anti-Slavery Society, 136.

Anti-Slavery movement, 22-27; in South, 43-55; workers in, 153. See Abolitionists, Free Soil party, Emancipation, Liberty party, Republican party.

Associationists, urge unity of reformers, 95; supported by Milne, 143. See Brisbane, Fourier, Greeley.

Bailey, William S., Southern abolitionist, 50; *The Free South,* 219, ci., 35, 50, 131-132, 164.

Barnburners, oppose extension of slavery, 113; join Free Soil movement, 143; return to Democratic party, 146.

Birney, James, abolitionist, ci., 62; *The Philanthropist,* 109, 125, ci., 43.

Bledsoe, Moses, on unequal taxes in South, 42.

Bray, John Francis, *Labor's Wrong and Labor's Remedy,* 80.

Bright, John, views on Civil War, 197.

Brisbane, Albert, on abolition, 86.

Brownson, Orestes A., on abolition, 88-89; favors alliance of labor and slaveholders, 104.

Buchanan, James, hostility to labor, 151-152; vetoes Homestead bill, 163-164; criticized by *Irish-American,* 173-174.

Burritt, Elihu, Liberty candidate for Vice-President, 139.

Businessmen, opposition to slave-power, 24-26; Southern, opposition to slavery, 30; alleged insincerity of anti-slavery advocacy, 67; conflict with planters, 95-96; relation to slaveholders and laborers, 103-107; slaveholders appeal to against abolition, 107-110; alliance with slaveholders, 114, 138; and Free Soil party, 142-143, 146; and Republican party, 148, 154-155, 165, 168-169; fear uprisings in case of war, 172; gains during Civil War, 183, 202-203; anti-labor and anti-Negro practices, 187, 205.

Cabet, Etienne, Utopian socialist, 20.
Calhoun, John, 123, 143, 152; on democracy, 40; defines slavery, 100; on alliance of slaveholders and laborers, 105-106; positive good doctrine, 130; on free labor, 204.
Cameron, Andrew C., urges labor party, 210; represents National Labor Union at First International, 211; urges cooperation of white and Negro labor, 213; *Workingman's Advocate*, 210, 216.
Capital, capitalists. See Businessmen.
Cass, Lewis, candidate for President, 145.
Catholics, and slavery, 69; attacked by Helper, 163; and emancipation, 195.
Civil liberties, of abolitionists, 74-76, 109, 124-126; of Negroes, 207.
Civil War, 24; efforts to avoid, 173-180; labor's participation, 180-201; opposition, 183-186.
Clay, Cassius M., on effect of slavery on workers, 28-29; on slave competition with labor, 31; on oppression of Southern labor, 51; supported by German-American socialists, 54; press destroyed, 75; on unions, 92; *The True American*, 50, ci., 38.
Clay, Henry, suggests anti-abolition tract, 67-68.
Cobbett, William, compares laborers and slaves, 79.
Coffin, Levi, abolitionist, ci., 109.
Colton, Calvin, urged to write anti-abolition tract, 67-68; ci., 63.
Communists. See Socialists.
Compromise of 1850, 118, 119, 143, 146-147.

Confederacy, 193, 195-196, 199, 200.
Conscription, law, 189; labor's attitude, 189-194; draft riots, 190-193; in South, 193.
Considerant, Victor, Utopian socialist, 20.
Copperheads, 183-184, 190, 200, 201.
Crittenden plan, 177, 178, 179.

Davis, Jefferson, 193.
DeBow, J. D. B., ci., 57.
Democracy, in South, 40-41, 60; slavery a menace to, 70-76; slaveholders' attitude to, see Slaveholders.
Democratic party, 22, 121, 135, 148, 184, 191; and Irish labor, 68-69, 151; instrument of alliance between slaveholders and workers, 103-104; becomes party of slaveholders, 143, 162-163; dissension over slavery question, 143-145, 147; and free labor, 151-152; and German-American workers, 153; rejects businessmen's program, 154; opposes Homestead law and tariff, 163-164; in secession crisis, 172-173, 176, 180; Peace Democrats, 184; election of 1862, 185. See Barnburners, Buchanan, Calhoun, Cass, Douglas, Johnson, Milne, Van Buren, Walsh.
Douai, Adolph, Southern socialist and abolitionist, 54; in election of 1860, 168.
Douglas, Stephen A., 165, 166.
Douglass, Frederick, hires out his labor, 32; on race prejudice, 59; on discrimination, 65-66; on Walsh, 82; resented by Garrison, 135; on passive resistance, 136; *The North Star*, ci., 52.
Draft. See Conscription.
Dred Scott decision, 127, 134, 154; condemned, 127.

Pro-slavery, forces, 22; arguments, 57-60, 96-103, 130-131; position of labor spokesmen, 81-82; *Southern Quarterly Review*, ci., 102. See Calhoun, Estes, Fitzhugh, Grayson, Hammond, Harper, Las Casas, McDuffie, Pickens, Ruffin, Slaveholders, Toombs, Van Deren, Walsh.

Purcell, Edward, favors emancipation, 195.

Purcell, John B., favors emancipation, 195.

Randolph, John, on alliance of planters and laborers, 105.

Raymond, Daniel, political economist, ci., 28.

Rayner, Kenneth, on taxes in South, 42-43.

Republican party, and land reformers, 21; formation, 147-154; election of 1860, 154-169; pro-business policy, 183; appeals for labor's support of emancipation, 199; and Negroes, 208. See Emancipation, Fremont, Greeley, Lincoln, Schurz, Seward, Sumner.

Rogers, Nathaniel P., abolitionist editor, 73.

Ruffin, Edmund, opposes universal suffrage, 40; defines slavery, 100; on secession, 171.

Schools, public, in South, 41-42; demanded, 207.

Schurz, Carl, and nativism, 163; and emancipation, 195; ci., 126.

Secession, threatened, 108, 154, 164; crisis, 170-180.

Sedgwick, Theodore, political economist, on slavery and labor, 64.

Seward, William, on sectional balance, 112; on Fugitive Slave Law, 126; "irrepressible conflict," 128;

on conflict between slaveholders and freemen, 149, 162.

Simpson, Stephen, compares laborers with slaves, 80.

Slaveholders, on free society and free labor, 38-40, 101-102, 105-106, 150-151, 160, 199-201; rule in South, 55-60; fear growth of capitalism, 95-96; alliance with Northern workers, 103-107; appeal to capitalists to oppose abolition, 107-110; alliance with capital, 114, 138; and Democratic party, 143; demand for confiscation of their land, 207. See Slave-power, South.

Slave-power, 111 ff., 117, 118, 120, 143, 146, 149, 150, 155, 156, 182, 183, 191, 193, 194, 202, 204; "conspiracy," 122-133, 152-153, 160. See Slaveholders, South.

Slavery, effect on Southern labor, 28-43; effect on Northern labor, 61-65, 150; menace to democracy, 70-76; compared with wage slavery by labor reformers, 77-81; by Southerners, 96-101; Republican policy, 147-149; extension, see Expansion, Territories, Slave-power "conspiracy." See Anti-Slavery movement, Abolitionists, Emancipation, Pro-Slavery, Slaveholders, Slaves.

Slaves, resistance to slavery, 22-24; in Southern industry, 46-47, 57; in Civil War, 181-182, 193-194. See Slavery.

Smith, Gerrit, land reformer and abolitionist, 138, 147; Liberty party candidate for President, 139.

Socialists, Utopian, 20, 99; on abolition, 86-88; on annexation of Texas, 114; *The Harbinger*, 92, 114; *The Phalanx*, ci., 86, 87,

The University of Illinois Press
is a founding member of the
Association of American University Presses.

University of Illinois Press
1325 South Oak Street
Champaign, IL 61820-6903
www.press.uillinois.edu

Printed and bound by CPI Group (UK) Ltd, Croydon, CR0 4YY

09/06/2025

14685783-0001